OPE!

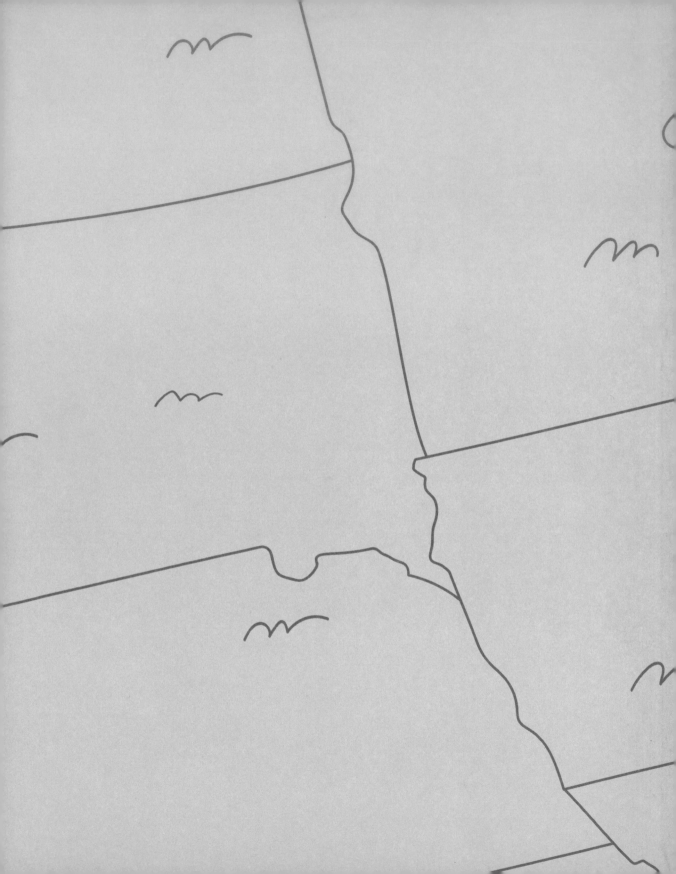

The Midwest Survival Guide

The Midwest Survival Guide

HOW WE TALK, LOVE, WORK, DRINK, AND EAT . . . EVERYTHING WITH RANCH

Charlie Berens

WILLIAM MORROW

An Imprint of HarperCollins*Publishers*

FIRST EDITION

Illustrations by Vanessa Montano

Library of Congress Cataloging-in-Publication Data has been applied for.

ISBN 978-0-06-307495-8

21 22 23 24 25   WOR   10 9 8 7 6 5 4 3 2 1

For Grandpa Bob

(1935–2019)

If all perch go to heaven
It's a little awkward for Grandpa Bob right now . . .

Contents

**Intermission:
Midwest Gallery
120**

Introduction: Life in the Midwest...

For years as a comedian, I've been touring around and telling stories about the greatest place on Earth, the Midwest. Wisconsin, Minnesota, Michigan, Iowa, Illinois, Indiana, North Dakota, South Dakota, Ohio, Kansas, Nebraska, and Missouri stick out like a silo in a skyline. As a guy born and raised in Wisconsin, I've had the privilege of witnessing the quirks of the Midwest up close. I'll be honest with you. This is a weird place, but that's what keeps it filled with the world's best-kept secrets. And we can't just keep these secrets buried deep inside, because that's where our feelings go. Rather, like the bag of frozen fish from the bottom of my garage freezer, we must share these secrets with anyone who asks, but especially those who don't. And that's what inspired this book.

Throughout my years onstage, I've noticed Midwest audiences like stories about sunken ice shanties and church-sponsored bar crawls. That's expected. We're a unique and close-knit club, bound by April snow, wallets lost in cornfields, and lying about the best-colored jig to catch a walleye so there's more in the lake for the liars.

But I never expected this thing would take off across the country. (Apparently there's a big demand for freezer perch.) Oddly enough, my Midwest-themed *Manitowoc Minute* character, inspired by the time I spent working in local news, first debuted onstage at the Comedy Store in Los Angeles. During the show I'd asked, "Is anyone from the Midwest?," and one guy (who may or may not have had a couple two-tree beers) says, "Oh yah, me! I'm from Manitowoc." We had a good back-and-forth in that bit, so I named the *Manitowoc Minute* series after him. But he wasn't the only Midwesterner to raise his hand that night. Turned out, a quarter of the room in that L.A. comedy club was from the American heartland.

So I reawakened my native accent (which I'd spent years trying to remove for my budding journalism career) and delivered local and national news, and self-deprecating jokes, through the lens of the quintessential Midwesterner. I thought I'd release one video and that would be it. But after the success of the first video, I knew I had to keep making more.

At first, I was concerned I wouldn't have enough material, but then I remembered that the Midwest is like an onion. And not just any onion. It's the one you forgot about in the back of the crisper that started to sprout. It's full of layers and complexity. It looks a little funny. It makes you cry sometimes when you pull back those layers. And when you plant it, you get another crisper full of onions for your liverwurst. In other words, the material has been heartfelt, bizarre, and endless.

The *Manitowoc Minute* soon turned into a live show and social brand. I released the Midwest album *Unthawed* with Adam Greuel from Horseshoes and Hand Grenades and it topped the bluegrass charts, I collaborated with comedians across the United States, and I even created a beer. Eventually the fan base grew to millions. In short, I got luckier than a buck that just crossed I-94.

I've thought about why Midwest life resonates with the rest of the country, and here's what I came up with. First, because everyone is either from the Midwest or knows someone from the Midwest. Second, because the Midwest has largely been underrepresented, or falsely represented, in pop culture. We've been flown over culturally, and most people only seem to notice us every four years when we take an outsize control over the political landscape. In truth, the Midwest is an old dried-up lake bed just waiting for the dam to break. A complex and diverse region that *is* empirically, despite what those on the coasts might think, more exciting than vanilla extract. No offense to vanilla extract.

Sooner or later everyone's coming to the Midwest. It's unavoidable. Maybe only for a quick visit, but forty years can go by quicker than a pike snapping through your monofilament line. Like brandy through a supper club, these are the days of our lives.

Yes, there's a lot of camouflage here, but at least you can't see it. And where you went to high school usually matters more than where you went to college. And yes, "Midwest nice" is a real thing, but it can get pretty treacherous if you don't know what you're doing. And so our guests from the South and the East and West Coasts can sometimes get a little bewildered.

That's why I've assembled this official guide to the Midwest—a collection of how-tos, tall tales, vocab lessons, etiquette, and advice that gives you everything you need to know about living your best life in America's heartland.

I'd call this guide an ode to my favorite region in the world, with its cornflake casserole, Kwik Trips, and hours spent finding ways to leave someone's house politely. Other than my years traveling the country as a newscaster and a stand-up comedian, I've spent my whole life in America's heartland. I've walked across Lambeau Field with my dad, drunk beers on water skis, and woken at 4:00 A.M. to enjoy a balmy fifteen-degree day sitting in a deer stand, only to see more deer taunting me as they crossed the highway on my ride home. When someone asks me if I wanna drive forty-five minutes to a Friday fish fry, there's only one answer: Perch or walleye? I've milked cows (and goats), I've drilled holes in the ice to fish (and drink beer). When someone says I have something nice, my instinct is to tell them I bought it with a coupon. When my first girlfriend said she loved me for the first time, I hesitated and just told her to watch out for deer.

This book is, at its core, a tribute to life in the American Midwest: the good, the bad, and the Chicago Bears. The point of the *Manitowoc Minute* has always been to make people laugh—at themselves and at another way of life. And, whether online or during our live shows, my hope has always been to bring people together. When everyone is laughing, we forget what divides us.

For years, people have asked me what it was like growing up and living in the middle of America. *The Midwest Survival Guide* will answer that question, but the short answer is: It's a trade-off. Yes, it gets cold enough that our lakes freeze for months, but how else would we ice-fish? Yes, there are biblical swarms of mosquitoes, but without mosquitoes there'd be fewer hummingbirds. Brutal winters make for euphoric springs. In many ways, the inherent attitude of the Midwest is something the rest of the world may want to borrow: Find joy in the lows of life, because the lows lead to the highs. Fully embrace the good *and* the bad. Don't be afraid of discomfort; joke about it. Sure, the weather is better in California, but I guarantee you they'll never appreciate the sunshine like we do.

Okie dokes, let's keep 'er movin' . . .

—Charlie

How Well Do You Know the Midwest?

A PRELIMINARY TEST

Before we begin, let's see how much you *already* know with a little quiz. At this stage, could be a lot or next to nothing. But, no matter how you do, you're a winner. If you're a newbie who bought this book to learn, it'll be a fun exercise to reveal all the great things you'll soon be discovering. And if you nail every question, this quiz proves you're among family here and should enjoy this celebration of all things Midwest.

1. How do you show someone in the Midwest you love them?

a. You say, "I love you"

b. You clean their gutters

c. You say, "Watch out for deer"

2. Your neighbors' lawn has been taken over by dandelions. These people are:

a. busy

b. botanists

c. deeply *deeply* troubled

3. Your mom tells you she's "just had the most amazing three-way." How do you respond?

a. *Wait . . . What?! What in the name of Sam Hill is wrong with you?*

b. *Well, aren't you just full of surprises.*

c. *So jealous. Wish I'd been there with you.*

4. How many schools are in the Big 10?

a. 10

b. 8

c. 14, obviously

5. "Lake-effect snow" is:

a. when snow looks like a lake

b. the name of an indie trap-folk duo from Cleveland

c. when Canadian winds get caught in a Midwest goodbye over the Great Lakes

6. You have the left *and* the right. You should:

a. go straight down the center

b. trust your partner for one trick

c. be cool and give one of them back

7. Ranch dressing is best used on:

a. salads

b. pizza

c. yes

8. A "bubbler" is:

a. something you used once in Colorado and forgot the question

b. a delivery device for water

c. the poorly parented child in front of you at the Brewers game

9. Which of these is *not* people food:

a. runsa

b. chislic

c. puppy chow

d. chippers

e. lefse

10. Which of these is a famous comic book villain?

a. Ypsilanti

b. Knockemstiff

c. Wauwatosa

d. Mxyzptlk

e. Ipswich

11. When you remove your bratwurst from the freezer you:

a. defrost it

b. thaw it

c. unthaw it

12. When approaching a four-way stop you:

a. Roll and go

b. What stop sign?

c. Wave everyone by a minimum of three times each before finally proceeding

How'd You Do?

Self-score and total your correct answers.

0–3 Correct	Ope! This is the right book for you . . .
4–6 Correct	Not bad, but there's still some work to be done. This is the right book for you . . .
7–9 Correct	Impressive. You've clearly spent time here. This is the right book for you . . .
10–11 Correct	You're a heartland authority and you've almost perfected your casserole. This is the right book for you . . .
Perfect 12	Eminent Midwesterner. This is the right book for you!

OPE!

The Basics

The States of the Midwest

Before you learn how to fillet a walleye or call a loner without the right bower, let's first nail down where da heck we're even talking about.

Illinois, Indiana, Iowa, Kansas, Michigan, Minnesota, Missouri, Nebraska, North Dakota, Ohio, South Dakota, and Wisconsin.

In alphabetical order, so no one gets their feelings hurt. (Which is the last thing *anyone* wants to do in the Midwest.) Each one of these twelve proud states lays an arguable claim to being the "most Midwest." But how to ever resolve such a thing?

Is it proximity to the Great Lakes? Snowfall volume and duration? Longest goodbye? Most corn? Most lakes? Most unnamed roads? Most crappie hooked? Most growlers purchased? Holiest fish fries? Best jerky? Most sacred church bar crawls? Biggest racks? The most-pronounced *You-betcha!* accent? Or, strangely, the *least*-pronounced try-to-sound-like-you're-from-Dayton-if-you-want-to-"sound-generic-American"-and-get-a-job-in-broadcasting accent?

Should coordinates resolve this debate of the "most" Midwest? If we were a dartboard, hitting Cedar Rapids might get you twenty-five points, but don't write off everyone on the outskirts. Nebraska may sound like a stretch, but once you've driven past eight *billion* acres of corn or scarfed down a classic Omaha Reuben, you might as well be in Indiana. And Cincinnati may teeter mere feet from the American South, but play euchre against one of their West Siders and they'll win with off-suit nines and queens *while* finishing a case of Pabst like they worked the beer lines in Milwaukee.

A wonderful hodgepodge of history, topography, weather, industry, location, community, and deer all combined in a way to create the American heartland out of these twelve states. And while these twelve may give each other guff every now and again, collectively there's a shared experience in everything from the way we raise our kids to the cheese on our pie.

Why Is the "Midwest" So Close to New Jersey?

Before deciding where the Midwest is, or *should be*, we should first figure out the location of Dead Center USA. Since 1918, a town called Lebanon, Kansas, has laid claim to being the geographic center of the United States. The scientists at that time used rather sophisticated technology to reach this important conclusion: they cut out a cardboard map and balanced it on a nail. I shoot you not. When the board achieved perfect balance on that nail, they knew they'd found Dead Center USA: Lebanon.

When Alaska was added, Dead Center moved five hundred miles west, to Belle Fourche, South Dakota.

In any case, during the American Revolution, Cleveland, Ohio, was considered the Wild West to colonials. Fort Wayne, Indiana, was an actual fort. Guys dared their drunk friends to cross the Ohio River. Only the very bravest, deranged, and desperate folks in the colonies watched the sun set behind Pittsburgh and thought: *Huh, wonder what's out that way . . .*

Ohio, Indiana, Iowa, Michigan, Minnesota, Missouri, and so on were "the West"—a catchall term for all those woods and open plains that Americans of European descent often kept away from but talked about with a strange combination of disinterest and yearning that continues to this day. A hundred years later, there were another forty states, and "the West" had moved two thousand miles and into the Pacific.

But by then, *generations* of Americans had grown accustomed to thinking of these states as "the West," and it was not a custom easily dropped. (Consider how well we took to the metric system, which the entire rest of the world adapted to in a couple weeks.) So easterners started calling the middle states "the Middle West," and our new western states and territories now became "the West." Calling Indiana or Michigan the "Eastern West" sounded odd, so "Middle West" worked best for everyone. Always looking to speed things up, Americans eventually dropped a demanding syllable and just went with "the Midwest."

Someday, probably, we'll become simply "the Mid"—which, evidently, if you balance a piece of cardboard on a nail, ain't so far from the truth.

The Middle

Brothers & Sisters from Another Mother

Yes, topography and weather and proximity to the closest brat stop are all very important, but the "Midwest life" is principally a state of mind. You don't have to live here, or even be *from* here, to embrace and enjoy the lifestyle. You may be that one guy in Atlanta who wears shorts in thirty-degree weather or the gal in Hawaii who instinctively knows to put cheese on her apple pies. Or that family in Anaheim who says "Good morning" and "Hey, how you doing?" to everyone they pass, *especially* strangers.

There are whole cities thousands of miles from Shakopee, Minnesota, who've taken on enough Midwest qualities to become honorary members of our special club. If you can't get to the real thing, or are from here and feeling homesick, here are some alternatives to get you a comparable-enough Midwest experience.

Assisi, Italy

Billings, Montana

Chestertown, Maryland

Chiang Mai, Thailand

Clarens, South Africa

Cork, Ireland

Delaware (entire state)

Dire Dawa, Ethiopia

Fairhope, Alabama

Haddonfield, New Jersey

Hoth

Isla del Sol, Bolivia

Juneau, Alaska

Kuala Lumpur, Malaysia

Latrobe, Pennsylvania

Liechtenstein

Lilongwe, Malawi

Madrid, Spain (*if* you like Chicago)

Rabat, Morocco

The Shire

Ukraine

The very top of Mount Fuji

Toronto, Canada

Winslow, Arizona

"THE CITY"

Let's deal with the windy elephant in the room.

For one hundred years, Chicago was the second-largest city in the United States—it's now a comfortable third behind NYC and L.A.—and, then and now, when Midwesterners speak of "moving to the city" or "visiting a relative in the city" or "ya know, to 'heck' with that city," we don't mean St. Paul.

We're talking only about Chicago.

Chi-Town. The Windy City. Paris on the Prairie. The White City. Chicagoland. Sweet Home. The City by the Lake. City of the Big Shoulders. City of the Century. City on the Make. The City That Works. The Big Onion. I Will City. New York Done Right. The Heart of America.

Nice nicknames, but if you live anywhere in the Midwest that *isn't* the City by the Lake, you may think of Chicago (with close to ten million people) as rude, aggressive, condescending, ostentatious, and worst of all . . . Bears fans. Some think those who dwell there are bad-mannered terrors on the highway who only wave with one finger and root for sports teams only a mother might love. Chicago is so loathed that some Midwest states (okay, *one* Midwest state—cough, Wisconsin) commonly use the term "FIB" for describing *all* folks from the state of Illinois. (Example: "And then some FIB just let the door slam right in my face.") *F* for—well, you can figure out yourself; *I* for Illinois; *B* for—well, seven letters, not four. This is getting more complicated than the Zodiac cipher. Just know it isn't pretty. But can you blame the rest of us?

Chicago is where your ex goes to live with that architect who was "just a friend."

Chicago is where you talk about moving to "really make it," but then you start tabulating what rent will be each month and another seven years passes . . .

Chicago is where they have the audacity to charge $6 for a PBR instead of the traditional $2.50. And it doesn't even come with a free shot of Jamo.

Chicago is that older sibling who moved off and made it big, and every Thanksgiving you have to see their Tesla and hear about their latest trip to Burning Man. But, like all insufferable siblings, Chicago is *our* big brother/sister. And though *we* might give our city a hard time behind closed doors, outsiders better keep their unfavorable comments to themselves.

Chicago, truth be told, is one of the great cities of the world.

Ever since 1780, when the Founder of Chicago—Jean Baptiste Point du Sable, a free Black man from, most believe, somewhere in the Caribbean—built his farm at the mouth of the Chicago River, immigrants from around the world have come to the "swampland beside Lake Michigan" and built it into a looming powerhouse of manufacturing and retail known across the world. North, South, West, Downtown. Take your pick from seventy-seven diverse and distinct neighborhoods, from Wicker Park to Hyde Park, Lincoln Square to Bronzeville. Shop on Michigan Avenue or Oak Street, or in the lovable shops in Bucktown. Foodies will enjoy grub from the whole world via Chinatown or one of a hundred-plus restaurants gathered on the West Side. St. Patrick's Day. The Crosstown Classic. Spend Friday night in the Theatre District or hearing live jazz and blues in Uptown. Visit one of Chicago's sixty-plus world-famous museums or catch one of its ten orchestras. Lake Michigan's bike paths, beach volleyball, and inebriated whirlyball battles. Blackhawk fever, Soldier Field, White Sox vs. Cubs. And so on.

Chicago is no "Second" city to us. It's "The" city.

And we're dang proud of you.

(Now, a little wave on the road every now and again wouldn't kill you FIBs, would it?)

Lights, Camera . . . Corn!
10 Movies to Watch After *Fargo*

Need a crash course in Midwest life for an upcoming trip to Dubuque, or perhaps you're a native feeling a little homesick? Here's some flicks you can check out to go with this book. The Coen brothers (born and raised in St. Louis Park, Minnesota, a suburb of Minneapolis) have set many of their films in the heartland and crafted the gold-flannel standard with *Fargo*, forever capturing the perfect blend of Midwest snow, talking through your nose, and wood chippers. After you've given that one a look, make a big bowl of puppy chow or grab a bag of BBQ chips from Guy's Snacks or Lutz's and plop down for another Midwest classic. As a proper study guide, included are all the MBCs (Midwest Basics Covered) and the MMM (Most Midwest Moment).

Purple Rain

Ordinary kid from Minnesota works hard to make his music dreams come true. **MBC:** ~~Velvet pants, cravats, and silk ruffle shirts.~~ Great local bands, dressing in layers, scarves, empty downtowns after six P.M. **MMM:** The most Midwest first date: "You have to purify yourself in the waters of Lake Minnetonka."

The Rider

Brady Jandreau is a Lakota Sioux cowboy who suffered a traumatic brain injury riding in the rodeo. His real-life story became the plot for *The Rider*, which was filmed on the Pine Ridge Reservation in South Dakota. It's best to watch this movie in spring so you can say "Geez Louise, something must be bloomin'" when you're crying your face off. Nobody will believe you, but it's customary. **MBC:** Ignoring doctor's advice. **MMM:** Removing your own surgical staples with buck knife.

Super 8

Five years *before* the *Stranger Things* kids were dealing with aliens and government cover-ups in Hawkins, Indiana, a group of Ohio kids dealt with the same in J. J. Abrams's Spielberg ~~rip-off~~ homage *Super 8*. Fun fact: while both stories *seem* to be set in the 1980s, they're actually both set in present time. **MBC:** Sidewalks, politely declined dinner invitations, local shops on Main Street, kids nostalgically riding bikes without helmets, a cop in the family. **MMM:** Having your plans thrown off by a passing train.

Barbershop

A Chicago man sells his barbershop, only to realize how much it really meant to his neighborhood. **MBC:** Money doesn't make you rich, people do. **MMM:** Accidentally leaving the bumper to your pickup truck behind after a botched towing job.

Escanaba in da Moonlight

A middle-aged Michigander (played by Michigan native Jeff Daniels) must bag his first deer or risk being the oldest person in his family's history not to have a buck notch. Captures the spirit of Opening Day and time spent with family and booze in the woods. "It's like Christmas, with guns": the brother encapsulates so much of the Midwest in just five words. **MBC:** Plaid, outhouses, drinking deer urine, group cabin sleep destroyed by that one guy/gal who snores/farts all night. **MMM:** Getting plenty done in only long johns and a good hat.

Field of Dreams

Guy builds a baseball park in his Iowa cornfield and is haunted by ghosts. **MBC:** Playing catch with dad, hearing weird stuff while in the corn, choking on a hot dog, good-looking men. **MMM:** Locals openly mock the main character for not being good at yard work.

The Wiz

The Wheat State and Motown combine to share the whole Midwest in one story. **MBC:** Disorienting snowstorms, faithful hardy dogs, great music, making new friends easily, long travels. **MMM:** Original musical's Kansas setting yanked to New York City for movie.

Road House

Local tavern owner in Missouri hires a consultant to improve customer service. **MBC:** A dress that was once a picnic table cover, McMansions directly next to farms, mullets that totally work, reading James Harrison. **MMM:** Neighbors unite to murder town bully, then chuckle about it.

Cedar Rapids

A Wisconsin insurance agent who's never stayed in a hotel or flown in a plane is chosen to represent his company at a convention in the big city . . . Cedar Rapids. **MBC:** Knowing the airport's only TSA agent by name. **MMM:** The out-of-focus pool boy is also the host of the *Manitowoc Minute*.

The Blues Brothers

They're on a mission from God. After Jake Blues is released from prison, he and brother Elwood get the band back together in order to save their childhood orphanage. **MBC:** Not paying 116 parking tickets, helping friends, utter appreciation for the Queen of Soul. **MMM:** Jumping an open drawbridge in Chicago to demonstrate the power of a Dodge Monaco.

Grumpy Old Men

Neighbors in Minnesota torment each other passive-aggressively for decades and then fight over visiting redhead. **MBC:** Grudges that last thirty-plus years, shoveling snow, talking about love in a bait shop. **MMM:** Attempted aggravated assault with a frozen walleye.

Twister

Okay, so it's set in Oklahoma, and only Midwest-adjacent, *but* not since Dorothy has a film captured the unique delight of foolishly storm chasing or waking up a visiting in-law in the middle of the night to say, "We need to get down into the basement now. Like, *right now*! Come on, it'll be fun . . ." The United States averages more than twelve hundred tornadoes a year, more than any other country. The Midwest—with a respectful nod to the kings in Texas—accounts for half of them. **MBC:** Total disregard for storm safety, pickups. **MMM:** Passing cow while driving (even one soaring through the air) and reflexively having to say "cow" out loud.

Planes, Trains and Automobiles

Bears fan wants to fly straight from New York to Chicago and skip all that crap in between. Instead, he's forced to drive from Wichita, Kansas, to Jefferson City, Missouri, and St. Louis before finally heading north to Chicago. It's like Dante's *Inferno* without the poetry. **MBC:** Long drives, ice scrapers. **MMM:** Customer service turkey call.

The Revenant

Non-bears fan wants to find his friend in the Dakota woods. (Even when being mauled to death, still sneaks in the SKOL chant; respect.) **MBC:** Snowy breath, grit, lots of trees, playfully catching snow on the tongue, great bear story. **MMM:** Goes full tauntaun with a horse to survive a blustery night.

Hoosiers

Locals support the high school sports team. **MBC:** Locals supporting high school sports team, making out in the woods in a knit hat, old school is still the best school, being suspicious of new guy for most of the school year, actually knowing the name of the high school basketball coach and/or caring, backboards attached to sides of barns. **MMM:** Jimmy Chitwood says, "I'll make it." Does.

Honorable Mentions: *The Music Man, Children of the Corn, The Bridges of Madison County, Tommy Boy, My Friend Dahmer, Reindeer Games, Ordinary People, Meet Me in St. Louis, Abraham Lincoln: Vampire Hunter, Heathers, A Christmas Story, Rudy, Superman* (1978 version), *The Wonderful Wizard of Oz* (1910 version), *Starman, Wayne's World, A Nightmare on Elm Street 3: Dream Warriors, Grosse Pointe Blank.*

Also check out Vision Maker Media: Hollywood has typically fallen well short of accuracy in films about Indigenous Peoples in the past, but Vision Maker Media (based in Lincoln, Nebraska) supports, funds, and streams Indigenous-made films. They even do a Halloween film fest! Check them out real quick once (visionmakermedia.org).

The Best Midwest TBR Pile

Billboards along any Midwest highway can provide miles of light reading. But for those of you looking for plot points beyond "Hell is Real," "Jesus Saves," "Cheese and Moonshine," and "Adult Super Store Next Exit," we've got you covered. Here are a few books about the Midwest or by Midwesterners to distract you from the bucks passing by your deer stand:

Giants in the Earth by Ole Edvart Rølvaag. A family that drags out its vowels and adds "cha" to every fourth word does yard work and struggles through snowstorms from October through April. (And don't miss the sequel, *Peder Seier*, in which Beret understandably goes crazy and locks herself in a trunk. The seas of grass are neverending and Midwest isolation sometimes gets the best of us. Fortunately, people of the plains are . . . resolute and resilient.)

Drive: The Story of My Life by Larry Bird. The classic tale of a Midwesterner who grows up in small-town Indiana, goes to college in Indiana, gets a job in the East for a while, and moves back to Indiana.

The Westing Game by Ellen Raskin. This slim, compelling mystery could be found in every fifth-grade classroom library from 1978 to 2005 and may yet be there today. Set in a high-rise tower on the shore of Lake Michigan, just north of Milwaukee, the mystery pits parent against child, husband against wife, stranger against stranger—all for the fortunes of a paper tycoon, presumably one who made his fortune in the Fox River Valley. It is remembered fondly for its vast, rich palette of characters and for teaching legions of fifth graders all the words to the first verse of "America the Beautiful." *May God thy gold refine.*

The Lakota Way by Joseph M. Marshall III. Sicangu Lakota Sioux member Marshall blends history, folklore, and memoir to write about how we are supposed to live in the world. In personal, accessible essays that redefine history, Marshall writes about each of the Lakota qualities: humility, perseverance, respect, honor, love, sacrifice, truth, compassion, bravery, fortitude, generosity, and wisdom.

Mudbaths and Bloodbaths: The Inside Story of the Packers-Bears Rivalry by Gary D'Amato and Cliff Christl. Like *The Odyssey* and *The Aeneid*, this one tells a story of ancient history: a time when the Packers and Bears had a competitive rivalry. Written in 1997 (before Favre in purple, 4th and 26, and da rise of da Rodgers), the story chronicles every late hit, eye gouge, and missing tooth that marked the inglorious and frequently lopsided rivalry.

American Gods by Neil Gaiman. Speaking of ancient history, *American Gods* tells a story of a group of all-powerful and forgotten gods who scheme to maintain their own immortality after being threatened by new gods. A pivotal and unforgettable scene set in Spring Green, Wisconsin, might make this the grandest version of a story even older and grander than Thor and his hammer: the story of some Midwestern transplants with chips on their shoulders, afraid of being passed over.

Sugar Man: The Life, Death and Resurrection of Sixto Rodriguez by Craig Bartholomew Strydom and Stephen "Sugar" Segerman. A worthy companion to the 2012 documentary *Searching for Sugar Man*, this book chronicles one of Motor City's most famously overlooked singer-songwriters, Sixto Rodriguez. A Dylanesque poet of the workingman, crusader against the establishment, and weaver of sad, transcendent tales of grit and redemption, Rodriguez tried nobly to ignite a career that ended up being a B-side to the more bankable, danceable, and iconic styling of Motown. But the story didn't end there.

The Audacity of Hope by Barack Obama. The inspiring story of a Bears fan who ran for president just so he would know what victory felt like.

The Great Gatsby by F. Scott Fitzgerald. A polite guy from Minnesota moves to New York City to try and make some money. He connects with some old family and friends, who hang out with him because he's too nice to say anything rude about them, and he ends up listening a lot. He makes friends with another polite guy from North Dakota who has become very wealthy with the help of some friends from Detroit and Chicago and who frequently has people over to his house for hors d'oeuvres and supper club drinks.

The Clubhouse Mysteries series by Sharon Draper. For younger readers, a group of friends in Ohio go on various adventures of exploration and mystery and history. Adults, like most kid adventures in the Midwest, are optional at best.

More Midwest Manuscripts!

The Bridges of Madison County (Robert James Waller), *A Map into the World* (Kao Kalia Yang, illustrated by Seo Kim), *The Round House* (Louise Erdrich), *Murder on the Little Oconomowoc River* (Agatha Christie), *A Thousand Acres* (Jane Smiley), *You Can't Win Them All, Charlie Brown* (Charles M. Schulz), *Tom Sawyer, Detective* (Mark Twain), *Where the Sidewalk Cracks* (Shel Silverstein), *Where's Waldo? Cornfields IV* (Martin Handford), *The Bluest Eye* (Toni Morrison), *O Pioneers!* (Willa Cather), *American Dervish* (Ayad Akhtar), *Rez Life: An Indian's Journey Through Reservation Life* (David Treuer), *Broom of the System* (David Foster Wallace), *The Ope in Our Stars* (John Green), *The Beautiful Ones* (Prince), *The One-Room Schoolhouse* (Jim Heynen), *The Cat in the Camouflage Yukon Tracks TrueTimber Alaskan Fur Hat* (Dr. Seuss), *Winesburg, Ohio* (Sherwood Anderson), *Little Second House in the Big Woods* (Laura Ingalls Wilder), *Choose Your Own Adventure: $20 at the State Fair* (H. R. Pufnstuf), *The Road Home* (Jim Harrison)

"Midwest Nice" . . .

There are nice people everywhere, but the American heartland has always had its own special brand. And understanding this is the key to understanding where the Midwest is . . . existentially. It goes far beyond just saying hello to everyone you pass at Walmart or apologizing sincerely when someone steps on *your* foot. In these very special states, we also say hi to the stranger two stalls down in a public restroom. And, if a friend-of-a-friend mentions he's catching a flight to Dallas, and you're driving from Madison to Chicago that same day, it's not out of the question to offer him a ride to Texas because it's "on the way."

This is why "Midwest nice" is an expression recognized and ratified across the world. People from Miami to L.A. know what to expect when you say you're "from the middle" of America. Think about a few of the Midwest's biggest ambassadors: Captain James T. Kirk (Riverside, Iowa), Steve Urkel and Carl Winslow (Chicago), Dorothy Gale and Clark Kent (Kansas), The Fonz (Milwaukee), Tia and Tamera Landry (Detroit), Leslie Knope (Pawnee, Indiana), or even Jack Dawson (Chippewa Falls, Wisconsin). Minnesota alone has Bullwinkle J. Moose; Charlie Brown; Gatsby's only real pal, Nick Carraway; and Mary Tyler Moore. Nice folks, right? Kind. Sharing. Hardworking. Quick with a genuine smile. An "aw-shucks" innocence that borders on foolish but still proudly plagiarizes from the

Dalai Lama: *Be kind whenever possible; it is always possible.* As if, in twelve states, millions of people are still living in some kind of colorized Frank Capra movie. (Pleasantville—by the way, if you know the movie—is a real place in Iowa.)

But these small acts of gratefulness, courtesy, and thoughtfulness are the oil that make the Midwest engine run smoothly. Speaking of cars, there are horns in Midwest cars, but they're really only used to give a double toot and a wave to the Johnsons.

If you take a Midwesterner out for dinner, you might already be seated and ordering while your date is *still* holding the restaurant door for total strangers. Two grown men will politely debate for six minutes who should take the last deviled egg. The intersection of a four-way stop sign can sometimes take half an hour to get past as all four drivers wave each other on and then laugh because everyone waved at the exact same time, and then all four restart the whole routine. (Cars have run out of gas doing this.) If a guy in Indianapolis has got a couple free hours between taking a pal to the airport and helping a coworker move, he might be cutting the neighbor's lawn because he already had the mower out anyways. A proper Minnesotan will help paint a friend's house for five hours, even volunteering for ladder duty, and then she'll apologize for not staying longer.

There can be, of course, consequences for all this niceness. Loans you'll never get back, missed opportunities, some heartbreak, hours and months spent doing things you really didn't want to do. But it's always worth it. Midwesterners love to be nice and help others because it's ~~what gets you out of Purgatory quicker~~ what makes us truly happy.

Practice Makes Perfect

It helps to be born directly into it, so you're learning "nice" from the very start via osmosis. From the Midwest doctor who first yanks you free from the womb to your third grade teacher, you'll be enclosed in a seamless cone of niceness that should provide all the patterns and real-world examples you need to get the swing of things by the time you're eight.

However, if you're not born here, these skills can also be acquired over time (years, usually, but still quite doable) with preparation, patience, and practice. Just like learning a new language, there are several things you should be doing to help develop your emergent "nice" skills:

1. **Buy this book, but tell everyone you got it on sale.**

2. **Hold doors. Especially when the person you're holding the door for is half a mile away.**

3. **Make flash cards with the following words and phrases: Ope. Sorry. Geez. Can I sneak right past you? Sorry. And yes, sorry should be in there twice.**

4. **Remove Siri from your phone, download the iOpeS app.** It doesn't have Siri, but it does have Sheryl . . . Sheryl Lizinski.

5. **Read Irish drinking song lyrics.** Take notes.

6. **Apologize to every car that cuts you off.**

7. **Apologize to your car when you run over a pothole.**

8. **Creative writing.** Rewrite *The Godfather*, but imagine Vito Corleone was brought up in Sheboygan.

Of course, the ultimate key to achieving Midwest nice is to recognize and harness the core values behind, or beneath, the "nice." These values are the enduring and rock-solid foundation upon which the nice, and our deserved reputation for it, is built. Now, like all our roads, these values will crack and develop potholes now and again—but, our sense of tradition and community and spiritual guilt will quickly descend like a sixty-person work crew to repave right away. Lock these steps down and the only thing left to say is "sorry."

TRUE MIDWEST STORY #1: "THE SHAKEDOWN"

I was in Wisconsin doing a comedy show at the Fond du Lac Fairgrounds. Now look, I'm not trying to brag, but I sold enough tickets to switch venues from the Cow Palace to the Rec Center. And, they rewarded me with my own private bathroom! At intermission, I had to go dehydrate the jerky and headed to my five-stall Taj Mahal. Wouldn't ya know it, the men's public restroom had a line so long it could catch a lake trout. (I guess a lot of folks were tying one on.) So I did the Midwest nice thing and I opened "my" bathroom to the public. I approached the urinal like Aaron Rodgers approaches the line of scrimmage: a man on a mission. But then I get asked for a selfie. So I called an audible, zipped it up, and says "Cheese!" Well, before I knew it, the whole bathroom turned into a meet-and-greet nobody paid for. About five minutes into this, Grandpa Bob—who'd come to the show with Grandma Sue and their friends—walks into the crowded bathroom. He shook his head as he saw me taking pictures by the crappers. "Unreal," he said as he did his best Bart Starr to the third urinal on the left. I let him run the play and then I says, "You doin' okay over there, Grandpa Bob?" I accidentally blew his cover. Well, the gentleman in the neighboring stall turns and says, "Oh, you're Grandpa Bob?" And then this guy pulls up his free hand for a shake hello. Grandpa Bob obliged, put down his beer, shook the guy's hand, and gave a "How are ya?" midstream. The perfect Bart Starr audible. I was so proud. Because that's where I got it from. And Grandpa Bob probably got it from his grandpa before him. A long line of Midwesterners that dates back to the earliest hunters and gatherers, just happy to see another person in the woods. Anyways, the point of this story is that Midwest nice is a "be nice first, ask questions later" kinda deal. It knows no bounds . . . just like the guy who shook Grandpa Bob's free hand. And I wouldn't have it any other way. 🌽

The Midwest Values System: 5 Rules to Live By

1. **Apologize.** There is no "when in doubt" here; simply accept blame and seek forgiveness. The waiter brings you the wrong meal, *you* say sorry. (And, genuinely feel bad he has to go all the way back to the kitchen.) Another boat recklessly runs over your fishing lines, cup your hands together and give a loud and hearty *"Mmmyyyy baddd!"* Even when you did everything you could to avoid the situation and the other person is—by all conventional standards—the wrongdoer, still proceed as if the difficulties are/were your fault. Remember: You could *maybe* have done more to avoid them running off the road and into your house. Isn't that right?

2. **Help.** Midwesterners are among the most self-reliant people on the planet. It's a tradition that dates back to the Indigenous Peoples in the Midwest, whose self-made and self-sustaining attitude defines the Midwest we know today. What fun is fixing the shingles if you can't pull yourself up by your bootstraps . . . and watch YouTube videos until you figure it out yourself. That independence often spills over onto our neighbors' property. It doesn't matter if you know, or even *like*, this person. As the Iowans explain in *The Music Man*: "We can stand touchin' noses for a week at a time and never see eye-to-eye, but we'll give you our shirt and a back to go with it if your crops should happen to die." So help stain their other fence. Mow their lawn. Back their boat into the lake after they jackknife it for the third time. Doesn't matter if you've been neighbors for twenty years or are just now meeting in line at the Kwik Trip. Help and expect nothing in return. Help even though they'd never dare ask for it. Help because what the heck else are we here for.

3. **Be nice.** Just as they practice at the Double Deuce in Jasper, Missouri, it's nice to be important, but more important to be nice. Midwest guru Dalton (Patrick Swayze) explains it simply: "If somebody gets in your face and calls you a @@#***, I want you to be nice. Ask him to walk. Be nice. If he won't walk, walk him. But, be nice. If you can't walk him, one of the others will help you, and you'll *both* be nice." You may be fuming on the inside and/or detest the person you're interacting with, it doesn't matter. Dig deep and find that "heartland smile"—the fake one will look exactly like the real McCoy—and say something pleasant. It's cold enough out here without the extra chill of your expressed hostility. Instead, bottle that anger deep in your heart to keep warm at night, treat yourself to another round, and maybe take it out on your dryer the next time it leaves your slacks a little damp.

4. **Work hard.** Whatever you want to call it—resolve, grit, grind, diligence, hard work, stubbornness, Midwesterners have a stick-to-itiveness and drive recognized around the globe. Starts when you're around three years old and need to help shovel clear the driveway all day, only to discover that, during the night, another nine feet of snow appeared and it starts all over again. It's how Greek gods used to punish each other. Over time, you come to accept that there's always more snow to shovel, ice to scrape, leaves to rake, fish to clean, Kroger bags to carry. Eventually you'll even *embrace* the struggle. It's what makes our backs strong and time on the couch at the end of the day so much better, and it lays the foundation for a fierce and powerful tenacity for when the real crap hits life's fan.

5. **Keep your word.** Missouri may be the Show Me state, but the whole Midwest is the Show Up state. If you said it aloud, do it. If you make a commitment, keep it. If you promised the gang fried catfish, you noodle until your arm feels funny. There are no "something suddenly came up" opportunities here. If you're not showing up for something you promised, you better have a first child to show for it. Second child won't cut it.

Quiz: What Would/Should You Do?

Below are a series of social scenarios you will likely find yourself in while in the Midwest. For each, provide your best guess for how to adequately handle the situation. You'll find the answers below.

1. You're at Target on a Saturday night and notice someone deliberating aloud to themselves between two cans of cream of mushroom and cream of chicken.

a. Suggest they use both and then text them your favorite hot dish recipe.

b. Quickly move to another aisle and avoid eye contact.

c. Hold the two cans behind your back and make them choose a shoulder.

2. A family of deer is making a ruckus in your garage late at night. You:

a. Flash the garage lights and shoo them away.

b. Nudge past them to get to the dehydrator.

c. Tell them they get "just one night" and back the car out so they have more room.

3. You purchase a bratwurst-studded Pac'n'Cheese at Lambeau Field and drop it on the way back to your seat. You:

a. Scoop it up as best you can and toss it out; head back to chair hungry.

b. Get back in line and buy another—*and* another beer in celebration of you.

c. Scoop it up as best you can and head back to your chair with a bratwurst-studded Pac'n'Cheese; buy another beer in celebration of you.

4. You're at a party and the bonfire needs more wood. You say you'll go grab some but find the woodpile is surrounded by several belligerent coyotes. You:

a. Bypass the woodpile and find a tree to chop down.

b. Grab some logs anyway and invite the coyotes to join the party.

c. Come back empty-handed; watch the fire die out.

5. You're getting a cup of Joe at Caribou Coffee and the guy in front of you is angrily shouting: "You're the worst barista ever!" You:

a. Tip extra to make up for his behavior.

b. Assure the man everything will work out and then offer to pick up his coffee.

c. Ask what a barista is.

6. Your friend is moving for the fourth time in a year. You've already helped the previous three moves. She refuses to use a moving company or rent a U-Haul and she owns a piano, four kitchen tables, and more than ten thousand books. As usual, she is not at all packed when you arrive. You:

a. Hire a moving company for her.

b. Block her calls and texts the day of the move.

c. Help pack, wrench your back, make seven trips to the new place, and apologize for not having a bigger car to more safely carry the piano.

Answers: 1. a, 2. c (b *also* acceptable), 3. b or c, 4. a or b, 5. c, 6. c (a is no good, you know they'll never do as good a job as you will)

Famous Midwest Arguments

Yes, we may have just established that "Midwest nice" is a very real thing, but that doesn't mean arguments won't break out now and again, on anything from fish-frying techniques to which team should rank fourteenth in the Big Ten. Recognizing and understanding these conflicts is a big part of Midwest acuity and sophistication. From Ogallala to French Lick, here are the top six heartland squabbles you'll need to be aware of, and enough information to maybe even choose a side.

1. Hot Dish vs. Casserole

Meat. Cheese. Sauce. Starch. And vegetables . . . if you're trying to prove something. Put it in a dish that can serve twenty. Or two, for a week. Who could possibly argue about such a perfect example of humankind's capacity for awesomeness? Lots of people, it seems. What to call this scrumptious concoction, and which of the two is better, has been hotly debated for centuries. If you're thinking "hot dish, casserole, what's it matter?" then you've clearly never called it a casserole in front of one of those hot dish zealots. It matters because these one-dish meals are frequently served at family reunions, church potlucks, bridal showers, sobriety checkpoints, graduation parties, wakes, bar mitzvahs, fantasy-football drafts, bingo nights, office Christmas parties, sorority mixers, euchre tournaments, Thursday night team dinners, and union strikes. Confucius, who never made it to Minnesota, said, "The beginning of wisdom is to call things by their proper name."

While the words *hot dish* and *casserole* are often used interchangeably, there *is* traditionally a difference between the two: Usually, **casseroles** are cooked uncovered and use white meats (chicken, tuna, fish) and get their carbs via pasta, rice, or pumpkin. Usually, a **hot dish** is cooked covered and uses the red meats (beef, pork, Bambi) and typically gets its carbs via various forms of potato (see: Backer's potato chips, hash browns, tater tots, and so on). The casserole binds with flour, stock, wine, cider. The hot dish gets baptized in gallons of cream of mushroom soup, creamed corn, and so on. Over time, cross-pollination has occurred, and a casserole maker in Fond du Lac will dump cream of broccoli all over their chicken and rice. And a hot dish wizard in Mankato will bake uncovered using beer, gin, and vegetable juice to get their venison bake just right. Thus, the confusion now on what to call this deliciousness. As far as which of the two *tastes* best . . . *de gustibus non est disputandum*; it's an argument that will never be settled, and doesn't need to be.

2. Who's on Top? Tots vs. Cornflakes

Another casserole/hot dish argument. (Told you it was an important dish.) This one focuses entirely on the best way to top your masterpiece. Above all that meat, carbs, cheese, and juice goes, believe it or not, one more reason to live—a crispy top shelf for some extra salt and crunch. Breadcrumbs, tortilla strips, potato chips, crushed nuts, cornflakes, granola, Red Hot Riplets, pumpkin seeds, croutons, chow mein noodles, French's fried onions, Ritz crackers, Rice Krispies, caramel popcorn, rolled oats, bacon bits, riced cauliflower, flavored Pringles, Mikesell's Spicy Dill Pickle Chips, or *another* layer of tots. We could do this all day, and often do. You never know until you try. In this argument, everyone's a winner.

3. The Mitten State: Michigan vs. Wisconsin

Michigan and Wisconsin have long argued over which state looks more like a mitten. Now, you're probably thinking, *This is exactly what happens when we legalize da weed*, but these arguments date back to the late 1800s. Seemingly a moot squabble, as Michigan is commonly called the "Mitten State" (mostly by people from Michigan), and if you ask a Michigander where they're from, they'll actually often use their hand to show you where Saginaw is. Strong argument. *But what if you live in Sault Ste. Marie?* Then, what do you point at? The air somewhere about three inches past your pinkie finger? Michigan has that whole Upper Peninsula to explain, an area that makes the full state look *nothing* like a mitten. Wisconsin, meanwhile, is fully contained within the shape of a hand and would also serve you well on a snowy winter's day. Thus, the debate continues.

(Later, we may need to address the "Which State Looks More Like a Cutting Board?" argument. Hint: Kansas, North Dakota, and South Dakota are deeply involved.)

4. Who Has the Most Lakes? (Size Matters . . .)

When you live ten or more hours away from the nearest ocean, lakes take on an importance all their own. Lakes are where you swim, ski, fish, play hockey, ice-fish, and boat. Possibly all in the same week. Minnesota, in this regard, is known far and wide as the "Land of 10,000 Lakes." It's even on their license plates. They've actually got 11,842 lakes and are being modest about it to not rub in their lake supremacy. *But hold on der*, says Wisconsin. *We've got 15,000 lakes!* And Michigan says: *Hang on now both of ya, don't go putting extra curds in your Bloody Mary just yet. We've got 11,000-plus lakes **and** twenty-five million acres of lake* (twenty-two million more than Minnesota, thanks to some help from the Great Lakes), *which would plunge half of Minnesota underwater.* Interesting arguments, but, as Midwesterner Mark Twain coined: "There are three kinds of lies: lies, damned lies, and statistics." Minnesota counts a lake as a body of water ten acres or more that's full all year. Wisconsin counts basically anything as a lake; most are far smaller than ten acres (for you Minnesotans, that converts to twenty-seven hockey rinks), and 60 percent aren't even named. They even consider ponds you can jump over with a good running start and a couple of Schlitz. Using Wisconsin criteria, Minnesota would have more than twenty thousand lakes. (But we don't recommend you do that, Minnesota, because then you'd have to name them all, and that's no easy task; just ask Wisconsin's Random Lake.) Using Minnesota's system, Wisconsin has only 5,898—not substantially ahead of *New Jersey's* 1,700. So we're declaring Minnesota the official winner in this essential matchup. As to Michigan's claims, which are chiefly associated with total acreage, sorry, no one cares; the Caspian Sea (a lake so big they misnamed it) is *ninety-one* million acres (enough to cover *all* of Michigan), and no cares about that fact either.

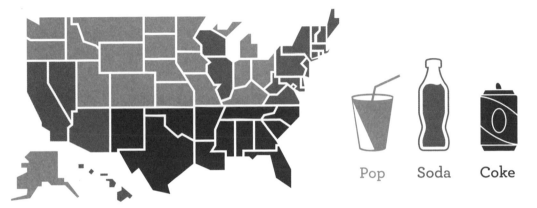

Pop   Soda   Coke

5. Soda vs. Pop

For decades, you could quickly uncover the Midwesterner by how they ordered their carbonated sugar water: "I'll have a pop, please!" Clearly someone from Aberdeen, Indiana, or even Chicago. In contrast, folks from the coasts generally go with "soda" and southerners lean toward "coke," a nod to soft-drink titan *Coke* based in Atlanta. Simple enough. However, in the twenty-first century, it's getting a little syrupier to tell who's who. There are now Midwesterners who swear they've *never* once called their soft drink a "pop" and get offended by any suggestion otherwise. A study was conducted that shows where the special pockets of "soda" Midwesterners dwell. (Special thanks to Matthew Campbell and Professor Greg Plumb of East Central University in Oklahoma.) Just clip this map out and keep it on hand and you'll know what to safely order. When in doubt, just say "soda pop" and count the blank stares.

6. Who to Root For

Speaking of carbonated sugar water, centuries before the European settlers, Indigenous Peoples were using sassafras root to make water more delicious. It also had, it was believed, medicinal purposes and was later sold as syrup by pharmacists for that purpose. In 1875, pharmacist Charles Elmer Hires was the first to successfully market a commercial root tea but called it "root beer" to interest his target audience: coal miners. More than a hundred years later, the blarney over the "best root beer" in the land continues: BuckSnort (Idaho), Sprecher (Wisconsin), Stewart's (Ohio), Tree Fort (Minnesota), Dad's (Indiana), Lost Trail (Kansas), and Frostop (Ohio) top the list but there are dozens to choose from.

7. Cheap Beer

Miller Lite, Bud Light, Busch Light, PBR, Coors, Schlitz, Hamm's, Red Dog, Milwaukee's Best, Natty Light, Blatz . . . (No, this isn't a grocery list.) To some, these may all sound the same. But to a Midwesterner, each of these "reasonably priced" beers offers its own marginally identifiable taste *and* identity. There's no wrong answer when it comes to which beverage you decide to make your go-to . . . unless you pick a hard seltzer. (For more, you'll find a helpful brew guide in Chapter 9!)

Midwest History

2,462,000 BCE to 650,000 BCE—On the Rocks

Giant glaciers say "Let me squeeze right past you der" and move over a continent, flattening every mountain in their path, creating thousands of lakes of various sizes, and establishing a chill in the air that's still freezing pipes and hearts today.

13,004 BCE—The First Midwesterners

Tribes like Kickapoo, Sac, Potawatomie, Ottawa, Ojibwe, Illinois, Huron, Dakota, and Sioux made the Midwest their home. They've watched others come in and try to survive in the land. The newcomers need to be tough in order to make it long term. Two words: Big. Coats.

10,000 BCE

Two Indigenous hunters meet on an isthmus the Ho-Chunk Nation will later call "dejope," and that, MUCH later, a real estate developer will call "Madison." They spend the next three hours sharing recipe ideas, fishing lies, and fresh deer jerky. They both tell the other to tell their folks they says hi. Both agree to do so. Neither told the other's folks they says hi. (Learn more about the Ho-Chunk and other Indigenous Nations of Wisconsin at Wisconsin-firstnations.org.)

1144—The First Midwest Metropolis

Cahokia was a Native American city of 20,000-plus (a people today recognized as the "Mississippian culture") that thrived for centuries in what is now Illinois, just across the river from today's St. Louis. To put in some context, that's larger than *every* colonial city during the American Revolution and almost twice the population of colonial New York. Mass flooding, it seems, chased folks to other places in the 1300s.

1541—No Gold in Wichita

Spanish explorer Francisco de Coronado and a squad of five hundred-plus heads north up from Mexico pursuing rumors of cities of gold. He arrives in Kansas and is thoroughly disappointed.

1679—The "Michigan Triangle" Strikes Again

August 11, 1679, a top-line French shipping vessel, *Le Griffon*, vanishes somewhere in Lake Michigan and is never seen again. Not the first time or last for the lake to disappear things—though usually it only claims fishing poles, baseball caps, and E10 fuel. If you ever want to get away from it all, there's no need to travel all the way to Bermuda. Between Michigan and Wisconsin in an acute-angle triangle that covers a large portion of Lake Michigan and connects the three points of Ludington and Benton Harbor, Michigan, and Manitowoc, Wisconsin. Within this space, boats and airplanes have mysteriously vanished for hundreds of years. Ice is reported to fall from the skies on cloudless days; strange lights are seen. And, to really creep you out, they've recently discovered a Stonehenge-esque circle of stones at the bottom of the lake.

1767—Sweet Meat

How can you have any cinnamon roll if you don't eat yer meat? April 18 in Cape Girardeau, Missouri, young Walter Vesper defiantly grabs a cinnamon roll from the dessert plate before dinner has even begun. Hoping to teach him a lesson, his mother, Dorothy, forces him to eat dessert *with* his chili dinner. By the end of the meal, the entire family of fourteen has set the crackers and bread aside and are dipping cinnamon rolls into their chili bowls, and the Midwestern world is changed forever.

1810—Fowl Moves on the Dance Floor

The setting: Munich, Germany, on October 12 at the reception of King Ludwig I and Princess Therese of Saxe-Hildburghausen. Family, friends, and total strangers all stood in a circle and danced like chickens, a tradition that spread like Marek's disease across northern Europe and ultimately, via Scandinavian and German immigrants, directly into the American heartland. The current world record is seventy-two thousand people at the Canfield Fair in Canfield, Ohio. The "chicken dance" would remain the dominant dance move in the Midwest for the next 170-plus years; to be usurped in 1993 by the electric slide—still performed in bars from Goshen (Indiana) to Yankton (South Dakota), regardless of the decade or song actually being played.

1816—First Lay-down Loner

May 22, 1816, in Marquette, Michigan. Bathilda "Betty" Pflueger called hearts after being dealt the queen, king, ace, and both jacks in euchre's first-known lay-down loner. The quick four points won Betty and her sister the match, but turning over all her cards at once proved confusing to all, and her brother-in-law argued—for the next sixteen years, until he was killed by a moose—that doing so was "cheating" and that she'd actually *lost* two points.

1835—Michigan Declares War on Ohio . . . for Toledo

If you're not willing to lay down your life for Toledo, you just haven't spent any time there. In the spring of 1835, Michigan and Ohio decided it was a town worth fighting over. The Buckeye State brought six hundred heavily armed soldiers and Michigan arrived with a militia of a thousand-plus men. According to the ever-reliable historical source of Wikipedia, "the single military confrontation of the 'war' ended with a report of shots being fired into the air, incurring no casualties." I hate to be the one to say this, but "shots being fired into the air incurring no casualties" isn't called a war, it's called duck hunting. After the gunpowder smoke had cleared the field of battle, Ohio kept Toledo, and Michigan was *granted the entire Upper Peninsula* by the US government as a parting gift for their troubles.

1837—Watch and Learn

Oberlin College (Ohio) becomes the first university in the United States to formally declare students of all races welcome. Two years later, it was the first university to officially admit women.

1842—The Center of the World

Copernicus notably argued that Earth was *not* the center of the universe and was put in jail for the rest of his life. Meanwhile, Randall Wilmot proclaimed Trumball County, Ohio, was the "center of the world." Everyone was like, *Sure, okay, whatever.* The town Center of the World still exists today.

1864—The Midwest Torches Atlanta

As General Sherman and the Union forces marched into Atlanta in November, the majority of his one hundred thousand soldiers were from Ohio. Okay, Missouri was pro-Union and pro-slavery, *but* every other Midwest state sided with President Lincoln and the battle for a more unified and free nation.

1869—Threeways in the Oval Office

Ohio-born Ulysses S. Grant takes office March 4, 1869. Six of the next nine United States presidents will also be from Ohio.

1890—America's Roller Coast

The Griswolds may have gone to Wally World, but since 1890, more Midwest families have instead made the pilgrimage to the top of Sandusky, Ohio, for three-hundred-plus acres of whiplash, vertigo, and sunburn. The Cedar Point amusement park was converted from barracks built for Union soldiers who were prison guards for captured Confederates. The first attraction at the park was a water toboggan ride consisting of a ramp that launched riders into Lake Erie. (Please *please* bring that one back!) These days, the park features a world-record seventy-one different rides, including seventeen roller coasters.

1911—Turning Left at 75 MPH

When we think auto racing, we think the South, but let's not forget the "International 500-Mile Sweepstakes Race," first held at the Indianapolis Motor Speedway on Tuesday, May 30, 1911. For several years, the speedway mainly featured balloon races, but they soon decided cars might prove a better draw. Forty cars qualified that first year, mostly for their ability to maintain 75 mph on the straightaway. Still the premier racing event in the United States today, the Indy 500 pulled 60,000 spectators to its first race in 1911; the track now comfortably holds 230,000.

1918—Kenneth Steve Henson Is Born

February 14 in Thayer, Nebraska. A date and place to be revered and taught to every schoolchild in America. Thirty years later, this man would invent ranch dressing.

1945—Japan Attacks Nebraska

As World War II was wrapping up, Japan filled nine thousand balloons with hydrogen and tiny explosives and floated them eastward in an effort to create panic in the States. One got as far as Omaha and exploded on April 18 in a flash of light that most assumed were fireworks or farting cows.

1951—The Pot Roast Hash Cure

January 27, Sioux Falls, South Dakota. Greg Pedersen was fighting a massive hangover and decided to try breakfast at the new Bob Evans in town. His finger randomly landed on the listing for pot roast hash. He felt better within three bites and was heavily drinking again just ten hours later. Pedersen's miraculous cure would soon be shared with the entire world. (It *has* been suggested that Jonas Salk's vaccine, which came out only two years later, was partly inspired by Pedersen's gift to humanity.)

1995—For Those About to Rock

September 2, the Rock & Roll Hall of Fame opens in Cleveland to forever capture the raw sound and defiant spirit that epitomizes rock 'n' roll. Celebrated Midwest acts include Prince, The Supremes, Patti Smith, Bob Dylan, Buddy Red Bow, Chuck Berry, Alice Cooper, and more.

2021—*The Midwest Survival Guide* Is Published

Author Charlie Berens struggles over decision about best coupon to offer potential buyers.

To be continued . . .

The Language

Learning a new language is a lot like ice fishing. It's terrifying at first. But if you go ass over tea kettle enough times, eventually you get the hang of it. These days there are apps that make learning a new language even easier. Unfortunately, there's still no Babble for Yoopernese, Duolingo for Wisconsinese, or Rosetta Stone for Minnesotan. Not to fear. From ope-offs to the long Midwest Goodbye and every "uff da" in between, we've got you covered . . .

Saying Hello (Not As Easy As You Think)

Saying hello to a stranger often confuses, or even scares, a surprising amount of people. Apparently it's not big-city etiquette to wave at everyone you pass and compliment their electric scooter. But that's how Midwesterners are brought up. Eye contact, smile, wave. It's how you show your fellow man you're the kinda person who'd clean their gutters without asking. There are plenty of ways to say hi. When in doubt, here are a few winners:

Any of these or a variation is fine. The trick is to (a) act as if it's part surprise you just ran into someone (even if standing in a crowded supermarket or a Michigan State game) and (b) use it on *everyone* you pass. Total strangers, especially. When it comes to greetings, there are no strangers in the Midwest, just proudly strange people.

The Long *Goodbye* (Even Harder)

A respectable Midwest goodbye isn't complete without five attempts to leave, six beers, and a bag of fresh rhubarb stalks. It doesn't matter if you've spent the whole day together or will see each other again next morning or have a four-hour trip ahead of you. Spouses and significant others *not* from the Midwest may get furious for the first couple years but will eventually get the hang of things. (It'll help if they come from Italian or Latinx families—or are from Boston; basically *all* Catholics are good at this.) The Midwest children learn quickly: when Mom says "ten more minutes," it's only another hour, and they'll be pretty excited about leaving soon.

You must plan in advance and do the math. If you want to leave before midnight, start saying goodbye around 8:15 P.M. After that, it's a series of steps and social graces that take years of practice, or this easy step-by-step-guide. Clip it out or take a pic on your cell phone for future use.

The 12 Steps to Saying Goodbye

1. Announce Your Plan to Leave (Round 1) This is fake. No one, including you, yet believes it. Your sham pronouncement will, in fact, be completely ignored, as if you never even said it. That's okay. You still have to get it out there to formally start the full procedure.

2. Announce Your Plan to Leave (Round 2) Said more emphatically. For accent, you can tap your leg gently. (Save the *hard* slap for later.) Things you might say:

"Well, I s'pose it's about that time . . ."
"Welp . . ."
"All right, then . . ."
"Okay, well . . ."

The ellipses are everything here. It lets everyone know you plan to see them again and expect to spend another few hours. At this point you will be offered another beer, something to eat, a recipe from the kitchen, or to check something out in the basement.

3. Accept Invite to Stay for Another Coffee, beer, slice of rhubarb pie. It doesn't matter. Have another. Why? Because you have no choice, that's why. This has been predetermined by your creator. You say: "Okay, one more . . ."

4. Repeat Steps Two and Three The knee slapping should get stronger. You might even stand. The ellipses get shorter. Toss out some more absolute lines like "See you guys tomorrow" and "I'll tell Grandpa you says hi" and "We'll get you on the boat this year." Do this until you are standing up with your coat on. Remember: It doesn't count until you say "I'm going" *at least* three times, but not too quick, because that could be mistaken as rude. Whatever you do, don't let your host know how you really feel.

5. Refuse Gifts You will be handed vegetables, pies, gardening equipment, and old coffee tables. "I have plenty of _____ at home, thanks!" You will need to politely turn down recipes for whatever you just ate (Watergate salad, toasted ravioli, Scotcheroos, and so on). Locating those recipes will be impossible and likely lead to your host finding you another beer instead. If that happens, you'll be spending the night. This lasts two rounds. Stay strong. You'll still be in a coat, and it's getting warm. Whatever you do, don't take it off . . . or you may never put it on again.

6. Accept Gifts Third time. Agree. This is God's plan. "Guess someone's making a pie!"

7. Announce Your Plan to Leave (Round 3) This means shouting "Goodbye!" to those still in the house, out back, or who have snuck upstairs to sleep because it is well past midnight.

8. Stand in the Doorway and Talk for Another 20 to 30 Minutes This is where the *real* conversations will begin. Family scandal, medical issues, financial concerns, playoff hopes, and so on. It's the doorway that brings out secrets like: "Oh, did you hear about Uncle Gene and the thing with the cartel?"

9. Stand on the Porch and Talk for Another 30 to 40 Minutes Relax, you're doing great. You've gotten outside the house. Warm your hands for emphasis, rub your shoulders. Feeling bold, rub *their* shoulders. "Best get goin'" is a sign you might be freezing to death. If it's summer, say something to note your discomfort, like, "Ya know, it's not the heat, it's the humidity." Still, keep talking.

10. Stand in Parking Lot or Driveway and Talk Another 15 to 45 Minutes You can scream as soon as you get in the car and drive a block away.

11. Get in the Car and Talk for Another 15 to 45 Minutes You've gotten that coffee table stowed on the roof or in the back. Now you've got two options: car door open, using it to lean *on* casually while you talk or sitting *in* the car with the window down to let them (and yourself and your family) know you're serious about leaving.

12. Leave You did it. Graciously. You can't imagine spending one more minute with these people, but everyone involved now feels like they got the most of your time together. (Note: make sure you grabbed the rhubarb when you left or you'll have to go back in and start over somewhere around Step 3.)

"I'm gonna bring the Shop-Vac out here and clean out them cup holders, Bill."

Alternatives to Cuss Words

The Sopranos is not set in Kalamazoo. While the rest of the world got R-rated, the Midwest still has plenty of bars of soap on hand for those who can't take a little of that edge off when cut off in traffic or watching the football game or dropping a pumpkin on their foot or while voting. This is not some aww-shucks *shtick* (pronounced improperly as "stick" by many Midwesterners) but how people of all ages actually cuss. Not saying a good old "F word" doesn't come out every now and again, but you should make sure you're in trusted company before letting it fly. Some Midwesterners get a pass on dropping the F bomb. (For instance, in Wisconsin you're allowed to say F*** only when it's immediately followed by "da Bears"; you don't even have to confess it to Father Tom.) But, when in doubt, here are some legit alternatives to traditional profanity:

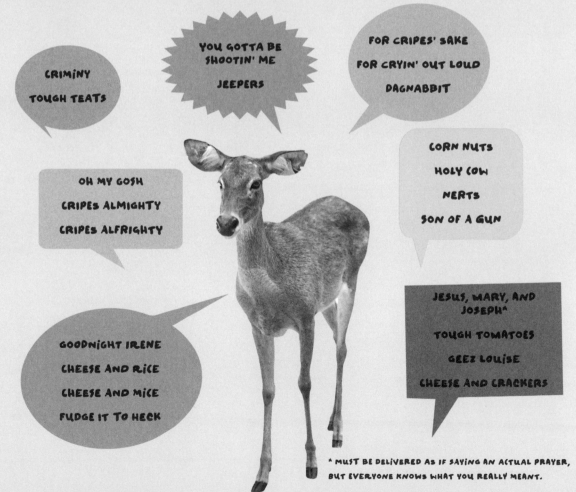

CRIMINY
TOUGH TEATS

YOU GOTTA BE SHOOTIN' ME
JEEPERS

FOR CRIPES' SAKE
FOR CRYIN' OUT LOUD
DAGNABBIT

CORN NUTS
HOLY COW
NERTS
SON OF A GUN

OH MY GOSH
CRIPES ALMIGHTY
CRIPES ALFRIGHTY

JESUS, MARY, AND JOSEPH*
TOUGH TOMATOES
GEEZ LOUISE
CHEESE AND CRACKERS

GOODNIGHT IRENE
CHEESE AND RICE
CHEESE AND MICE
FUDGE IT TO HECK

* MUST BE DELIVERED AS IF SAYING AN ACTUAL PRAYER, BUT EVERYONE KNOWS WHAT YOU REALLY MEANT.

Baby's First Words . . .

Fortunately, Midwest nice starts with very rudimentary language: *Sorry. Please. Thank you. Sorry.* We put sorry twice for good measure. Kids will start babbling these three words by the time they're six months old. They are the glue that binds all Midwest interaction and conversation.

"Sorry"—Someone once said, "Love means never having to say you're sorry," but that guy was from Brooklyn. (No, seriously. The author of *Love Story* was raised in Brooklyn and then learned about love at Harvard.) A proper Midwesterner says "sorry" fifty times a day, to the people we love and the people we just met. It's a great catch-all term with many nuanced meanings for almost any social situation (like *aloha* in Hawaii) and subtly covers all the modesty and decorum anyone could possibly need. Remember: when in doubt it's probably your fault, even when it's definitely not your fault. So ask the person you didn't wrong to please accept your apology. Then, thank the person for their understanding. If they're from the Midwest they'll reply with "Oh no, you're fine." If they're from anywhere else, they'll still be staring at you. (*See "ope" below for variation on "sorry."*)

"Please"—Said almost as often as "sorry"; over time, these two words have become almost interchangeable. (Example: You ignored what someone just said; merely say "Please" and they'll say it again. Reach for the same Pabst in the cooler there and say "Sorry!"; the other guy will hand it to you.)

"Thank you"—The mighty spirit at the center of the Holy Trinity of Midwestern courtesy. Our thank-yous include a hundred spoken options, from "That was real nice of ya" to "Jeepers creepers, ya shouldn't have" to "Oh . . . real good then." Beyond the words, one would need to travel to feudal Japan for something approaching the number of different ways to tangibly express appreciation. Pick up a friend's coffee at the gas station (note: they'll refuse the first four offers, just keep going); they'll likely come to your house the next day with a handwritten note and a fresh-baked cobbler. Now, in turn, you'll probably give them Grandma's secret casserole-and-cornflakes recipe and clean their gutters, and then they— And so on, for several weeks.

Special Phrases to Learn

"Ope"—When in doubt, Ope it out.

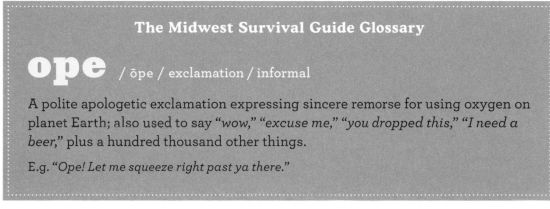

The Midwest Survival Guide Glossary

ope / ōpe / exclamation / informal

A polite apologetic exclamation expressing sincere remorse for using oxygen on planet Earth; also used to say *"wow," "excuse me," "you dropped this," "I need a beer,"* plus a hundred thousand other things.

E.g. *"Ope! Let me squeeze right past ya there."*

One of the most important words/sounds you'll need to know for playing nice in the Midwest is "Ope!" It's like a Harry Potter spell. You need to get down with O.P.E. (*Yeah, you know me.*) It's typically said with a combination of surprise and childlike naïveté. Yes, this is a strange sound coming from big bearded guys in flannel. But that's what always makes it so disarming and authentic. Here's everything you should know about this magic sound, in my ope-inion . . . sorry, I had to.

Pronunciation: Rhymes with rope or soap.

Part of speech: Noun, adjective, or verb? Yes.

Etymology: Middle English *opeswound*, from Old English *meopeswound*, from *me-* + *obbens*, to apologize; akin to Old English *obberbadden*, to act contrite for beer, from Latin *oparthos*, the name given by the Romans to the people who called themselves the Apologia Socraties, which according to Aristotle was the prehistoric name of the Dutch.

To use "Ope" in a text: ☺pe

Examples in Context

Someone cuts you off in traffic?
You: *Ope, sorry.*

You walk into the public restroom as someone's walking out?
You: *Ope, let me squeeze right past you.*

You order an MGD and the bartender brings you a White Claw?
You: *Ope, sorry. If I wanted this, I'd go to the bank, get one of those free suckers, and then dip it in a La Croix.*

Whoops, there it is!
You: *Ope, there it is!*

Oops, I did it again.
You: *Ope, I did it again.*

Your friend's ferret dies.
You: *Uff da! (trick question; more on this word on page 46)*

Where to use: Only in the Midwest.

Special rule to remember: We've all heard "I before E except after C"—in this case, it's "Ope before Sorry except after Geez." So, rather than "Geez, ope!, sorry," the proper order is always: "Geez, sorry, ope!" Make a notecard like you did for Spanish class and practice bumping into things.

Can You Match These Global Words of Apology?

Afrikaans	jagh yIbuStaH
Arabic	Sajnálom
Bosnian	Lo siento
Dutch	آسف
French	ごめんなさい
German	Oprostite
Greek	对不起
Japanese	Ope, sorry!
Klingon	désolé/désolée
Korean	Het spijt me
Mandarin Chinese	Es tut mir leid
Midwestern	Jammer
Spanish	Συγνώμη

˙If you really wanted to check your answers, sorry.

TRAPPED IN AN OPE-OFF

SEEN HERE MID-OPE WITH RYAN REUBL

I was walking through Wausau, Wisconsin, and this guy was coming directly toward me and so I tried to get out of his way, but then he went in the same direction, and so I says "Ope!" But then things got strange. The guy says "ope" right back to me at the exact same time. So I says "ope" back again. And he says "ope!" yet again. But I had to make sure he'd heard mine, so we did it all over again.

Yes, we were stuck in a classic Midwest Ope-off. I had no idea what to do. I tried switching to "Ope, sorry." We both did. Then I switched to "Can I squeeze right past you?" He had the exact same idea. This just kept going for hours, until he got bit by a rabid raccoon. To which I says, "Ope, we gotta get you to the doc's office."

uff da! / ōof duh / exclamation / informal

A common Midwest phrase typically used to express disbelief or dismay, but occasionally used to convey relief or a sudden shock to the senses; appropriate in any situation, however most often used after receiving bad news, especially as it pertains to sports, fishing, hunting, or family issues.

E.g. *"I just missed a 12-pointer in the stand but hit one on my way home in the Corolla!"* *"Uff da!"*

"Uff da!"—*The Catchall Howl Against Life*

When responding to the various slings and arrows of outrageous fortune, especially in the most northern states of the heartland, you may only need one single phrase to express your human condition: *Uff da*. An approach to life similar to the way many people attach themselves to patchouli or astral projection or flagpole sitting, it is the Uff-yang to da world's yin. It is the final and stout grumble of heroic surrender.

A wonderful phrase defined by expressing surprise, bafflement, dismay, relief, fatigue, or a sudden shock to the senses. In other words, *Uff da* means . . . everything. *Uff da* is like your NFL team's Zubaz, appropriate in any situation: wear 'em to work, to bed, to church. It's all good. In the same way, *Uff da* is appropriate in *every* situation.

Car won't start? *Uff da!*

You're making Bloody Marys and ran out of Worcestershire? *Uff da!*

Your mule dies in a snowstorm? *Uff da!*

Your mother, the queen, marries your uncle after only three weeks? *Uff da!*

Long day at work and collapsing into the couch? *Uff da!*

Stub your toe on a deer? *Uff da.*

A baby is being born? *Uff da!*

A baby is being made? *Uff da!* (Technically, the guy says *"Uff!"* and the gal goes *"daaa"* . . . but it still counts.)

Brought to the Midwest more than a century ago by Scandinavian immigrants, Norwegians today still use "huff" or "uff" as exclamations for "wow," "oh my!," or misfortune, and the Swedish *still* say "*ojdå*" when expressing "wow," "that sucks," or "oopsie." (Hint: any situation a Jewish person might say "Oy vey," *Uff da!* can be swapped in nicely.) It's an impeccable substitute for any profanity you might use in other parts of the country.

Now, imagine you've flown into Uff-Da Airport (a real airstrip in Stoughton, Wisconsin), then made your way to visit UffDa Fest! (an annual event in Spring Grove, Minnesota) and Uff Da Days (in Ostrander, Minnesota), and then the cherished Uffda Day Fall Festival (in Rutland, North Dakota), but you forgot to pack your favorite Zubaz. Yup, *Uff da!*

The Midwest Survival Guide Glossary

keep 'er movin'

/ keep er mōōvin / exclamation / informal

Both a metaphorical and literal phrase to convey a physical, emotional, or (especially if walleye are involved) spiritual movement forward; a Midwestern form of encouragement, mantra, or simple request.

E.g. If you're fishing and go ass over tea kettle because you stuck your foot in a walleye hole ya can't give up, ya gotta keep 'er movin'.

"Keep 'er movin'"

This is a philosophy. A mantra. A sacred utterance that captures the infinite and reminds Midwesterners "Life is short, but let's not dwell on it." The best way to fix it—whatever *it* is—is to keep 'er movin'. If you make the wrong decision (from stepping on thin ice to unwisely swiping right or joining a cult connected to aliens from Venus), life always has a way of guiding you back to the right path. But the only way that happens is if you keep 'er movin'. Don't overthink, don't fret too much, apologize when you need to, laugh when you don't. Moved to Seattle? Bought a pet anaconda? Told your boss the truth? Tossed a snowball at a moose? There are no wrong paths, just scenic routes. And *your* path will always reveal itself . . . as long as you just keep 'er movin'.

er no /er-noh / expression / informal

Derived from "or no"; a dependent clause often used by people from the Midwest to offer an alternative option to any question they ask; usually extends decision-making by at least fifteen minutes.

E.g. *"I got some extra perch in da freezer and a jar of pickled green beans from da garden for ya. You wanna stop by and get 'em, er no?"*

"Er no." [sometimes spelled "or no"]

You will find that many questions in the Midwest are followed by "Er no."

> You wanna go to the mall with me? Er no.
>
> I'm gonna send you home with these fish we caught. Er no.
>
> We should leave. Er no.
>
> I'm going to kiss you now. Er no.
>
> Would you please pass the salad bowl? Er no.
>
> Do you take this man to be your lawfully wedded husband? Er no.

It's essential the "Er no" is delivered as a statement, not as a second question. (That'd be pestering.) This implies your question has no wrong answer and that whichever option they select is perfectly fine to you. No feelings will be hurt. No damage done. You are a paragon of affability. Nothing proves this more than a two-word phrase that pledges an easy way out of anything you just proposed.

Rules for Speaking with a Midwest Accent

If you are a Midwesterner, you will be unreservedly shocked when someone suggests you have an accent. This is an outrage and a gross error in their comprehension and listening skills. Don't make a big deal of it; just laugh it off. So silly. You have no accent. The Midwest has no accent. And *Fargo* was a ridiculous Hollywood exaggeration. You speak "normal," and it would be impossible to imitate you. But in a pinch, the following rules can be used by outsiders to approximate the accent we don't have.

1. **Speak mostly through your nose and the top of your head.** Imagine your face doesn't exist below your upper lip. The area up top is where your spoken communication should come from. Your lower jaw should not ever move (you'll get too much snow in your mouth!). Push the words out from that space between your eyebrows and the top of your nose. Do this as if you had a terrible cold.

2. **Drop that "th" sound.** Your ancestors were too busy to pick up English's interdental fricative, and so are you. The word *think* is putting a lot of unnecessary heavy lifting and teeth tapping on your tongue. Ditto with *these*, *them*, and *those*. *Dees, dem, dos* takes half the effort and will get the point across just as well.

3. **Replace "still" with "yet."** This becomes a math problem: Drop the "still" and turn it into "yet," then move it to the end of the sentence. Example:

   Not Midwest: *She's still down at the lake.* **Midwest:** *She's down at the lake yet.*

4. **Add vowels whenever possible.** Elongate "cat" into "c-ea-t." "Bag" becomes something closer to "byeag." When in doubt, try and imitate a Boston accent; you'll fail but will probably land on a passable Minnesotan.

5. **Use Midwest lingo with confidence.** Unsure if you're using a phrase correctly? Use it anyway. Make something up. Odds are you'll be fine—and if you're wrong, no one would be rude enough to correct you. Don't take my word for it. Just ask the guy who started saying "screwed the pooch."

6. **Use spoken words only to be considerate or passive-aggressive.** Anything in between is a waste of your nose.

7. **Be unreservedly shocked** when someone suggests you have an accent.

Specific Tips for Guests from Other Regions

East Coasters: Slow down, calm down, lower your voice real quick (if you don't mind). You're scaring the cows. Treat your emotions like a moldy basement wall. Paint over it and hope for the best.

West Coasters: Good news! We *do* have sustainably harvested, grass-fed meat; it's in the back of the freezer marked "Venison—St. John's Meat Raffle." And *when* we say hello to you, remember that we're *not* trying to murder you. (But if we were, we'd also say "hello.") The main difference is there is no hidden agenda in what we're saying, so you can turn off your Bing Crosby "Everybody's got an angle" switch; there's no angle out here, only people trying to be genuinely polite and friendly.

Southern Charm: We're genuinely polite and friendly, but could you pick it up *just a little*? Endurance is forged in the cold and on the assembly lines. But so is/was a touch of impatience.

MILWAUK DA TALK

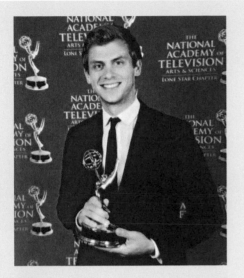

Figuring out you have an accent is kinda like a Lake Winnebago perch getting caught for the first time. Accents are like water; you have no idea you've been swimming in it your whole life until a fella in an XXL Packers hoodie, camo cargo shorts, and Crocs flops you into his boat. For me, that fella in the Packers hoodie was a broadcast news instructor.

This guy had one of those golden NPR voices we all hope for. "From NPR News in Washington, I'm going to judge you . . ."

Our first assignment was simple. Just write one paragraph to read off the teleprompter. I sat behind the anchor desk, and waited for my countdown. 3 . . . 2 . . . 1 . . . "In Maaaaynasha today, police pulled over a maaan from Ashwaubenon for not stapping at da stap-and-go light. He got arrested real quick once after police found weapons in his baaayyyyyyyyyyyg."

I looked over to my esteemed mentor with a proud grin on my face.

He wasn't smiling back. Instead he just stared at me with this pained expression . . . as if he'd just discovered a fresh hemorrhoid.

"Charlie," he said in that golden voice, "has anyone ever told you . . . you have a voice . . . for print?"

Then he walked over to the window and just stared out. "I can see your whole career right in front of my eyes." He was looking at the guy trimming the hedges.

So that's when I knew I had an accent. But my instructor's beautifully resonant emotional abuse did actually inspire me to find a voice coach. And word by word, phrase by phrase, I learned how to talk like a Cubs fan. I ended up getting some jobs in local news; even won an Emmy. But just because you change your accent doesn't mean your accent changes you.

I remember one hot day anchoring in Dallas, Texas. I encouraged viewers to make sure they find a bubbler. Many of you may refer to it as a water fountain. But for me, a water fountain is where I go to get change for the meter, so I just call it a bubbler. It's a Milwaukee thing.

Unfortunately, the rest of the country hears "bubbler" and thinks of the device one may use to partake in the devil's lettuce. I had an interesting conversation with my boss that night. Point being—you can leave home, but home will never leave you. 📣

The People

The Midwest is basically a big ol' hot dish of people from all over the world. From Indigenous Peoples to immigrants descending from Scandinavia, Ireland, and Germany. From the Great Migration of Black Americans northward and the Appalachian Migration from the east to our newer Midwesterners from the Middle East, Latin America, Africa, Asia, and everywhere in between—all these folks call the heartland their home. Each group has helped shape the culture here as they were brought together by the shared experiences of our unique landscape. It's a chicken-egg riddle. Did the Midwest land shape the people, or vice versa? After digging out from four feet of snow or surviving a deer stampede, maybe it's not such a puzzle after all. In any case, sixty-eight million people live here, and you'll soon find that no matter where we come from, how we got here, or when we started calling it home, there's a quality and way of life that's unique to the region. (Except for that one guy in Ames, Iowa. What's with him?) This next section will give you all you need to know to walk among the locals and even, I hope, become one yourself if you're not already!

Who You Will Meet . . .

From Swamp Angel, Kansas, to Watersmeet, Michigan, there are tens of millions of Mid-westerners with more personalities than I-80 potholes. That said, a few recurring characters tend to pop up every now and again. But this is far from something bad. In fact, it's kinda comforting when that Evansville taxidermist reminds you of Grandpa's fishing buddy from Oshkosh. It's a nice reminder that though we're all different, we all still double dip our onion rings in ranch. Just nod your head and pretend that analogy was profound while I list off a few personalities that perhaps you've encountered yourself.

The Big Fella (Bratwurstus Maximus)

This fella (who doesn't even have to be a fella) appears standoffish or even grumpy at first. But that's only because he's focused on making sure your brats don't burn. He's first to volunteer his grilling expertise for the Walleye Weekend concession stand or 4-H fundraiser at the State Fair. This guy's a giver. And few will make you laugh as hard, drink as much, or be as quick to re-shingle your roof if he notices a few got shook loose in last week's hailstorm. He's got his ear to the town and knows all the best gossip. But he'd never share it. Unless you bring him a beer. Then you'll get the scoop on how the Galanskis' sewage ended up in the Johnsons' basement.

Family: BYOB, That Guy Over There, people named Ray

Distinctive features: cargo shorts, belly, boat

Habitat: church festivals, tailgates, backyard cookouts, Supper Clubs, golf carts

Nesting: within fifteen miles of where they went to high school

Feeding behavior: bratwurst, grilled steaks, nationally advertised beers, *really* good scotch from someone else's liquor cabinet

Songs and calls: "Have another," "I ever tell you about . . . ," "I love you, man!"

Migration: Gulf Shores, Vegas, parents' lake house now shared with sibs

The Hunter *(Asleepis Treestandus)*

Vegetarian, they'll tell you, is an old Bavarian word for "terrible aim." Hunting season may only run from September through December, but for them, it's a year-round commitment. There's always another boat show (even if it's a five-hour drive away), a new pup to be trained, a fancy new duck call to try out, or some homemade jerky to be made. When in doubt, fishing is *always* an option. He got married in a camo tux with a blaze-orange tie and still doesn't regret it.

Family: backpacker, Sasquatch

Distinctive features: camo, blaze-orange, glove box full of expired season tags, smells of doe pee

Habitat: wandering in Fleet Farms; full range extends to one and a half tanks of gas or nearest open body of water

Nesting: tree stands, friend's 100+ acres

Feeding behavior: anything you can wrap in butcher paper and freeze; known to pull over, inspect roadkill, and roll the dice

Songs and calls: "Get downwind," "Just look at that rack," "That buck is a shooter for sure."

Migration: rotates seasonally among open bodies of water, public lands, and firing ranges

The Slugger *(Wannaplay Catchius)*

Often related to the Big Fish or the Hunter, she grew up playing sports, hunting, and feeding goats. When there was work to be done or a sixth player needed for a pickup game of backyard football, she was there—gear on and ready to go. Now, she still climbs, hikes, fishes, and is the best player on all of her company-sponsored sports teams. She doesn't just play fantasy football in a family league; she knows what college the local pro team's third-string TE went to.

Family: fantasy football organizer, gym rat, people who stretch

Distinctive features: a vast and diverse collection of knee braces, straps, sleeves, thumb supports, ice packs, painkillers, fading scars, and baseball caps

Habitat: hiking trails, tennis and basketball courts, sports bars, and backyards with soccer goals

Nesting: walking distance from stadium, apartment above Anytime Fitness

Feeding behavior: whatever can be hauled to the side of the soccer field or carted to the company picnic, provided there's enough room for the cleats and nets; expert-level players have multiple slow cookers and serving platters for an impromptu potluck over a mean game of cornhole

Songs and calls: "You're on," "Rub some dirt on it," "It's just hair."

Migration: wherever their team has Spring Training, Vegas for March Madness

The Transplant *(P&Gius Resumethis)*

Not raised in the Midwest but has moved here for career opportunities.

Family: workaholics, post-Boomers

Distinctive features: still uses a Franklin Planner, *WSJ* print subscription, framed portraits of the Chesapeake throughout house, unchanged cell phone number reveals area code not from the Midwest

Habitat: boardrooms, country clubs, local gym

Nesting: They congregate in preestablished nesting regions with other employees of their corporation, within easy reach of shopping, restaurants, and paved walking trails. The longer term their prospects of remaining in the area are, the bolder they become and the farther they will likely nest from their place of work.

Feeding behavior: any restaurant within sixty miles that's not a chain restaurant

Songs and calls: "I miss the ocean," "What a great place to raise a family," "I didn't really expect to stay, but . . . that was twenty years ago."

Migration: particularly known for lavish, short-term trips anywhere but here, then grateful recovery in a place where the cost of living won't blow their entire paycheck every month

The Big Fish *(Bigusfishush Smalluspondish)*

While "the Big Fish" glories in the down-home vibe of his Midwest city, this species presents in style, delivery, and mindset as if they actually are living and thriving in L.A. or Manhattan. To ever point this out would be rude and pointless. In *this* town, they're king of all they survey, even if this town is fourteen square blocks. After all, they *have* had dealings with the outside world and *have* crossed paths with the rich and famous. They *could* be a fifth fiddle in Miami or Seattle but choose to remain maestro of the Midwest. From social chairs and local philanthropists to small-town politicians and professors who genuinely seem to love their job, you will never meet anyone as hospitable or content.

Family: debutante, kingpin, grande dame

Distinctive features: half-finished bottle of sake in fridge, personal business cards, voguish glasses, unremitting and genuine smile

Habitat: Halloween parties, book launches, family reunions

Nesting: sensible home in suburbs

Feeding behavior: mixed cocktails with outlandish names; anything catered—they may even own a catering company, or be friends with the owner

Songs and calls: "I met him once," "You simply have to come join us at . . . ," "The grand opening is next week!"

Migration: frequent trips to any large social hub, for shopping, cultural experiences, and appropriation of outside experiences that can be later tailored to their local constituency

The Farmers' Marketeer (*Communis Plantus*)

While fairly quiet during the week, this species displays full plumage on the weekends, congregating in minivans full of home-canned goods or handmade jewelry, or truck beds stocked with fresh-picked tomatoes, green beans, and zucchini. May extend their natural attraction to DIY efforts and craft projects to include homeschooling and church volunteerism.

Family: granola, flower children, dude

Distinctive features: weathered skin slathered in a relatively new layer of mineral-based sunscreen, bright, clear eyes, big smiles; often accessorized by home-brewed kombucha and hemp bracelets, smelling faintly of honey

Habitat: farmers' markets, flea markets, rallies, and art fairs

Nesting: several acres "just outside" of town

Feeding behavior: hand-stuffed sausages, fresh vegetables, craft beer they got from a neighbor's homemade stash, fresh meat never treated with chemicals, bottled water

Songs and calls: "Try one," "I never get sick," "That rug really tied the room together."

Migration: same as habitat, but in cities/states outside their home range

The Returner *(Sempregohomeagain)*

They've worked in Chicago or Boston or London or Tokyo for decades but have now returned "home" again to raise a family or enjoy the golden years in a place where Mom met Dad and Aunt Minnie still hosts Labor Day parties and Super Bowl night. Formerly a major CEO or judge or journalist or network TV showrunner, they now run a small nonprofit or a local business and sit on several local boards. Differentiated from the Big Fish species in that they have very little patience for small-town politics.

Family: entrepreneur, 30 under 30, Most Likely To

Distinctive features: well-made clothes classic enough to weather being out of fashion, quietly luxurious brands and vehicles

Habitat: gated communities, historic home refurbished while back visiting coast, one of the four penthouses "downtown"

Nesting: a home with a view—of a river, a lake, or a wealthy neighborhood; have earned the right to live in the house of their long-ago dreams

Feeding behavior: eastside restaurants and country clubs

Songs and calls: "Let me make a call," "Interesting . . . ," "Good for you."

Migration: Travel to see their kids, who are them, but a generation younger, and take their parents to bucket list locations all over the world

The Urban Explorer *(Downtownus Gentrifices)*

They grew up in the suburbs but are now ready for life in the big city. No, not Chicago. More like downtown Wichita, or Dayton, or Fort Wayne—where the streets are alive late at night (at least on a couple blocks) and where friends, neighbors, and vaguely lost tourists are out peering at galleries still open past six P.M. or bellying up to the bar for a craft beer or a matcha tea latte. Coworkers are often surprised to learn members of this species live "downtown," and their invites to visit, try the new restaurant in the converted church, or do a paddle-wagon tour of the bar district are often politely ignored for years.

Family: hipster, bohemian

Distinctive features: fedora, beret, or tweed flat cap; comfortable shoes; thriftwear, or expensive clothes that look like thriftwear

Habitat: micropubs, rallies, obscure bar where friend's band is playing, anywhere they sell coffee

Nesting: small apartment above local business or converted row house with six roommates

Feeding behavior: cheap wine, expensive beers, espresso

Songs and calls: "Have you tried the new place on Vine?"

Migration: micropub crawls, nervous bike tours in Spain, urban farmers' markets

And, What They'll Be Wearing . . .

Fashion on the coasts is like a first-time sailor on Lake Michigan—blowing with the wind and capsized somewhere because they tripped over a Vera Bradley bag. On the other hand, fashion in the Midwest is like an anchor. And attached to that anchor is a fishing boat. And in that fishing boat are three people with plaid shirts, jacket layers, and jeans. The fish are biting and they're not going anywhere. And neither is their fashion.

If you're unsure how to dress in the Midwest, look no further than the notoriously fashionable Paul Bunyan. Regardless of gender, Paul Bunyan has set the gold standard for fashion in the Midwest—and I think that's something we should all strive for. Man, woman, or child. Beards and flannel are "in" right now across the whole country. You probably have one or both so you're already well on your way. The fact that hipsters have made beards popular again and that plaid flannel is woodsy chic is merely a fleeting countrywide understanding of comfort, practicality, and austerity. For the Midwest, this understanding will endure forever. It's how we garbed in 1840 and it's how we'll garb in 2040. Clean-shaven faces and velvet jumpsuits may be the popular look in a decade, but you can rest assured your favorite buffalo-check top or neckbeard will always be welcome in the heartland. Here are some other tips to keep in mind.

Layers

Seattle may be the birthplace of grunge and the accompanying layered look that came with it, but we've been rockin' this pragmatic look for centuries. Men and women will craft a combo of four to five shirts, sweatshirts, and jackets of various weight and material as dressing can become somewhat like a medieval knight preparing for a joust. While grunge rockers layered to, somewhat ironically, prove they didn't care how they look, folks from Topeka to Joliet go with layers for a very practical reason: the weather changes every ten minutes. It can be sunny and mid-70s in the morning and start snowing by

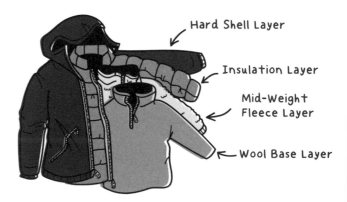

Hard Shell Layer

Insulation Layer

Mid-Weight Fleece Layer

Wool Base Layer

dinner time. Windstorms appear randomly. Lightning strikes in the middle of a sunny day. Rivers have caught on fire. (Sorry, Cleveland, it's a tough one to forget . . .) Scientists have ascertained the ten US cities with the most unpredictable weather, and every single one is located in the Midwest. (Sioux Falls, South Dakota, and Minnesota's Minneapolis and St. Paul top the list.) Apparently, the oceans regulate the weather. We don't have those. So we gotta dress for the possibility and option of a rapid Vegas-esque costume change into *whatever* the next few hours will be.

Five Years "Behind"

Mark Twain once said, "When the end of the world comes, I want to be in Cincinnati . . . because it's always twenty years behind the times." Good line, but (a) he probably didn't say it and (b) Mark's from Missouri, so he was good for another fifteen years anyway. Look, this is not a slam. It's just a fact: the Midwest *is* "behind" the coasts on any number of things. Nowhere does this reveal itself more than in how we dress. If cargo shorts were "in" circa 2010 in Boston, they'll be popular in St. Louis or Sioux Falls between 2015 and 2025. This, of course, has a couple practical advantages. (1) There is almost zero chance of going after a fashion that will be gone in a few weeks. (See: "harem pants" or Dorothy Hamill haircuts.) Historically speaking, only the tried-and-true fashions successfully make their way from the coasts into the American heartland; only the hardiest survive the trip inland. And (2) by the time capris and Vera Bradley bags make their way here, the prices have been slashed in half. That foldable clutch Carrie Bradshaw flashed in 1999 cost $600, but you'll find one on the Rhinelander Craigslist for a cool $80. So what if it got burned on the stove? And that one hip guy wearing Vineyard Vines ten years before anyone else paid $100 for that shirt; you'll get one on sale for less than half that price at Kohl's and look just as good. (Better, because you can pair it with a nice Members Only jacket for some top-notch layering.)

Team Colors

Nothing identifies you to your people faster than colors. When in doubt, wear the tints and pictograms of your local sports team: NFL, NHL, college, high school, or neighborhood KinderCare. Worst case, you'll know exactly what to wear 43 percent of the week.

On Fridays, visit any Midwest side of town and you *will* find a sea of red/purple/gold/and so on, as everyone in town pulls out their local high school team's gear. It doesn't matter if they actually have kids at the school, are alum, or just know where the school is. Most supermarkets and drugstores will have the local high school colors on racks in the front of the store. Saturday, you can switch easily to ~~scarlet and gray~~ (sorry, ruby and porpoise), blue and orange, crimson and cream, navy blue and gold, blue and maize, black and yellow, white and cardinal, or what have you. Sunday, of course, is for the big boys. Packers, Chiefs, Bears, Lions, Colts, Vikings, the Browns, and even the Bengals . . . You won't have to even watch the game or know the name of the starting QB. Just throw on a winter hat with the little colored pom-pom up top or your trusty Brett Favre jersey and you're good to go for a trip to the supermarket or to mass. Bye weeks or a missed postseason won't matter; still dress for Sunday.

Function Over Fashion

Coco Chanel declared: "Fashion is not something that exists in dresses only. Fashion is in the sky, in the street; fashion has to do with ideas, the way we live, what is happening." Which is why you won't see a whole lot of Chanel tags in the Midwest. It doesn't matter how "ugly" that twenty-year-old snorkel parka is when it's cold out. Sweatpants and cargo shorts aren't a surrender flag here, but a practical realization of Coco's quote. If the choice is to look good or tactically gear for the cold or the next four things on the to-do list, that sweatshirt with the paint stains and frayed cuffs *is* coming on. There's work to be done (at home or *work* work); no point in getting all gussied up for that. It should take a single week to know your boss's five outfits, and it should take them a couple days to know yours. The kid who wins "best dressed" in the high school yearbook each year is *always* from somewhere else, and probably not much use when there's heavy raking to be done.

Shorts

Thirty degrees out? A light dusting of snow on the yard? Nose icicles? It doesn't matter; shorts are always in season and generally the preferred option. The idea of wearing shorts below with a fleece jacket or thick hooded sweatshirt and hat on top might seem very high school prom queen in February, but it's a look Midwesterners of all ages are particularly fond of. Any opportunity to wear shorts is a celebration of how much worse and colder it could be. It also provides the *illusion* that it's warmer than it actually it is.

Sandals or Flip-Flops *and* the Right Boots

Like shorts, sandals, flip-flops, and Crocs *can* still be worn in January. When it's warm out, you'll notice cold feet; but when it's cold out (as it usually is in the Midwest), you kinda don't think about your feet at all. Yes, because they're numb. So the ease of tossing on some well-trusted flip-flops is often the quickest and most trouble-free way to get to that mailbox or grocery store, or to shovel snow if it's just a dusting. You may want to consider adding socks, not for warmth, but for fashion. That said, you *will* also need a good pair of snow boots if you plan on spending the day outside. Good winter boots should be high, waterproof (both outside *and* inside), and well insulated, with rubber soles and deep lugs for the best traction. If you can't afford boots, the time to "borrow" them from your siblings' basement is in July. This will leave you a solid month before the next snowfall. When you go to return the boots the following year, said sibling should have already purchased new boots. You, of course, will feel guilty about this for the next decade, which will lead you to bring your bro or sis one casserole per week for the duration of your life. But at least you have warm feet.

Camo

Midwesterners are deliberately humble and discreet, not wanting to stand out in the crowd. Nothing captures that retiring spirit like the ability to literally hide in your immediate surroundings. Camo is also for hunting prime parking spots, free coffee, and getting a good deal on mulch. It doesn't even need to be hunting season; camo shines (discreetly) when used on baby parkas, skirts, yoga tights, and earmuffs. Camo confirms you are one with nature, and not too far removed from going Leo DiCaprio on some bear if ever called upon.

Dressing for Bugs

Speaking of hiding from wild creatures—how's your entomology IQ? It's not all cheese curds and bike paths in the American heartland. With all those thousands of lakes and creeks and gallons of rainfall comes a whole bunch of bugs. Floodwater mosquitoes, ticks, midges, fleas, monkey slugs, chiggers, fungus gnats, cow killers, sawflies, lake flies, June bugs, berry bugs, camel crickets, home-invading weevils, botflies, more mosquitoes . . . you get the point. But not all bugs are equal. Here are the two insects Midwesterners most loathe and plan their wardrobes around.

Ticks: If you're going deep into the woods, *or* into a park to use the swings or picnic tables, watch out, 'cause that's tick territory. In the dog days of summer, you'll see Midwesterners hiking with their pants tucked *into* white socks (it's easier to spot ticks on white). However you dress, it's important when you get home to check for ticks before they sink their head into yours. If we're catching Lyme disease, it'll be from undercooked venison and not from some unwanted bite in the night.

Mosquitoes: How come the Bible doesn't mention when God created mosquitoes? The answer is: Because God didn't. The devil did. And Midwesterners agree it'd be a better world, and life, without these vampiric bloodsuckers (though that's somewhat debatable, because bats eat mosquitoes and bats pollinate agave, and agave makes tequila, but let's not let facts get in the way of our frustration here). Wisconsin and Minnesota have gone as far as claiming the mosquito as their state bird.

The Hat for *You!*

The notion that we lose almost half our body's heat "through our head" is a dad-perpetuated and nonsensical myth started by some US Army field manual in the 1950s. It's more like 7 to 10 percent. But, when the frozen tundra hits twelve degrees, that 10 percent ain't nothing to sneeze at. So, before you climb on that toboggan, you gotta cover that noggin. In the Midwest, it's the ~~cooler~~ *warmer* heads that prevail. Selecting the right hat for you is like a young wizard picking their wand; the *hat* kinda picks *you*. The only way to know for sure is to try each of these out for a spell and see if they've got that fall/winter magic. Here are the primary options to look for:

Beanie/Toque

Timeless. Simple. Cheap.
Pros: Comes in orange.
Cons: Always goes missing and turns up later in weird places.

Trapper Hat

Constructed solely for reliable, flawless function.
Pros: The warmest hat you will ever own.
Cons: Weighs seventeen pounds and you can't hear a thing. The latter may be a pro, depending on who's trying to talk to you.

Pom-Pom/Bobble

The playful cherry atop your winter hat sundae.
Pros: Tells the whole world you're still fun!
Cons: You look like you're six.

Stormy Kromer Cap

A semipro baseballer-turned-railroader asked the Mrs. to make a warm hat that'd stay on his head. She modified a baseball cap.
Pros: Respect for history.
Cons: Very Holden Caulfield.

Fur Hat/Cossack

Unique charm and craft fit for a world traveler.
Pros: The whole *Dr. Zhivago* vibe.
Cons: Ears red, brittle, and clogged with ice.

Slouchy Beanie

Youthful alternative to the classic beanie.
Pros: Comes in cashmere.
Cons: 90 percent of the hat is doing nothing. Like, seriously, nothing.

Ski Hat

Ageless perfect combo of warmth and levity.
Pros: Earflaps
Cons: Can get caught in the wood chipper.

How to Look Flan-tastic!

From Paul Bunyan to the Brawny paper towel man, there's no mistaking, or ignoring, the time-tested splendor that comes with wearing a plaid flannel shirt.

It says you are ready to get the job done—whether that job is chopping down a tree, playing the guitar, or watching Netflix for six straight hours. It should be the cornerstone of your Midwestern closet.

First marketed in 1850 to railway workers and lumberjacks as a dependable winter shirt, the pragmatic style quickly spread to cowboys and farmers and truckers to eventually become an everyday option for hipsters, hippies, feminists, grunge rockers, gangsta rappers, and soccer moms in Peoria.

Plaid and flannel are often used interchangeably but *are* two different things that meet with the same passion and you-complete-me-ness as fried fish and coleslaw.

Plaid is the pattern: Colored bars and stripes that cross at right angles can be traced back at least three thousand years. The design was found on the remains of a Caucasian guy found in northwest China. (No, for real; the Cherchen Man.) It became popular, of course, with the Scottish clans (when plaid was called *tartan*) and was crafted as heavy traveling cloaks worn to handle Scottish winters. The multicolored tartans got banned for almost a century after Scottish forces were defeated at the Battle of Culloden in 1746 but, as Andy Dufresne says, "no good thing ever dies." Today, you can't walk down the street without seeing someone (or some mortified dog) dressed in plaid. Red is the preferred color.

Flannel is the material: It began with Welsh farmers in the 1600s, peaked in Seattle in the 1990s, and comes in patterns other than plaid, but we've never seen them.

The combination remains the perfect apparel for an active lifestyle and quickly changing weather. As needed: Roll up the sleeves, pop open two or all buttons, take it off completely and wrap it around your waist, blanket-drag a deer with it, wear it over the jacket, under the jacket, whatever you like.

WHERE TO WEAR

Thanks to the internet and unremitting catalogs, you can effortlessly pick out/up all *your* Midwest fashion from the comfort of your own davenport (that's a Midwest couch!). While Costco is where you'll ultimately end up, here are some homegrown heartland couturiers to also help dress the part:

Alchemy Detroit
www.alchemydetroit.com
headquarters: Detroit, MI

Arrow Boutique
www.shoparrowboutique.com
headquarters: Aberdeen, SD

Askov Finlayson
www.askovfinlayson.com
headquarters: Minneapolis, MN

Beyond Buckskin Boutique
shop.beyondbuckskin.com/about
headquarters: North Dakota

Bizaanide'ewin
www.bizaanideewin.com
headquarters: Wisconsin

Duluth Trading Company
www.duluthtrading.com
headquarters: Belleville, WI, and Mt. Horeb, WI

Great Lakes Northern Outfitter
www.greatlakescollection.com
headquarters: Minneapolis, MN

Hackwith Design House
www.hackwithdesignhouse.com
headquarters: St. Paul, MN

Haystacks.net
www.haystacks.net
headquarters: Suttons Bay, MI

Heart Berry
www.heartberry.com
headquarters: Minnesota on the Rez

Hideside Outfitters
www.hideside.com
headquarters: Fish Creek, WI

I Am Anishinabe
www.iamanishinaabe.com
headquarters: Walker, MN

Kileidoscope Clothing Co LLC
www.thekileidoscope.com
headquarters: Cleveland, OH

Kiwi's Boutique
www.kiwisboutique.com
headquarters: Chicago, IL

Lands' End
www.landsend.com
headquarters: Dodgeville, WI

Lee Jeans
www.lee.com
headquarters: Merriam, KS

Makwa Studio
www.makwastudio.com
headquarters: Minnesota

Moose Apparel
www.opeoutdoors.com
headquarters: St. Louis, MO

Stormy Kromer
www.stormykromer.com
headquarters: Ironwood, MI

Thrive
www.thriveunltd.com
headquarters: South Dakota

Wigwam Mills
www.wigwam.com
headquarters: Sheboygan, WI

Wildflower Boutique
www.thewildflowerboutiques.com
headquarters: Evansville, IN

Wolverine Worldwide
www.wolverineworldwide.com
headquarters: Rockford, MI

The Midwest is a heck of a lot easier with a car. You can thank Detroit for that. As Ford and GM boomed, towns were designed around the car, which became a symbol of good old American freedom. The automobile is to the Midwest what air-conditioning is to Florida: strongly preferred. So it's extra important to get all the driving rules and regional idiosyncrasies down. In due time, you'll realize that the eyeglasses holder is also the perfect brat holder, but first you'll need to nail some regional basics. Whether you're visiting for a week or staying for the rest of your life, you'll quickly discover that there's driving, and then there's Midwest driving—and knowing the difference is going to save you a whole lot of headache, heartbreak, and middle finger fatigue.

What to Expect

Long Drives. There's not a whole lot of walking to the store, school, or job when living out here—there's just so much space. It'd take most folks six hours to walk to work. Add to this the fact that a lot of places don't have the most reliable public transportation. (Cleveland, Indianapolis, Cincinnati, and Detroit all have NFL teams but no easy way to get downtown to see a game.) Search for a subway on your smartphone and you're sent to a subpar sandwich shop. If you want to see *actual* subways in most of our towns, you'll need to buy tickets to some ghost tour and explore the unfinished projects from the 1930s now covered over with highways. That's why getting in the car to cover some distance doesn't really bother anyone out here, and it becomes second nature when you can drive for five hours and *still* be in the same state. (Visitors from the American West will get it.) A Midwesterner is prepared to drive an hour to get to the closest Olive Garden. And this isn't a sixty-minutes-sitting-in-traffic kinda thing. This is driving 70 mph for 45 minutes. East Coast in-laws will stare in wide-eyed amazement when you pass the thirty-minute mark when driving to a nice dinner out and will eventually break out with, "Where in the heck are we going?" The answer is a confused expression from their local driver: "Right down the road." As for longer travel, why hassle with an airport when you can just drive there in twelve to fourteen hours?

"Passive" Drivers. There's a reason there are one hundred *Fast and Furious* films and not one of them is set in the Midwest. Although *Fast and Furious: Sheboygan Drift* screams box office smash, the truth is that speed isn't the primary motivation of the Midwest driver. We're more interested in pointing out deer and cows. And if we have to slow down to fifty-five in the fast lane to mark some turkeys . . . well, them's the breaks. Rain and snow aren't a problem, but we sure as shoot are gonna follow Dad's advice and go slow enough for a passenger to fillet a walleye without getting accidentally circumcised. We were born with a yield sign on our face. So, roundabouts can be paralyzing. (*Who decided to put those here?*) When in doubt, we *always* give the other guy the right of way—even when it doesn't make sense. Take a four-way stop, for instance: just because you were there first doesn't mean you need to *go* first. That's the thinking out here, and to drivers from the coasts where more assertive driving is needed for survival, you're just gonna have to flip that switch to a gentler cycle. No matter how big that pickup truck is in front of you or how the guy driving it looks like a 250-pound Jeremiah Johnson, always imagine he was your grandma on a Sunday drive. Because that's what he's doing. (Exception: Do *not* expect this in Chicago, where local motorists have intimidated hardened drivers from New York City, Beijing, and NASCAR.)

Waving. If a car or truck passes you and the driver, passenger, or a kid in the back seat waves, it is *not* because they mistakenly think they know you. They're just being nice. If you have out-of-state plates, expect "welcome" waves from other vehicles you pass. And once you wave back, you'll never go back. It will become second nature in no time. Every vehicle comes with features for safety, but there are very few features for politeness. You must use what the good Lord gave you. Any time you have to scoot by someone, you give 'em a wave. This wave means: "Ope, sorry, no, you're driving real good; I just gotta get somewhere a hair sooner than you! Hope you don't mind." A wave can mean all that. It's Midwest magic. Once you officially pass someone and get in front of them, you must wave again with your right hand. Extend it just below the rearview mirror. If they return your wave, you can be assured they aren't from Chicago. If they flip you off, the plates will be from New York or New Jersey. If someone cuts you off, wave as if it were your fault somehow. Nothing wrong with yelling out "Ope, sorry!" as you do.

Patience with Parallel Parkers. We may drive everywhere, but that doesn't mean we've learned to parallel park. Because of our abundant parking space, this maneuver doesn't come up too often. When it does, expect several failed attempts followed by a quick embarrassed drive away; we'll find a better parking situation blocks away and walk back.

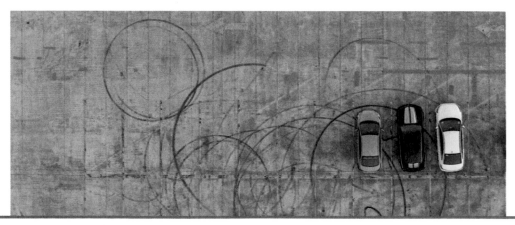

Driving Etiquette

1. **Wave at every passing vehicle.** (See "What to Expect," above.) Other places, driver's ed starts when you're fifteen. In the Midwest, the rules of the road begin in the womb. (In fact, my birth took fourteen hours because I kept waving ahead all those pedestrians dressed in surgical gowns before leaving my garage.)

2. **If you see someone with a nice twelve-pointer hanging off the back or hood**, it's customary to one-up the wave and roll down the window to shout over something like "Nice buck!" He'd do it for you. If you're anti-hunting, a simple wave is a fine compromise.

3. **When you want to change lanes, roll down the window and ask permission.** Three easy steps: First, turn on your blinker. Next, hold your left hand out and wave. Finally, wait for a nod or wave back. This all happens pretty fluidly *as* you're passing, but it's important to wave *before* passing. If you don't, they'll think you're from Chicago.

4. **After you pass two Culvers, never pass a third.** It's bad luck. Stop and buy custard or something. If you go during Lent, don't pass up the walleye.

5. **For highway driving,** use the on-ramp to get up to speed, make your way over to the fast lane, then immediately slow down so the car behind you can read all the sports teams on your bumper.

6. **Plan ahead.** Light a candle at church so construction will go away. Summers are spent fixing the potholes we make in the winter. When the barrels come back, just light another candle.

7. **If the sign on the bridge says "Be careful. Could be icy!,"** take care, even in July. Ya never know . . .

8. **Gaps in conversation must always be filled** with chat about construction or the last animal you saw.

9. **Remember the rules of four-way stops:** The only way you automatically get to go first is if nobody else is there. Even then, make sure there are no deer hiding in the woods. The last thing you want to do is kill Bambi's dad at an intersection. (First off, that'd bruise the meat and make for bad jerky. Second, if you kill too many Bambi daddies, then what are you gonna miss when you shoot your rifle once a year in the fall?) If another car rolls up to this four-way stop, wave 'em by at least a couple-two-tree times. Michigan, Wisconsin, and Minnesota folks will need at least three waves before they know you mean business.[*] Do *not* attempt to pull forward after your second wave. This will be viewed as rude. Now, if the other car waves you by three times, take your foot off the gas slightly, but be aware that the other driver may do the same, as they believe you are sincere in *your* invite for them to go and take you up on it. Do not get frustrated! Think of this less as an inconvenience and more as a ritualized dance. Sometimes you lead and sometimes you follow. In these situations, I recommend acting the way I would on any dance floor . . . avoid finding any rhythm and bite your bottom lip.

10. **Research the more-specific local laws.** (For instance: In Missouri, you can't honk someone else's car horn. It's illegal to run out of gas in Youngstown, Ohio. And, in Kansas, you can't transport dead poultry.) Yeah, no, seriously . . .

---

[*] You won't need to worry about folks from Chicago, as they rarely use stop signs.

Just Past the Third Deer on the Left

These days when it comes to driving, people are all about convenience. Most folks just plug in their phone and the GPS gives them all the directions. When you take a wrong turn your phone immediately reroutes you. You'll never get lost. Where's the fun in that? That's why we make directions way more confusing here. Because in the Midwest we believe if you never get lost, you'll never find yourself.

Rule 1: Time = Distance

Ask someone how far away the nearest hospital is, they're not ever going to give you miles. They'll say "ten to twelve minutes." In Midwest cartography, "five minutes" = one mile and "about ten to twenty minutes" = fifteen miles. (The speed limit is 70 mph but most folks still drive 55, plus you gotta stop for custard.)

Rule 2: Landmarks = GPS

Ask how to get somewhere, don't expect street names and route numbers. We don't really know or use those. We can visit family or a best friend once a week for a decade and have zero idea what street they live on. Instead, Midwesterners depend almost entirely on landmarks. "Over there by the railroad tracks, right off the main drag" or "Go ten minutes that way and take a right just past the second Dairy Queen. If you pass the three bars by the church you went too far." Street names are usually just some goofy name a developer added to the universe. It's kinda illusory. But that railroad track is a real and permanent thing. Something you can count on to get you to the *next* landmark.

Things That Can Be Used as Landmarks

- Train tracks
- Churches
- Gas stations
- A big rock
- A tornado
- A covered bridge
- The Mall of America
- Willis Tower

- A stop-and-go light (what thirty-eight other states call a stoplight)
- A billboard of the Ten Commandments (or REPENT! or HELL IS REAL!)
- Deer crossings
- Lake McConaughy
- That red-haired family

And so on . . .

MY FIRST CAR

"WHO'S RIDING SHOTGUN?"

Before I continue on about the distinctive practices of driving in America's heartland, I want to tell you the story of how I got my first car in distinguished Midwest fashion: I Dick Cheney'd my dad's minivan. That's right, I shot it. With a shotgun. But only once. Because it was an accident. I was fresh out of college, and still living in Wisconsin, but had just gotten a job as a production assistant in Los Angeles. (A production assistant is where you turn two college degrees into making six figures—I

mean six coffee decanters, a day.) Now, since I was moving to L.A., I was hunting for a car . . . but not like this. (Before we get to the incident, I gotta tell you about the minivan. This wasn't just any minivan. It was a certified preowned Silver Dodge Grand Caravan SXT. SXT stands for SEXY XT. This was the Cadillac of minivans. It had everything! A CD player. Bucket seats. Polyester. The only thing missing was wood paneling. I'm from a big family; we weren't used to a life of such luxuries.)

"OPE, FOUND SOME MORE BIRD SHOT . . ."

Okay, back to the incident. We were hunting pheasants, aka the sirloin of the sky! I was with two of my brothers, my dad, and our dog, Murphy, for one last hunt before I headed to L.A. Everything was going great; we got three or four birds (seven or eight if you ask my dad). We did everything by the book: before putting the shotguns back in their cases, everybody unloaded their guns and made sure the safeties were on. And by everybody, I mean everybody except my brother Andy. He'd just put his locked-and-loaded shotgun back in its case. (This is why you don't use lead paint in nurseries.) We drove all the way home with it lying in the back seat, and I was one pothole away from telling this story to St. Peter.

When we got home, my dad told me to unload the car. So I pulled all four shotguns from the van and BOOM! Blasted the polyester right off that back bucket seat. Pellet holes were now lodged in the front console, and riding shotgun had forever taken on a whole new meaning in our home. All I could think was *SHOOT, I just shot the Cadillac of minivans. Will Dad reload and target me next?* I tried blaming it on Andy, but that's a little hard when you're literally holding a smoking gun. (I'm just happy nobody died . . . especially me.) Instead of killing me, my dad decided to murder my bank account. That night, I bought the Silver Dodge Grand Caravan (now known as the Silver Bullet Van) at its Kelley Blue Book value with the condition "Excellent" because, according to my dad, there was no option for "interior has minor shotgun blast." On that day, my dad also instituted the "Andy Rule" for all future hunts: everybody checks the other hunter's gun twice to make sure it's unloaded and the safety is on. And by everybody, I mean everybody except Andy; he's not checking sh*t.

I was crashing on people's couches when I first moved to L.A., but when they stopped answering the phone, I slept fine in the back of the Silver Bullet Van. One morning, I let the sunrise wake me up. As my eyes fluttered they fixed on an old call sheet, Nature Valley granola bar crumbs, and two shotgun pellets. A wonderful reminder from where the minivan and I had come. 🛞

Practice Quiz One

You've pulled over to ask for directions to Route 51 North.

"Sure. Just head straight no more than ten minutes or so and after you've hit your twenty-seventh pothole, take a hard right at the Kwik Trip. Then just drive through a couple stop-and-go lights until you see the Farm & Fleet. If you see the Fleet Farm, you've gone too far. Okay, take a left at that Farm & Fleet and once you drive past this one block with eight bars and nine churches, you're gonna wanna take another right at the Culver's. Keep 'er movin' until you see the next deer-crossing sign, and then it's a final right to the highway."

You know you're just going to say "Got it" no matter what. . . . So now, without looking, how much do you remember? Will you ever see Route 51 North?

Practice Quiz Two

I Spy with My Little Eye: A True or False Quiz

(Answers below)

1. If you see cows, count them aloud with the other passengers.

2. If you see ice fishers, count them aloud with the other passenger

3. If you see a deer, say, "Ope! There's a deer."

4. If you see a turkey, say, "Ope! There's a turkey."

5. If you see roadkill, say, "Ope! That poor guy had a bad day."

6. If you see someone you know, honk and wave.

7. If you see a family of ducks, say, "Ope! There's a family of ducks!"

8. If you see a cornfield, make dad jokes *about* the corn as you pass. Examples: "You know what a buccaneer is? A terrible price for corn." OR "I've seen that same corn before; I think it's stalking us." You get the idea.

Answers: 1. True. It's been said you always have to say hi to the cows or they'll be insulted and stop making milk and dairy prices will skyrocket. **2. True. 3. True. 4. False.** Stop and see if it's a jake, hen, or tom, what they're feeding on, if it's on public or private land, nice beard, and so on. **5. True 6. False.** It's a double toot and a wave. Honk three times if there's a pregnant woman in the back seat and you need help. **7. False.** Stop the car, get out, make sure they all get across. **8. Corny, but True.**

Winter Driving

It's time for an awkward talk about the birds and the freeze. Five of the ten coldest states in America are in the Midwest, so every winter and fall proves a challenge to the best-laid plans of ice and men. It's key to plan ahead, know what to expect, and be willing to go cannibal if absolutely necessary.

The most important thing about safe winter-weather driving is **speed**—*you gotta go slow*. Get over into the fast lane and then drop down to about 40 mph. You'll want to keep about three fishing-pole lengths between you and the car in front—and not ice-fishing poles but cane poles (about fourteen feet each).

Never *never* slam the brakes—always pump like you're dancing to House of Pain's "Jump Around." This equals a safe landing every time.

If caught in a ditch, digging out is the last resort. First, call AAA and impersonate your dad, because you most likely didn't pay your bill.

Important Note: During inclement weather, all waving rules are changed. Full waves to other cars are not expected or considered safe. Instead, keep both hands on the wheel—and, lifting only two fingers with one hand, give the peace sign. (Never both hands—you're not Richard Nixon.)

Ice scrapers are serious business, and we select and wield ours with the same pride and consideration as the samurai once carried their katana. After all, you can't drive a car with a windshield covered in ice. That is, you can't drive *well*. That's why it's important to seek out and purchase a scraper that has the perfect blend of durability, balance, and honing for you. You'll need to try out many models to see which style and features fit your personal taste the best: double-bladed, built-in gloves, telescoping handles, heating elements? The broom is a whole other kettle: placement on the scraper, the number of individual brushes, their thickness, their position in relation to one another and to you. If you've loaned your favorite ice scraper to a friend because . . . of course you did, you *can* always use your credit card. Avoid using your Kwik Trip rewards card, as it likely has more financial value.

There is much debate on how much ice you should scrape from your windshield before attempting to drive safely. About the size of an ice-fishing hole should do it, and no more than the size of your head. To help with the effort, always remember to start your vehicle and get that Unthaw Button going. (Your vehicle probably has it marked "Defrost" button, but just because it's wrong doesn't mean you have to be.)

Scraping as therapy: It isn't all bad scraping ice off your vehicles with both doors sealed tight and the front windshield covered in four feet of snow. Professional therapy can cost $100 to $500 an hour, but a good ice scraper costs less than $10 and you only need to buy a few of those in a lifetime. Since the Model T entered the scene in 1908, drivers have gotten the enjoyment of scraping ice and snow off their vehicle as a safe, easy, and cheap opportunity to harness all the resentment built over the past twenty years (or twenty-four hours) and take it out on the dang windshield. Hate your boss—scrape! Get cut off by some guy from Connecticut—scrape! Didn't get a good wave—scrape! Spilled your flask at the ballpark and had to buy $12 stadium beers—scrape! Someone bumps into you without saying "Ope!"—scrape!

Will I Need a Pickup Truck?

Not at all. It may seem like everyone in the Midwest drives a pickup truck, but anything you can do with a pickup you can try with your Corolla and a bunch of ratchet straps. It's very important after ratcheting your wood/cooler/mattress/refrigerator down that you give it a slap and say, "Yep, that's not goin' anywhere." Definitely don't take the highway home.

The Midwest Uber Driver

Not many taxis out here (unless you're in Chicago or willing to schedule it and wait an hour), so you may be extra likely to employ one of the driver apps when you visit. Lyft, Uber, Curb, and so on. If so, here are some basics for dealing with your new friend:

1. Their trunk may be filled with cases of beer, bags of sheep feed for their kid's 4-H project, or folding chairs, so expect to load your suitcase in the back seat.

2. When talking with your driver, it can get confusing. To help, always listen/focus on the last word they say:

   "Oh no, yeah." = yes
   "Oh . . . Yeah, no." = no
   "Yeah, no, definitely." = yes

3. It is assumed/expected that you will help the driver look for and point out turkeys.

4. Many rideshare vehicles around the country will provide complimentary water bottles and a charger for your phone. A Midwest driver may offer you ranch dressing and fresh jerky. This is not weird; they're treating you like kin.

5. Always know what bar or church is closest to your destination. Many Midwest drivers won't trust or use the actual app to get to your location. How can you trust an app that can't pronounce Fond du Lac, Ypsilanti, or Chillicothe properly?

6. Your driver may invite you to go ice fishing or offer their *actual* cell phone number in case you need more info about town later. Again, they are not being creepy. After forty-five minutes in a car together, this person now sees you as a friend.

When You Hit a Deer . . .

Considering that "Watch out for deer!" is a genuine and long-standing form of farewell in the Midwest, it should not surprise anyone that finding one of these delightful creatures within range of your headlights at 50 mph is a very real possibility. Spend enough time in the Midwest and you *will* hit one. On some roads, you'll see enough deer sprinting across the highway that you'll wonder if they're taking part in some kind of woodland dare, or perhaps seeking revenge for Harold hanging on your basement wall. Assuming all in the car are okay, here's what you do next.

1. Pull over to the side of the road and assess the damage to both your car and the buck.

2. Take a picture of the car for your insurance.

3. Take a picture of the buck for your deer processor.

4. Immediately text a friend, "This one worth saving or no? Also, having some folks over for euchre Friday if you wanna come."

5. Toss the deer in back and pray it wasn't just sleeping.

SEEK AND FIND GAME:
CAN YOU FIND THE DEER?

Search the picture below and see if you can spot the deer.

When You Watch a Train . . .

They say patience is a minor form of despair disguised as a virtue. You will need this virtue when dealing with Midwest trains. In other parts of the country, they put their trains *alongside* major streets or in areas you don't ever actually see, or even above or under where cars go. In the flattest lands around, they apparently just pulled out maps and drew a long straight line across the states—and through the existing roadways. Thus, expect long delays sitting at train crossings, wondering what trains are like in other states. Also, expect the train to simply stop sometimes, blocking the road for fifteen to forty minutes. There will be no *apparent* reason for this, but you must trust it exists, and abide. This is all meant to teach you about God. You can attempt to drive away and find another road to cross over, but you'll very likely encounter the exact same train again, as it is clearly one hundred fifty miles long and now bisects almost the entire state.

Things you can do to pass time:

1. Imagine the graffiti or tag-name *you* would use if ever called upon (likely Ope).
2. Count the empty flatcars.
3. Turn off your car/truck. Save some gas. Maybe clean out the glove box.
4. Make a pleasant "What are you gonna do?" face at the car next to you.
5. Place bets on which car in line will break ranks first and head the other direction.
6. Imagine life drifting from town to town on a train, Tom Cruise running along the roof as it passes. Or imagine being somewhere trains run alongside the road.

Recommended Playlist

It may take an hour or more drive to get to work, a shopping mall, or your favorite restaurant, and nothing passes road-trip time (or a railroad-crossing situation) like a good playlist. Here are some recommended albums to get you in the proper Midwest frame of mind.

Hitsville, USA—The Motown Singles Collection, 1959–1971

When entrepreneur and composer Berry Gordy Jr. started a new recording and publishing empire in Detroit, he would forever change how music was made, sold, and sounded. From 1961 to 1971, his Motown Records produced more than a hundred Top 10 hits for megastars like Diana Ross, The Temptations, Smokey Robinson, The Jackson 5, and Stevie Wonder (Midwesterners all!). There *are* dynamic and metropolitan cities in the Midwest, and Motown shared its sound with the world.

Most Midwest Tune: "Ain't No Mountain High Enough" by Diana Ross. On a clear day, people in Wichita can squint real hard and see folks in Columbus, Ohio. Fact.

Bob Dylan (Self-Titled Album)—Bob Dylan

Dylan (né: Robert Zimmerman) first picked up his guitar in suburban Hibbing, Minnesota, and then attended the University of Minnesota, where he started playing in small coffee shops and figuring out how to adapt his orthodontic headgear into a fine spot for a harmonica. Dylan's recorded enough songs for you to re-create his drive from Minnesota to NYC without repeat.

Most Midwest Tune: "Highway 51 Blues." Bob Dylan knows this highway like he knows his hand. It runs "from up Wisconsin way down to no-man's-land." What more do you need to know?

4EVER—Prince

The Purple One. His Royal Badness. The Artist formerly known as Skipper (true!). When not looking for Lake Minnetonka, the maestro of Minnesota was putting out enough funk to fuel twelve states and then some. This one's got forty tracks, thirty-seven of which you can *already* sing along to. Every road trip is better with Prince riding shotgun.

Most Midwest Tune: "Take Me With U." In which Prince passes a long drive off as a date.

Coloring Book—Chance the Rapper

Born in Chicago, Chance the Rapper exemplifies the Midwest work ethic. He endeavored his way to the top with mixtapes like *10 Day*, *Acid Rap*, and *Coloring Book*. *Coloring Book* was nominated for three Grammys and became the first streaming-only album to win Best Rap Album. Chance's hustle and creativity in circumventing traditional music labels to achieve the highest levels of success have inspired a new generation of rappers.

Most Midwest Tune: "Juke Jam" is a nostalgia-laced hit that takes place at Chicago's Rink Fitness Factory. It's all about your first time dancing while *not* leaving room for the Holy Spirit.

The Red Road—Bill Miller

Bill Miller is a three-time Grammy-winning Native American artist from northern Wisconsin. *The Red Road* blends country with Native influence, delivering catchy tunes that reflect hope without losing sight of America's troubling past.

Most Midwest Tune: "Tumbleweed" creates a catchy American country ballad to address the complicated relationship America has with Indigenous Peoples.

New Favorite—Alison Krauss

The fiddle prodigy and bluegrass icon from Champaign, Illinois, teams up with her long-standing band, Union Station, for all the pickin' and harmonies you'd ever need to get past the *next* fifty miles of cornfield.

Most Midwest Tune: "The Boy Who Wouldn't Hoe Corn," about a guy who doesn't work very hard, so he dies alone and unloved.

The King of Delta Blues Singers—Robert Johnson

In the 1930s, Black musicians from the South made their way north to escape the oppression of Jim Crow laws. The Illinois Central Railroad offered cheap fares, allowing some of America's greatest artists an opportunity to redefine Chicago music. The likes of Louis Armstrong, Jelly Roll Morton, Sippie Wallace, Blind Lemon Jefferson, and of course Robert Johnson did just that.

Most Midwest Tune: In 1936 Robert Johnson recorded "Sweet Home Chicago," the Mississippi Delta bluesman's ode to escaping the racially oppressive South in the 1930s. "Sweet Home Chicago" helped define Chicago Blues. Without Chicago Blues there would be no Rolling Stones or Beatles.

Scarecrow—John Cougar Mellencamp

It's what most consider the best album by Indiana's favorite troubadour, with thirteen tracks about life in the American heartland. Safe to grab any Mellencamp collection, but this one is his Midwest magnum opus.

Most Midwest Tune: Copyright laws prevent getting too specific, but let's just say it has to do with a town that's not big.

Still Driving? Here Are Some Other Options

- *Fullfillingness' First Finale*—Stevie Wonder
- *Against the Wind*—Bob Seger
- "Hoochie Coochie Man"—Muddy Waters
- *8 Mile*—Eminem
- *Iowa*—Slipknot
- "Save Me"—Wanda Davis
- "Smokestack Lightning"—Howlin' Wolf
- "Come See About Me"—The Supremes

- *Mellon Collie and the Infinite Sadness*—The Smashing Pumpkins
- "Good Way"—Frank Waln
- "Fast Car"—Tracy Chapman
- *Violent Femmes*—Violent Femmes
- *Ain't No Mountain High Enough*—Diana Ross
- "Ope Nope"—Berens & Greuel

(Ope, sorry for the shameless plug.)

Vehicle Emergency Pack

It's always prudent to keep one close at hand, as you never know when you'll be stuck in a snowdrift, tornado, deer attack, or 3:00 A.M. construction zone, or at a railroad crossing. Your kit should include the following:

- Jumper cables
- Scoopie tokens
- A regulation football (there's time yet to make the Packers practice squad)
- Deck of 32 cards for Sheepshead
- A quart of Bloody Mary mix
- Badtree-powered socks (don't forget extra DDs)
- Gorilla tape
- One can of Vernors ginger ale
- Dice for craps

- A quart of motor oil
- Packets of ranch dressing
- A gallon of coolant
- A box of Mackinac Island fudge
- Some random Band-Aids
- Buck knife (to clean the deer you hit while you wait for AAA to come)
- Deck of 24 cards for euchre
- Backup packets of ranch dressing
- Fishing pole . . . stream close by, I betcha

8:00 a.m.

9:45 a.m.

11:30 a.m.

1:30 p.m.

4:45 p.m.

5:00 p.m.

The Setting

Location, location, location. Communities are always shaped by their settings, and the Midwest is no exception. The combination of landscape (far too much) and weather (far too random) have blended seamlessly over thousands of years to influence our food, clothes, work, play, children, pets, and general attitude. Yes, it's mostly flat but you will also encounter legitimate mountain ranges. Oh, and rivers and lots and lots of lakes, some so big they produce genuine waves. (Surf's up, Sheboygan.) From beachfront property to farmhouses on fifty acres to lofty chic penthouse apartments in Chicago, Columbus, or ~~Fort Scott, Kansas~~ Minneapolis, the Midwest has you covered. And, when you need some time away from home, all the best—and officially approved—vacation spots have already been picked out for you.

The Weather: Like a Box of Chocolates

Consistently, the top-ten United States cities with the most unpredictable weather are all located in the Midwest: Fargo, North Dakota; Sioux Falls, South Dakota; Rapid City, South Dakota; Kansas City, Missouri; St. Louis, Missouri; Minneapolis and St. Paul, Minnesota; Cincinnati, Ohio; Indianapolis, Indiana; and Houghton, Michigan. (Are there some lists that include places in Oklahoma and Texas? Sure, but this book isn't about those places.)

Turns out the oceans regulate temperatures and are too big to push around weather-wise. So, when the West and East Coast landscapes try to act up, the Pacific and Atlantic usually quickly put them back in check. They may let the temperature fluctuate a couple degrees a day or permit an unexpected rainstorm to move along its edges—or obliterate the seaboard with a Category 5 hurricane—but that's about it.

In Sioux Falls and Steubenville, however, it's come what may.

A robin, we say, needs two or more snows on its back before it's really spring here. Some nights bring savage hailstorms and sleeping in the basement when the tornado sirens go off. Sans oceans in the Midwest, it gets extra hot in the summer and extra cold every spring, fall, and winter, and the weather just kinda does whatever it wants all day long. No telling what tomorrow—or the next hour—will bring.

Midwest weatherpersons pretty much say whatever they want. Because it doesn't matter in the slightest. They know it. We know it. Sure, they can make predictions based on sound science. And everywhere else in the world they'd be right. But God has a unique sense of humor, and Midwest meteorologists can't figure out how they became the good Lord's favorite punchline. If they say we're in for five inches of snow, it could be sunny and seventy degrees the next morning. "Clear skies" = your patio cushions *will* get soaked. "Downpour" = fog and sandstorms. It's a little game we like to play. They pretend what they're saying actually matters, and we pretend to adjust our plans accordingly.

When you take an improv class at Chicago's Second City you learn this rule on Day 1. "Yes, and . . ." It means if your scene partner says something or does something, you never deny it. You accept it with a "Yes." You add to it with an "and." It's how scenes get built. God is your scene partner. The weather is your prompt. *Yes, and* it and this whole thing will be a lot more fun. Speaking of which, yes, I have some May snow to shovel and a May snow angel to make, too.

Tornadoes: Don't Get Your Flannels in a Twist

A guy in Saginaw, Michigan, once tossed a bowling ball, and it rolled across three states before hitting a deer just outside of Cape Girardeau, Missouri. Thanks to glaciers, the Midwest is that flat. And tornadoes love *love* flat. America's Tornado Alley runs from central Texas northward into northern Iowa, South Dakota, central Kansas, and Nebraska, and then turns east to take out Ohio. While these five take the brunt of the action, every Midwest state knows tornadoes and knows them well. Thanks to our tendency toward twisters, we have actual drills—monthly, and in some towns even weekly. When it's not a drill, we head to our cellars or storm shelters (or front porches with a beer or tree) and wait to see what Mother Nature brings this time. We've placed tornadoes in the "Things to Do" section because—drills and deaths notwithstanding—Midwesterners eventually take a remarkable "so what" attitude regarding a thing up to two miles wide that's spinning at 300 mph. It's how people living in Pompei once looked up at Vesuvius every time it rumbled. This leads to an awful lot of amateur storm watching, mostly done on the driveway or back deck, sharing objective wonder and memories and comparisons of *previous* storms with a neighbor who's outside doing the same.

Plan Ahead: How to Know If a Tornado Is Coming

Weather Situation	Chance of a Tornado That Day
It's windy out.	35 percent
There's a thunderstorm in the morning.	35 percent
It's sunny and warm.	35 percent
It's snowing.	20 percent
The birds are quiet.	35 percent
The birds won't stop chirping.	35 percent
You just ran away from home because the town bully wants to kill your dog.	72 percent

Steps to Take

When that alarm goes off, there are several procedural actions to take as that funnel cloud nears to ensure the safety of you and your family. Over time, with practice and real-world experience, these will become almost instinctual.

1. Check if it's noon or the first Wednesday of the month. It might be a drill.
2. Argue about when drill day is.
3. Text family about approaching storm.
4. Argue via text about when drill day is.
5. *Close* the windows (regardless of what your uncle says).
6. Close the cupboards (just good to do).
7. Make a *Sharknado* or Helen Hunt joke.
8. Gather food and snacks to take down into cellar.
9. Get everyone down into the cellar.
10. Go back upstairs to grab a flashlight and a euchre deck. Realize the dog is still upstairs.
11. Get the dog down into the cellar.
12. Head out in front of the house to see what all the fuss is about.

Once the twister passes—and it will; the only question is whether or not it takes your house or car as it does—there's still some satisfying recreation to be had. Gather up the debris so you can exchange patio furniture, fence gates, and gutters with your neighbors. Like finding that missing sock, it's fun to put it all back together again. And chances are the power will be out for a couple days, so you might as well have a cookout before the beer gets warm and the pork steak from the meat raffle unthaws. Can't let all that frozen venison and pork steak go bad. (Yeah, the power will probably come back in an hour or two—but why take the chance? Start grilling right away.) Also, be sure to finish the cellar euchre game you started; it's purportedly bad luck to abandon an unfinished game and no one needs that living within or near Tornado Alley.

Your Home on the Range

Speaking of tornadoes, Dorothy Gale of Kansas correctly surmised "There's no place like home," and so it's especially important to understand the major differences between housing in the Midwest and everywhere else. The disparity is pretty substantial. As a picture tells a thousand words, let's get to it:

In short, live wherever and *in* whatever you want—just do so more affordably than anywhere else in the country.

Per a recent *U.S. News* report (of course, there are other reports and things change), Ohio is the least expensive state to live in, and Indiana, Iowa, Michigan, Nebraska, Kansas, and Missouri all also made the Top 10 Most Affordable. Nowhere does that affordability play out more than in our housing situation. Visiting in-laws or parents from the coasts gape in wonder at "how well you're doing," assuming you've dropped close to a million for a house that cost one-third of that. If you've got one of those sweet "I can work remote" tech jobs, a single year's salary (for you LA and NY types) could have you mortgage-free *and* living in a great neighborhood "with parks, shops, and plenty of deer to dodge."

The notorious 2020 will *also* go down as the year America took a long hard look at their studio apartment in New York and reconsidered living in an expensive shoebox. It's the year many added up their rent, clicked on Zillow.com, and said, "You mean I could have an entire house in Michigan?! It isn't that cold in January, right?" And, assuming said individual didn't look up historical temperatures for January in Michigan, they may very well be sitting in Kalamazoo or Frankenmuth right now.

Apartment in Florida	Apartment in the Midwest
Starter Home in Maryland	Starter Home in the Midwest
McMansion in Colorado	McMansion in the Midwest
"Gentleman's Farm" in Texas	"Gentleman's Farm" in the Midwest
Vacation Home by the Water on the East or West Coast	Vacation Home by the Water in the Midwest

Your Lawn: How We Judge You

Lawns. Why do we have them? Well, in short, we stole the concept from the British. Lawns are traditionally a status symbol in the land of castles and funny teeth. And we still haven't found a way to outgrow them here in the Midwest. But as long as the lawns are here, we're going to take care of them. And that means cutting them once a week while telling the grass everything we would have told a therapist. But it's not just cutting grass that occupies our time and weirdest thoughts. That's just the tip of the iceberg lettuce growing in the back.

It may seem as if working on their lawn is the only thing your neighbors ever do. You may wonder if they actually have jobs. (They must be taking personal time.) Relaxing at home is for the weak. Surely there's something outside that can be upgraded. Some bush that needs trimming, some edging, another round of scrubbing the side of your house to keep the mildew and mold 101 percent away.

The alternative is your lawn looking shabby and in disarray. If you can't take care of the appearance of your own house, how is anyone supposed to trust your capabilities as a parent, citizen, or human being? Thus, it is common for one neighbor to mow their lawn, and the Midwesterner living next door to respond with a fresh mowing of their own—even though they just cut the grass with a pair of nose-hair scissors two days ago. (If we ever get invaded by aliens, it's possible they will mistake this as some sort of mating ritual.)

It's a lot of pressure, but it eventually becomes so routine that you do it instinctively. Until then, here's an abbreviated To-Do list, broken out by month to keep you honest.

Your Yardwork Calendar

January

Repair all lawn-care tools: sharpen blades, replace any broken parts.

Reclaim your lawn-care tools: casually mention items you've lent to neighbors and family. (*See The 7 Steps to Lending Tools, page 107.*)

Prune the evergreens; return any borrowed lawn-care tools.

Shovel or snowblow snow and/or ice from your sidewalk, porch, steps, and driveway.

Shovel or snowblow snow and/or ice from neighbors' sidewalks, porches, steps, and driveways.

February

Test your soil pH. Treat any issues you find.

Prune shade trees. Pluck lawn moss fastidiously with bare hands.

Flush with water all lawn patches that have been in contact with salt or pets to minimize harmful compounds from roots before the grass starts to grow again.

Shovel or snowblow snow and/or ice from your sidewalk, porch, steps, and driveway.

Shovel or snowblow snow and/or ice from neighbors' sidewalks, porches, steps, and driveways.

March

Rake the entire yard to remove mulch, worms, debris, sticks, squirrel droppings, ice, and dead grass.

Mow the lawn weekly (blade on high).

It's 7:00 A.M. Start any lawn tool that has a loud motor. (*8:00 A.M. on Sundays.*)

Manually pluck all crabgrass and other fugly weeds from lawn.

Vacuum the entire yard to remove any missed mulch, worms, debris, sticks, squirrel droppings, ice, and dead grass.

Shovel or snowblow snow and/or ice from the sidewalk, porch, steps, and driveway as needed.

Enough is enough; your neighbors are now on their own.

April

Start mowing twice a week (blade set to high).

Trim and shape all the bushes as if you were Mr. Miyagi with a bonsai tree.

Watch dandelions grow. Pass on the weed and feed. Why trade expensive chemicals for free flowers?

Edge everything that *can* be edged. If grass is touching any other material or matter: edge it.

Shovel or snowblow snow and/or ice from the sidewalk, porch, steps, and driveway as needed.

May

Begin leaving grass clippings on the lawn to benefit soil.

Manually remove all weeds and "goofy-looking" grass.

Begin mowing four times a week (blade set to medium).

Put snowblower away, but be aware you may need to take it out one more time.

June

Drill a spigot to an old garbage can and call it a rain barrel. Use it to water the brown spots.

Raise the mower blade again to three or four inches, so that the higher grass blades shade the roots.

Mow the lawn daily. Wait until the neighbors are home (and preferably swimming or eating dinner together outside) so they can see you doing it.

July

Treat lawn for newly hatched pests like chinch bugs, white grubs, sod webworms, bluegrass billbugs, and rabid deer.

Get more rain barrels. Continue watering schedule. Beaver now swim in your backyard every morning.

Begin to mow lawn daily and two nights a week. (Be careful of the beaver!)

August

Aerate your lawn. Walk on lawn with golf spikes. At least they're good for something.

Continue the supplemental watering schedule. Chase off beaver.

Mow the lawn on all days divisible by two.

Prune back hostas, sedge; pull weeds as needed.

Catch poison ivy.

September

Test the soil and make any necessary corrections before seeding.

Overseed the lawn and seed bare patches.

After seeding, keep the grass area consistently watered.

Design and carve out an intricate hedge maze somewhere on your property.

Lower mower blades to preferred height; mow lawn on all days divisible by three.

Catch poison ivy.

October

Rake and leaf-blow fallen leaves; mulch twice a week.

Fill up those pumpkin leaf bags. Keep them in yard until snow unthaws.

Reduce supplemental watering to eight inches every two weeks.

Mow lawn on all days divisible by four.

Sweep the first snow and/or ice and/or hail from sidewalk, porch, steps, and driveway.

November

End the watering schedule.

Rake fallen leaves and snow twice a week. Eye neighbors' trees indignantly.

Take apart lawn mower to tune it up for next season. Have a beer. Forget how to put lawn mower back together.

Do at least one thing, something, with a chain saw. (*Not* your neighbors' trees.)

Shovel or snowblow snow and/or ice from sidewalk, porch, steps, and driveway. (Ensure all pathways are cleared to keep people from walking on your lawn.)

Shovel or snowblow snow and/or ice from neighbors' sidewalks, porches, steps, and driveways.

December

Look at lawn mower pieces on garage floor. Have another beer.

Make sure your equipment is properly stored.

Tell everyone you're winterizing lawn tools. Install heater in garage, set up lawn chairs—this is now your winter escape.

Chase your son through the hedge maze with an ax.

Shovel or snowblow snow and/or ice from sidewalk, porch, steps, and driveway.

Shovel or snowblow snow and/or ice from neighbors' sidewalks, porches, steps, and driveways.

THE 7 STEPS TO LENDING TOOLS

Thanks to Taylor Calmus for the inspiration here!

You ~~may~~ will lend various tools and lawn equipment to your neighbors. Though your neighbors will be Midwest nice, that doesn't mean you'll get your stuff back soon, if at all. Some key steps in getting your chain saws and socket sets back:

Step 1. Lend. The potential joy of lending it out is part of the reason you bought the thing. Even if not asked, offer it.

Step 2. Ask. Months have passed. Start with "Hey, you done with that chain saw?" It's a nice straightforward hint.

Step 3. Hunt. Another month after the ignored ask/hint. Go to *their* house under the pretense of borrowing something or having a beer. Make sure to bring the beer. They'll ask if you'd like a glass. This is always obligatory and typically declined. But this time insist on it. Then, when they're in the kitchen smelling dirty glasses in the sink to make sure they're clean enough, you turn into 007 or Jessica Fletcher or Veronica Mars. Search high and low. If you locate the item, casually bring it up toward the last quarter of your beer. Then it's an easy grab and go. If not, proceed to Step 4.

Step 4. Confront. You'll have to openly say: "Hey, can I get that socket set back." They'll say "no problem" and promise to bring it over right away. They won't.

Step 5. Pledge. Swear to yourself you'll never lend anything out to anyone again. Buy a new socket set. Wave back and smile at your neighbor when they wave to you but inwardly glare angrily.

Step 6. Bribe. Your neighbor will bribe you with beer or a cookout. Despite your best efforts, all *will* be forgiven.

Step 7. Return to Step 1 when the neighbor asks to borrow something again. 🏠

Quick Quiz:
The Midwest Garage

What's the purpose of a Midwest garage?

a. Hoarding scrap wood

b. Collecting fishing poles from garage sales

c. Storing three broken minnow air pumps

d. Storing two freezers for venison

e. Storing your car so it won't get snowed on

If you chose storing your car so it won't get snowed on, you would be incorrect. In the Midwest, we view it as a sport to clean off our cars in the early morning hours. It's how we get our blood pressure to a properly chronic level before 7:00 a.m. (that plus mixing leftover brats into our eggs). If you chose the rest of the answers, you are correct.

You can tell a Midwest garage by its scrap-wood supply. If there's enough scrap wood in the garage rafters or stacked in the corners to build at least two other garages, there's a good chance you're in Kalamazoo.

But it's not just scrap wood. A good Midwest garage has an abundance of *everything* you'll never need. Two of everything you don't need, actually. It's like Noah's Ark if the animals were replaced with DD batteries, cracked five-gallon buckets, and old cane poles masquerading as curtain rods. On second thought, this is the stuff God *wanted* to drown. Regardless, it's now all in your garage.

However, if you think the garage is just for storing stuff, you'd also be incorrect. The garage is often the best seat in the house. There's no better way to watch the world go by than on a foldout aluminum lawn chair you rescued from the lake after a tornado in the early 2000s.

GRANDPA IN THE GARAGE

GRANDPA BOB AND MUSKIE BAIT—I MEAN REGAN

Grandpa Bob was my Midwest garage guru. He taught me everything I know about garages. He'd always be cleaning and reorganizing. I never understood how one man could find so many different locations for a drill press. I must have helped him rearrange it fifty times over the years, and the constant cleaning and rearranging never made sense to me . . . until I got a garage of my own. And then I started cleaning it. Every weekend. I'd move the fishing poles to a more efficient location, then the miter saw; I put up new hooks for my

bikes and then moved them. Time flew by. And when I was done, I felt better. No idea why, but I did. I came to realize that Grandpa Bob wasn't just reorganizing the garage; he was sorting out his mind. And it's good to do that at least twice a week. When I came to visit Grandpa, he'd always be sitting at the front of the open garage. Just sitting. Not on his phone. Occasionally a beer by his side. Just sitting.

The strangest thing about this was that Grandpa lived on Lake Winnebago. On the other side of the house, he had a porch with a beautiful view. Maybe Grandpa spent enough time on the lake fishing. (The freezer full of perch would certainly agree.) One time he turned to my brother and said, "I could do this all day long. I used to sit out here and watch the cows. Now I sit out here and watch the cars."

I guess there's just something about watching the world drive by. And what better place to do it than the comfort of your very own garage. 🏠

Fly Away, Little Snowbird

Now that you've got all that extra rent/mortgage money lying around from your cheap lodging costs, how about a nice trip somewhere else? From the middle of the country, you're in perfect striking zone of multiple destinations for your next retreat or holiday. Whether a new couple's getaway weekend, girls' trip, or the Griswolds (Illinois) taking to the road for a week-plus, you're never too far from an incredible escape. Long winters get tough for people in the Midwest, so when folks need a break, they head to a variety of homes away from home. Here are the most popular options.

The Ocean

Who doesn't love a trip to the beach? Good news. Sans plane, if you live at the eastern edge of Ohio, you can splash into the Atlantic in about seven hours. That's—*maybe*, if you're weak and/or didn't bring a Gatorade bottle—a one rest-stop trip. And from the western edge of Nebraska you can surf the Pacific in about eighteen hours. Missourians can reach the Gulf of Mexico in a short eleven-hour drive. From Ankeny to Evansville, families have been getting up at four in the morning to start the short road trip to Florida, Virginia, or Cuba. To help you choose, here's a little list:

$ Myrtle Beach, South Carolina

Other than maybe Purdue University, the "Dirty Myrtle" is where you can go to meet the most folks from Ohio, Indiana, and Illinois. For generations, a straight-shot highway with little interference from state troopers and the promise of endless blocks of buffet has provided the quickest (and cheapest!) means to white sands, the swish of surf, and putt-putt golf. It remains the undisputable number one vacation destination for folks from the Midwest. And why the heck not? A family of twelve can enjoy a week at the beach for the cost of an okay laptop. It's not called a Redneck Riviera for nothing.

$$$ Hilton Head, South Carolina

If you wanna get fancier, rent a place in Hilton Head, the Mecca of Midwest vacationers. There's golf and tennis, and the kids will get annoyed they have to wear a collared shirt to dinner and ask if Packers jerseys count. Give it a try. You're on vacation. For a week or two a year, you can pretend you live on the coast while baking in the sun, and also in the glory of knowing your family is the *best* family. To capture your annual excursion, make sure to slap that South Carolina palmetto-moon decal on the back of your car/truck. (You may live in Des Moines or Akron, but your family has a Hilton Head–worthy ledger and résumé.)

$$ Sanibel Island, Florida

A little farther south you'll find Sanibel and Captiva Islands, once a remote slice of paradise of pretty shells and bike paths for those with the portfolios and know-how to get there. Today, upscale Midwesterners still fancy themselves part of an exclusive club when they visit, but the fact that so many manage to do it should tell you something. Remember decades ago when Cozumel was a remote island only a few dared fly to upon escaping touristy Cancun? Well, in this metaphor, beautiful Sanibel is Cancun.

$$ Destin, Florida

An affordable beach town in one of Florida's most beautiful and weather-friendly zones. Blue waters, white sand, and loads of vitamin D that didn't come out of a bottle or cow teat. The badge of honor that comes with later explaining, "Nah, we just drove straight through," is akin to the pride of returning from the Holy Land in the ninth century.

$$ Panama City Beach, Florida

See: Destin . . . with more beer bongs.

$$ Gulf Shores, Alabama

The Alabama Gulf Coast offers thirty-plus miles of immaculate sandy beachfront, and a southern charm you won't get from the other destinations. It's where Midwesterners head for fried oyster po'boys and the Pink Pony Pub.

$ Ocean City, Maryland

They say "Maryland Is for Crabs," but it's also for people from Ottumwa and Bloomington.

$$ to $$$ Miscellaneous Distant Resorts

Yes, you will have to arrive at the airport at 2:06 A.M., but sometimes the best vacation is one you can't drive to. Bermuda, Mexico, Antigua. Barbados. The Dominican Republic. Costa Rica. Belize. Crete. You get the idea. Plan ahead, get those passports out for something other than Ireland or your distant "cousin's" place in Västerås, Sweden. Even though this is the most expensive option, Midwesterners will still find ways to save money: make a peanut butter and cheese sandwich for the flights and hit up the local spots for the best beer deals. You can always go all-inclusive where possible for convenience and likely savings; you *will* be sick of having the same thing for breakfast, lunch, and dinner six days in a row, *but* you're leaving tomorrow morning anyway.

A LONG WAY DOWN THE HOLIDAY ROAD . . .

As beautiful as Sheboygan is in February, Midwesterners occasionally get the itch to see other parts of the United States. My family was no different. One year, my parents surprised the whole family with a spring break trip to Alabama! Gulf Shores, to be exact. Something my dad had to specify after seeing the confused look on everyone's face when he said we were vacationing in Alabama. Nothing against Alabama; we were just bad at geography and didn't realize it had a waterfront.

"How are we gonna get there?" my sister Betsy asked.

"We're drivin'—it's gonna be fun," my dad shot back with the credibility of a political pundit.

To be clear, I believed the driving part. Big families don't fly. It's too much money and there are too many ways for one of the toddlers to find their way on a plane to Greece. I didn't step on an airplane until I was eighteen. Same for my brothers Andy and John. (My brother Bill first got on an airplane at nineteen . . . and jumped out of it twenty-five minutes later. Skydiving. It opened.) Point being, big family + Midwest = probably not flying for the first couple decades of your existence. Because driving is not only cheaper; it's also "fun." Even if your destination is fifteen hours and forty minutes away.

Okay, now to the trip. Was it "fun"? At this point in my life, my sibling count was up to ten. That meant twelve people were about to drive a thousand miles in a fifteen-seater van. Blood would soon be drawn over those three open seats.

Since we were told about the trip at Christmas, I'd had three months to shovel enough walks to buy a shockproof portable CD player. (An important detail, because between my CD player and the van, only one had adequate shock protection. I'm pretty sure Dodge just said, *Who needs good shocks? Most people are just gonna use this to carry lumber or dead bodies.*) As it turns out, twelve-year-old me had brilliant forethought in purchasing this CD player. I was the only one in the car who could escape the captive conversations of eleven other people, ages one to forty-five. The one-year-old did most of the talkin'—WAAAAAAAAAAAAAAAAAA. You get the picture. With my CD player, I could escape it all! But this genius decision also put a target on my back: everyone wanted what I had. By the time we got to southern Illinois, my older brother noticed that not only did I

have a CD player, I also had one of the extra seats. Andy decided my wealth needed to be equally distributed, so he appealed the seating decision to the Supreme Court (Mom and Dad). But Andy chose a poor time for his appeal; little sis Nora had just filled her diaper and was crying, so my parents kicked it back down to the lower court. That meant it was up to me and Andy to decide this for ourselves. After oral arguments had been made without any change, Andy resorted to a violent annexation of the extra seat.

Now, at this point I should mention that my CD player wasn't the audio oasis it seemed. You see, I'd left my CD book back in the garage. My shockproof Discman contained only . . . Creed. The year was 2000, and I was twelve, as we've established. We can't all be perfect. By the time we passed Champaign, I was ready to never hear Creed again. In fact, I was just using my headphones as earmuffs at this point. Meanwhile, Andy wasn't backing off his war on the open seat. So I decided to make a trade. If I gave him the CD player, I could keep the open seat for the rest of the trip. He agreed. Also, Andy hated Creed. I handed off the CD player. He pushed play. Then stop. He asked for my CD book and I told him it was back home in the garage, on the deer freezer. Then he threw the Creed CD at me.

And that's how I got the scar above my left eye. 🏠

Ocean-Free Options

Apparently the ocean isn't everyone's thing. Thanks, Spielberg. But don't worry—there are plenty of *Jaws*-less destinations to choose from when chipping ice off your gutters gets the best of you. So if you're still looking for a January jaunt, February flight, or March . . . march somewhere to break up the Midwest winter's monotony, I've got you covered.

$$–$$$ Arizona

This is where the Brewers, Cubs, Reds, White Sox, and Cleveland all do their spring training. And by spring training, these fans are knee-deep in their second winter. It's some fifteen hundred miles as the snowbird flies, or roughly twenty-seven-plus hours for those snowbirds who prefer driving to their destination.

$$$ Estes Park, Colorado

There are times it's nice to see something taller than a basketball hoop. In those times, go west, young Midwesterner. Estes Park remains the favored resort town for those heartlanders seeking whitewater rafting, horseback riding, skiing, or even a night in room 217 at the Stanley Hotel, featured in *The Shining*. Remember: "Every mountaintop is within reach if you just keep driving."

$ Gatlinburg, Tennessee

Imagine a typical family vacation to some touristy beach: the shops and amusement rides, the petting zoos and kitschy souvenirs, the miniature golf and long walks, the minor injuries and arguments, the trip to the local supermarket to marvel how different it is from the one at home, the schedules, the adult feel of making a reservation for dinner. Now, just take away the beach. Replace it with trees and fog. (*See also: Pigeon Forge.*)

$$ Chicago

Yes, we make a lot of jokes about Chicago in this book, but bet your best liar's poker dollar that we enjoy the heck out of that city. And too many Midwesterners have never been. It's packed with restaurants inspired by every region on the globe and constantly entertaining with comedy, music, and theater. If you want to shop, you can do it. Want to visit great museums, you can do that, too. Beautiful skyline? Check. Easy public transportation? Check. Waterfront views? Check. A giant reflective Bean? Check. Wait, what?

OUR NECK OF THE WOODS

HERE'S THE BERENS FAMILY DOUBLING THE POPULATION OF THE UP

Packing to go up nort' exists somewhere between skillful astrophysics and alchemy for my dad. What to pack always depends on what we would anticipate doing in the great North Woods: fishing poles, bags board, testicle toss (you may call it ladder toss if you wish), bow and arrows, golf clubs, skis, a chipped set of bocce balls (with a painted softball replacing one bocce ball that someone sent into the marsh last year), swimsuits, books for rainy days, inflatable swan raft with a small leak that needs daily replenishment, and so on.

Dad plays Tetris on his computer for months leading up to this day. Packing the trailer and van with all these "necessities" is not only a process—it's an art form. Dad considers himself the Picasso of Packing. The Monet of Suitcase Manipulation. It's a supply chain: a child brings an item from the garage, and Dad finds a place for it. He doesn't request items in any order, but he'll find a way to make it work. And then once the van is packed, Dad decides it's not good enough and refreshes his browser. He unpacks the trailer and the car and starts all over again. The smartest thing you could do in my family is ask your boss if you can work extra hours on packing day.

Why bring so much stuff? Because what if we want it? The closest store is twenty miles away! Did we use all this stuff? Absolutely not. But there's just something more relaxing knowing that if you get the urge, testicle toss is always in the trailer. 🏠

The Family Lake House

Growing up in the Midwest, there's a good chance you, your family, your extended family, or a close friend (or some guy you bumped into at the gas station) will end up with a lake house somewhere. These houses come in all shapes, sizes, and prices. A good rule of thumb is that this house should cost less than your main house; most ideally, you're just borrowing it from someone. You are either going "up" to the lake house or "down" to the lake house; never "left," "right," "over to," or any other directional. This is a rule of lake-house physics. Fighting with your adult siblings about who uses the house when, whether or not to sell it, whose kid brought the pot—it's all part of the fun. Anyway, once you get up or down to the house and settle in and scrape all that nasty green stuff off the landing deck, kayaks, firepit, and sandbox, you're good to go for a week of stepping on toads.

Lake house must-haves: the original Monopoly and Clue board games (untouched since 1974), framed pictures of ducks, a hanging bed or hammock, several decks of cards that clearly reveal themselves as euchre decks (with twenty cards still sparkling white, showing how truly gross we all are), a toilet-paper holder shaped like a moose, a floating pong table, floating coolers, a floating dock with a hammock, floating pillows, a floating refrigerator, a floating bookcase, a floating fireplace—you get the picture. And every room will also need signage and/or pillows that say things like: *Go Jump in the Lake* or *Relax, You're at the Lake* or *Sip Happens!* or *Life Is Better at the Lake* or *It's a Lake Thing*, or . . .

Speaking of which . . .

WHAT *NOT* TO DO WHEN YOU VISIT SOMEONE ELSE'S LAKE HOUSE . . .

My friend Mike went to my aunt and uncle's lake house. (I'm omitting actual names in case my Aunt Debbie actually reads this book.) Anyway, my aunt had a guest book in their beautiful cabin, and Mike wanted to leave the perfect message. Here's what he wrote: "Life is better at the lake. You never know how many friends you have until you have a lake house. If you haven't grown up by age fifty, you don't have to. In dog beers I've only had one . . ." This message continued on for two more pages. You see Mike had taken the guest book and walked around the house writing down the text from every decorative sign hanging in the cabin.

And that was the last time Mike saw the inside of that cabin. 🏠

To Charlie's Aunt and Uncle!
Life is better at the lake. You never know how many friends you have until you have a lake house. If you haven't grown up by age fifty, you don't have to. In dog beers, I've only had one. Women love me, fish fear me. This is a night. If it was a good night, I would be fish~
[cont.]

JEAN BAPTISTE DUSABLE
FOUNDER OF CHICAGO

Jean DuSable
State: Illinois
Artist: Naimah Thomas (2021)

Midwest Gallery

There's no way for one guy from Wisconsin to tell you everything about the Midwest. That's why I wanted to include the Midwest Gallery. We sifted through hundreds of incredible artist submissions and selected one piece of art by representatives in each Midwest state. They say a picture is worth a thousand words . . . which means there's at least a whole other book on these pages. So when someone compliments this book in your bathroom, you can tell them you got a two-for-one deal on it. We love them two-for-one deals in the Midwest.

Diana Ross on Sign
State: Michigan
Artist: Desiree Kelly (2018)

We Built This City on Cereal
State: Iowa
Artist: Tim Gallenbeck (2019)
Based on original concept by RAYGUN

Winnebago Camp
State: Nebraska
**Artist: Henry Payer,
Ho-Chunk (2019)**
**Mixed media and
collage on canvas
(28" x 33")**
**Photo Credit:
Aaron C. Packard**

Firefishing
State: Ohio
**Artist:
Brendan Wentz (2021)**

Ho-Chunk Appliques
State: Wisconsin
Artist: Christopher J. Sweet, Ho-Chunk/White Earth Ojibwe (2021)

Moonrise Flames
State: Kansas
Artist: Louis Copt (2006)

Pinnesota
State:
Minnesota
Artist:
Gigi Berry
(2021)

Screaming Corn Delivers Toasted Ravioli
State: Missouri
Artist: Abby Nami (2021)

*Indiana State
Bird Atop
Indiana State
Flower*
State: Indiana
Artist: Joe
Kintz (2021)

Standing Still
State: South Dakota
Artist: Dustin Twiss (2021)

Community
State: North Dakota
Artist: Bill Brien, Lakota,
Dakota, Chippewa,
Metis Art (2020)

The Goings-on

We live in a country consumed by work, status, bad news—and social media to distract us from it all . . . is exactly what a person who hasn't been fishing in a while says. The Midwest is far from perfect, but the people here have come close to perfecting the best ways to recharge their badtrees.

Ice fishing, tailgating, camping, cardiovascular exercises like cornhole, church festivals, and bar crawls—you name it, we've turned to it in times of trouble, joy, boredom, or bad weather.

Speaking of the weather . . . the colder it is, the weirder our leisure gets. Look no further than the lady walking to the port-o-pot-turned-ice-shanty with a chainsaw and a bucket of fishing poles. Her name's Jan. If you bring her enough beer she might just give you a walleye. When she does, tell her I says hi.

There are hundreds of options ranging from free to somehow dropping another $450 on a boat that's still broke. Here are a few options if you want to give it a go.

Boating

If there's ever a sequel to this book, it'll be about life on the lakes. From Traverse City to Lake of the Ozarks, there's an intricate and enduring civilization of millions who have their own language, traditions, food, mating rituals, and ways of binding a foolproof knot—sometimes all at the same time. They say, "A boat is a hole in the water you throw money into." But then again, you gotta do something with that money.

There are more than nine trillion lakes in the Midwest, conservatively speaking, and five of them are bigger than most seas; boats are everywhere. "Taking the boat out" can mean anything from an eight-foot Alumacraft that leaks like a colander to a sixty-year-old pontoon boat your grandpa converted to a houseboat that sleeps thirty (or six comfortably). You'll also find sailboats and center console fishing boats that cost more than most homes. Now obviously most people don't have the money for a boat. Luckily it's easy to make friends in the Midwest. If you hit the right bars and make enough small talk, you could be on a boat by 9:00 A.M. tomorrow morning. (Okay, maybe closer to noon because one of you ordered shots of Malört.)

Kayak vs. Jet Ski

Thanks to Myles Montplaisir for the inspiration here.

There are many types of boaters in the Midwest, and some couldn't be more opposite. Of course I'm talking about the kayaker and the jet skier. While a rare few people do both, choosing which of these options is right for you may take some time, real-world experience, and reflection. Here's a little chart to help get you started:

Kayak	Jet Ski
Connect with the blue gill	0 to 70 in half a Red Bull
Close your eyes, feel the sun on your face	Yell *whoooooooooo!* Lose voice, gain speed.
Organic granola bar in pocket for later	RockStar in free hand
Constructed from recycled ocean plastic	Two-stroke engine leaking unburned fuel
Sometimes mistakenly called a canoe; *very* annoying	Loose spark plugs; *very* annoying
Burns 280 calories an hour	Burns four tanks of gas an hour

Snowmobiling

The Midwest is most often mocked for two things: being flat and covered in snow. Well, that's why Darwin gave us snowmobiles. See "Jet Ski," above. Our forebears used sleds and dogs, but you have to feed dogs and pick ice out of their toes and whatnot. Today, if you want to get across a frozen lake or back to that deer stand or down to the grocery store when eleven inches fell the night before, the feel of 200

HP grumbling between your legs is a power and opportunity to be embraced . . . with a good term life policy. No grooming or care required; just toss the tarp back over it until you're ready to go again. Bonus safety feature: you'll never get lost, as people from twenty miles away will always know exactly where you are.

Fishing: The Ones Who Got Away . . .

There's a library of books written on fishing and it would be impossible to do this sport and craft proper justice in just a few pages. But if you're angling for some fish tales of your own, here are a few of the basics you need to know before tackling this sacred calling and heading out on the lake.

Your tackle box can carry at least ten beers. If it can't, you need to return it to the Fleet Farm. It's defective.

If you tangle your line, you untangle it. Biting the line is for quitters.

If you're still untangling your line, bite it. Life's too short.

If you snag Dad's lure, it's worth diving in for it. If there's too much muck in the water to see it, stay down there until you find *another* lure you can replace it with. There's one down there, promise.

Never bring a camera along. Your lies will be easier to believe without one.

Also leave the phone at home. Nobody should distract you from this. It's like church . . . except you leave your phone at home.

Know your fishing knots. You'll want to learn these before you learn to tie your shoes. Nikes never caught walleyes.

The Clinch Knot

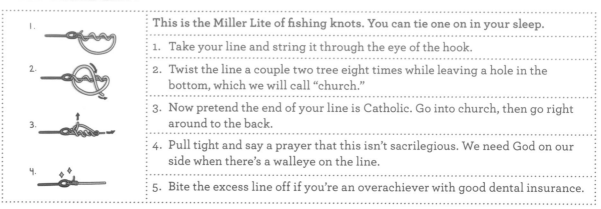

This is the Miller Lite of fishing knots. You can tie one on in your sleep.

1. Take your line and string it through the eye of the hook.
2. Twist the line a couple two tree eight times while leaving a hole in the bottom, which we will call "church."
3. Now pretend the end of your line is Catholic. Go into church, then go right around to the back.
4. Pull tight and say a prayer that this isn't sacrilegious. We need God on our side when there's a walleye on the line.
5. Bite the excess line off if you're an overachiever with good dental insurance.

The Palomar Knot

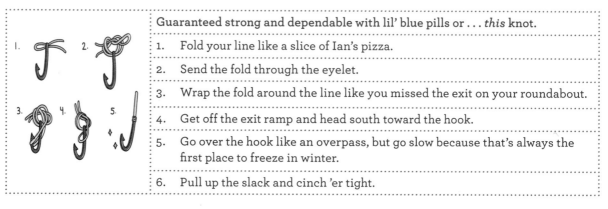

Guaranteed strong and dependable with lil' blue pills or . . . *this* knot.

1. Fold your line like a slice of Ian's pizza.
2. Send the fold through the eyelet.
3. Wrap the fold around the line like you missed the exit on your roundabout.
4. Get off the exit ramp and head south toward the hook.
5. Go over the hook like an overpass, but go slow because that's always the first place to freeze in winter.
6. Pull up the slack and cinch 'er tight.

The Turtle Knot

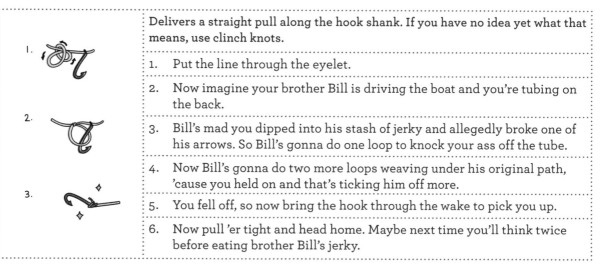

Delivers a straight pull along the hook shank. If you have no idea yet what that means, use clinch knots.

1. Put the line through the eyelet.
2. Now imagine your brother Bill is driving the boat and you're tubing on the back.
3. Bill's mad you dipped into his stash of jerky and allegedly broke one of his arrows. So Bill's gonna do one loop to knock your ass off the tube.
4. Now Bill's gonna do two more loops weaving under his original path, 'cause you held on and that's ticking him off more.
5. You fell off, so now bring the hook through the wake to pick you up.
6. Now pull 'er tight and head home. Maybe next time you'll think twice before eating brother Bill's jerky.

A FIN-TASTIC MEMORY

One of my favorite childhood memories is waking up with a surprise under my pillow. Was it money from the tooth fairy? Nope. This was worth far more. It was fishing gear. Each of my brothers got something different. Andy got hooks. Billy got bobbers. I got snap swivels, which I called "hook bites," and still do to this day. (Because if you look at a snap swivel when it opens up, it looks like it bites the hook . . . Kinda . . . sorta? I was dropped as a child.) Anyway, what I called them isn't important. What's important is what it meant: we were going fishing.

And, where did we go? Fond du Lac, where Grandpa Bob and Grandma Sue lived. We went to the park, to be specific. Where specifically in the park? I'd tell ya but it's a great fishing spot. And Midwest people may be generous with a lot of things, but information on their best fishing spots is not one of those things. Asking someone where they caught a fish is like asking someone their age, net worth, or thoughts on religion. . . . "It's just not polite."

On this particular fall day we were going for northern pike, the third-biggest fish in Lake Winnebago after sturgeon and the elusive muskie. Dad told me I should use a big bobber and a minnow or small perch as bait. But I didn't get bobbers under my pillow. I got hook bites. And that's what I wanted to use. Dad

WHO'S READY FOR BREAKFAST?

grew up in Fondy and knew the fishing. He recommended against my plan, but I tossed on that hook bite and a rubbery fish lure. Nobody expected me to catch anything, and after five casts I was bored and ready to believe them. So I sat there just jigging the artificial bait in my boredom, getting progressively colder and borederer, until Dad noticed I was bored and told me to try something else. I retorted, "No! I'm not bored. I saw this on a fishing show." The worst thing I could do was display, or admit to, boredom. That was worse than lying. So I committed to jigging this artificial lure. I started playing mind games; imagined a fish biting the lure. That didn't work. I said two Our Fathers. Nope, nothing. I started saying a Hail Mary but stopped because my dad had left *The Godfather: Part II* on the week before. I tried reciting the Packers' starting offense. Nada. I was soooo bored. My hands were now

freezing. I wanted nothing more than to get back in the car. I was to the point of never wanting to fish ag—

"I got one," I screamed. "I got one!"

I looked at Dad, who had that *You've got to be sh*tt*ng me* look in his eyes. You see, Dad had northern fishing down to a science, and here I was, messing around with a banjo minnow rig on a "hook bite." But it's in these moments you can tell a great fisherman. First they get that look of jealous rage, like they're gonna throw you in for getting the first fish. But then they'll scream those three magic words: "Get the net!"

And Dad got the net. And I caught a three-foot pickerel. It's the only one I've ever caught to this day. And it might be my favorite catch. Because as an impressionable child, I could feel my love for fishing slipping away with every freezing moment. But as soon as I felt that bite, I didn't just hook a pickerel—fishing hooked me.

And yes, it was three feet. And no, I didn't take a picture.

And Another Fishy Story

My mom and dad slept with a radio alarm clock next to their bed, and they'd wake up to the radio, not the alarm. On Saturday mornings Mom and Dad would greet the day with Tom Neubauer's fishing show. (Clearly the alarm clock was on Dad's side of the bed.) And on this one particular Saturday, here's how Tom

Neubauer woke up my parents: "All right, folks, let's go to the phones. We've got Andy and Charlie on the phone from New Berlin."

That was me and my brother Andy, just trying to become fishing famous. We didn't grow up like many do today, with celebrities on our cell phones. We grew up with Tom Neubauer on the radio. Tom Neubauer was our Justin Bieber. Andy and I would often wake up early on Saturdays to get Tom's fishing advice and, more important, gain his approval. One week we caught some minnows in a river we weren't supposed to go by because of flooding. You better believe we called Tom to help us identify our catch.

My parents proceeded to listen to their two oldest tell Tom that the "walleyes were biting in Lake Winnebago . . . right off Stinky Point, in fact." Tom asked where we caught the minnows and Andy said, "The river." What Tom and his dedicated listeners must have heard on the other end of the interview was a smack and a phone fumble. That was me hitting my older brother. We knew Mom and Dad sometimes listened in. Getting caught at the river would mean we'd be sitting in a minnow trap of our own.

I rescued the phone from the floor and told Tom we actually caught them in the pond. Tom told us we probably had bass minnows then. Our truth was concealed for the moment—but I still haven't forgiven myself for lying to Tom Neubauer. 🐟

YES, MY SISTER'S FISH IS TWICE AS BIG—THANKS FOR BRINGING IT UP.

The Fish You Will (Maybe) Catch . . .

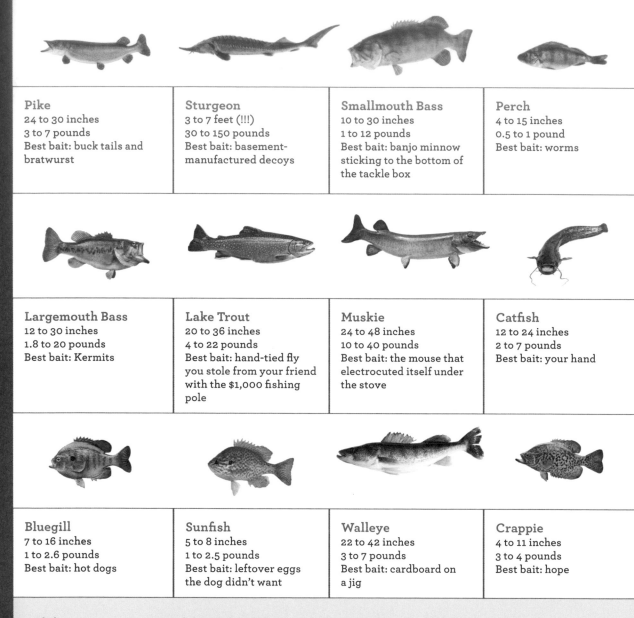

Pike
24 to 30 inches
3 to 7 pounds
Best bait: buck tails and bratwurst

Sturgeon
3 to 7 feet (!!!)
30 to 150 pounds
Best bait: basement-manufactured decoys

Smallmouth Bass
10 to 30 inches
1 to 12 pounds
Best bait: banjo minnow sticking to the bottom of the tackle box

Perch
4 to 15 inches
0.5 to 1 pound
Best bait: worms

Largemouth Bass
12 to 30 inches
1.8 to 20 pounds
Best bait: Kermits

Lake Trout
20 to 36 inches
4 to 22 pounds
Best bait: hand-tied fly you stole from your friend with the $1,000 fishing pole

Muskie
24 to 48 inches
10 to 40 pounds
Best bait: the mouse that electrocuted itself under the stove

Catfish
12 to 24 inches
2 to 7 pounds
Best bait: your hand

Bluegill
7 to 16 inches
1 to 2.6 pounds
Best bait: hot dogs

Sunfish
5 to 8 inches
1 to 2.5 pounds
Best bait: leftover eggs the dog didn't want

Walleye
22 to 42 inches
3 to 7 pounds
Best bait: cardboard on a jig

Crappie
4 to 11 inches
3 to 4 pounds
Best bait: hope

*fish sizes are average and depend on lake size and how honest your fishing buds are

Brazen plug time! For foolproof fish enticement, be sure to check out Grandpa Bob's Tackle Box—available at ManitowocMinute.com. *Fish beware!* Named for the Lake Winnebago legend himself, Grandpa Bob's Tackle Box is da key to successful fishing in da Midwest. Six lures with inspirational phrases, custom-made by Mepps over der in Antigo, home of the World's #1 Lure. Popular with fishermen worldwide for catching anything that bites. In the words of Grandpa Bob: *"Cripes Alfrighty, these soms a guns is really somethin'!"*

Ice Fishing

Fishing can be demanding enough. Now add 184 pounds of layering, Arctic winds, and two feet of solid ice between you and the fish—and you have a bit of recreation that many Midwesterners do all winter long. Whether participants are in tricked-out heated trailers watching the game with half a dozen friends or hunched alone on some five-gallon bucket, ice fishing accounts for a quarter of all fish caught recreationally in the Midwest. It's also a dangerous and often fruitless/fishless endeavor. But any chance—clearly *any* chance—to get outside is still better than a day wasted indoors.

There are dozens of tips we could give—from wearing camouflage to befuddle the fish to keeping the hole unthawed with a can of hot coals or a cooked brat—but it'd take six pages alone just to tell you how to distinguish if the ice is really *frozen* frozen. So, before you pull on those new shanty panties or get to experience the joy of watching a first-time ice fisher's face when they first hear that melodious crack of ice (which is actually usually proof the ice is freezing *more*—it's the quiet ice ya gotta worry about), here's all you need to know: *Go out with someone who really knows what they're doing. Someone with Korbel in their tackle box.*

Also, don't *ever* drive your car onto the lake. We legally have to say that, knowing you're going to anyway. That being the case, *always* keep your windows open when driving on said ice, for a quick James Bond escape if needed. Also, no seat belts. Out there it may be click it or ticket. But on the ice it's click it and sink with it. Remember, this *isn't* your grandpa's ice; the climate has changed a lot since he retrofitted that old Cadillac with fishing holes in the floorboards.

Hunting

Midwesterners hunt many birds, critters, and squeezles, including duck, rabbit, squirrel, pheasant, grouse, goose, and of course deer. And, for each species of animal, there's a species of hunter—each with their different quirks and attributes.

Now, some people don't like hunting, and that's understandable. If you fall into that camp, please keep in mind that I'm usually a vegan hunter due to my poor aim. Now that you know I'm on your side, you can continue reading without guilt. Also, according to an article I read online once: hunting deer (which *are* generally overpopulated) and wild pigs (which *are* an invasive species) *is* good for the ecosystem. (I'd explain why but I only read half the article online before getting distracted with the Big Buck Hunter app.)

When it comes to deer hunting, there are different seasons for the various methods of demise. There are also different clothes you have to wear. During bow season, you wear a camo coat. Gun season, you wear a blaze-orange coat. During muzzle loader season, you wear a red coat. (Yes, I wrote this entire paragraph for that punch line. I hope it was worth it.)

Deer hunters also like to spray themselves with doe pee. If that sounds weird, that's a good thing; it means you're not weird. But deer hunters have their rationale. You see, to bucks, doe pee doesn't smell nasty, it smells like . . . perfume. We have Chanel No. 5, they have Chanel No. 1. So hunters spray it on themselves and hope the wind will catch their scent and lure an unsuspecting buck. (Does it work? Well, one year I put on some doe pee, tossed the bottle in my car, and headed to my deer stand. I was up in that thing for five hours and didn't see one buck. But then, I got back to my car and realized the doe pee had spilled all over my back seat. The smell could only be described as: *a zoo in an oven*. I wisely rolled down the windows and headed home. It was unbelievable. I didn't see a single deer during my hours of hunting, but on the drive home five different bucks tried to mount my Corolla.)

Then there's the calls. When you're buck hunting, there's grunt, rattle, bleat, and snort-wheeze calls. Most of these calls are the hunter's attempt to lure in the trophy bucks looking to show their dominance. "Estrus bleats," on the other hand, are made by does when they're trying to mate.

I never thought about the calls until one year at deer camp. We were all outside on the porch cooking on the grill and drinking beers. Inside, my buddy Jeff turned on a *Game of Thrones* episode. The volume was loud enough that we could hear the TV, but not loud enough to understand anything that was going on. Then a "kissing scene" came on. Soon, a lady was moaning pretty loud. I watched as five of the six guys on the porch made a beeline for the television. I stayed manning the grill, as the steaks needed to be gently seared and a moment too long would ruin them. So, instead of following one primal drive, I tended another.

And then I began to ponder: What if one of those bucks mounted on the wall was real? And that fake wooden wall was his camouflage. What if Jeff didn't turn on the TV at all? What if that was the buck's practiced human call?! I abandoned my grilling duties and bolted into the house to rescue my friends from being viciously mauled to death by said buck seeking revenge for his other family members hanging in deer camp. As it turns out, I have a wild imagination. And we all had burnt steak that night.

Cooking Out

Speaking of grilling, a good cookout is the perfect amalgamation of all things Midwest: meat, friends, family, open flames, sipping beer, and standing outside (or in the garage *with the door open* if it's raining). These occasions can be thrown together quickly, as there's always meat in the old freezer in the basement or garage. You know that special feeling you get when the power goes out for four days and everyone comes outside to grill before the meat goes bad and— No? Well, you will. Anyhoo, there's no reason to wait for the next tornado to experience that sensation. Just fire up the grill—gas, charcoal, firewood, or that fancy pellet-burning thing you got on sale at the Fleet Farm—whichever you prefer, and get to standing/sipping. As your grilling skills and manners are one of the principal ways you'll be judged by neighbors, coworkers, in-laws, and your own kids, here are a couple basic rules to always keep in mind:

1. Never touch another griller's bratwurst. If it ain't your grill, your only responsibility is to bring the griller more beer, watch the broiler, and say things like "Looks real good" or "Can't wait" or "I gotta get one of these things. How much did it run ya?" Keep the kerosene kibitzing and back-seat barbecuing to yourself.
2. Have patience; it's the journey, not the destination. Have another beer. The meat will be ready when it's ready.

3. Spread the charcoal, wood, or flames unevenly; you want heat-zone options.

4. Treat your grill better than you do your kids—clean it often, protect it from the elements, and spend more time with it. This will all add up to a better grilling experience for you, the grill, and, ultimately, your kids.

Watching Sports

The Midwest is home to the greatest sports teams on the planet . . . unless you like soccer. Football, baseball, basketball, curling, hockey, and yes, *curling*; the list goes on and on. Watching on the TV is fine and all, but taking in a game in person is the preferred method when watching athletes between the ages of eight and eighty.

Fans are knowledgeable and passionate about their teams. Not saying other regions' fans aren't (we see you, Buffalo . . . and we're still sorry about those Super Bowls), but the heartland version is just a little more loyal and enthusiastic when it comes to getting behind the local team. Doesn't matter if it's the NFL, NFHS, NCAA, or ACO, Midwesterners take their professional sports seriously. And yes, ACO stands for American Cornhole Organization. If you haven't tailgated a professional cornhole match before, you're really missing out.

ALWAYS BET ON THE GREEN BAY PACKERS

I WON A BET WITH MY MOM AND GOT TO WEAR THIS TO CHURCH.

The year was 2010. The month was September. The city: Las Vegas. But first, the backstory.

Nine months earlier I had moved from Wisconsin to Los Angeles to try and make it in the entertainment biz. But I was mostly just making coffee. What I wasn't making was money. At least not a lot of it.

The Wisconsin Badgers were playing UNLV that weekend in Vegas. And a bunch of my Wisconsin friends were going to be there. But like I said, I was broke. Real broke. Rescuing bagels from the office garbage for dinner broke.

Luckily that weekend I just so happened to be more homesick than broke. I had a minivan full of gas. And a not-too-far-off city full of friends.

I was promised a prime spot on my buddy's hotel room floor. If that fell through, I knew I could always rely on the floor of my minivan.

Speaking of my minivan, I was really hoping I'd win enough gas money at the casino to get home.

So, I rolled the dice and headed toward the desert.

Now, even though the Wisconsin Badgers were the reason I went to Las Vegas, the Green Bay Packers are the reason I'm telling this story.

You see, I've been a die-hard Packers fan since I was a kid.

How die-hard?

I painted my face green and gold one hour before bedtime die-hard.

I tried to get a priest to bless my Reggie White toy locker die-hard.

I kept a kiddie cocktail spear from Major Goolsby's tavern in Milwaukee because it was

Packers green. I couldn't throw it out, it was good luck. So for the rest of the season I set it in front of me while I sat cross-legged in front of the TV and pointed the spear end toward the Packers' end zone each time they changed possession. *Die-hard!*

I really wish I was making that last one up. We'll get to the Packers in a second.

But first, back to the Badgers game. I didn't have enough cash to get a ticket, so I watched it with some friends at Caesars Palace. Then I took my last twenty bucks to the blackjack tables hoping to double and dump it into my gas tank, but I ended up on a hot streak. I was up $150. That was a record for me. It beat out my previous gambling record at Potawatomi Casino by $175.

Then the words of my Grandpa Bob echoed in my head: "When you're winning . . . walk!"

Grandpa was right. I was eating garbage bagels, for cripes' sakes. I needed to save this money and spend it wisely.

So I got up. I didn't want to. I wanted to play more. But I listened to that voice of Grandpa Bob. "When you're winning . . . walk!"

Then I walked past the sports book.

And the words of my Grandma Sue echoed in my head: "Maybe just one more."

Enter again the Green Bay Packers.

Even though the Packers' season had not yet started. And even though my heart still hadn't fully mended after their Super Bowl XXXII loss to Denver thirteen years earlier. And even though the Packers' odds of winning the Super Bowl were either 13 to 1 or 18 to 1 . . . I forget, but it didn't matter. They could have been 100 to 1—I was still dropping almost all the money

I just won playing blackjack on the Packers to win Super Bowl XLV.

Now some might call this a dumb financial decision. Not me. I called it an investment opportunity.

In fact, I called Uncle Denny to give him details on my recent investment, in case he might want to buy in.

Uncle Denny: *Charlie, that's a crazy bet. What were you thinking?*
Charlie: *I know, it's a little dumb, but—*
Uncle Denny: *I want in.*
Charlie: *How much?*
Uncle Denny: *$50*
Charlie: *Done.*

It's always nice to share some risk with a fellow die-hard Packers fan. I believe the financial terminology for such a transaction is "the ol' Wisconsin cheese hedge."

This was going to be a great uncle/nephew bonding moment. We'd have a new reason to stay in touch all season long. Yeah, $150 was a lot of money, but the Pack would win the Super Bowl. . . . I mean, why wouldn't they? Aside from the fact that they hadn't won it in thirteen years.

Okay, worst-case scenario, the Packers don't win. That's why the hedge is in place. And at least I remembered to set aside forty bucks for gas—oh shoot. I didn't pull those twenties out of my winnings before placing my bet.

"Excuse me, miss? I just put a $150 bet on the Packers to win the Super Bowl. Is there a chance I can return this ticket and bet forty bucks less? I just need gas home. Actually, I drive a minivan, so let's just make it $50—why are you laughing, miss? Ope, no refunds . . . welp, I s'pose the sign does say that. I understand this is a casino and all bets are final and whatnot. But in Wisconsin, if I asked Larry over there at Oneida nicely, he wouldn't have a problem refunding my ticket. I'd just buy him an old-fashioned as a thank-you. Have you ever tried a brandy old-fashioned? Okay, no need to call security, I'm leaving."

Die. Hard.

So there I was. Seven hours into my Las Vegas vacation. Broke. Or as I liked to say, cash poor. (I was worth a lot on paper.)

That night I hung out with my Wisconsin friends. They knew I didn't have much money, and they bought me drinks. I offered to get their next ones, but they never let me. We drank and laughed for hours. I don't remember the specifics, but I'll never forget that feeling. With friends like these, you don't need gas home. Because you're already there. (Of course you still run out of gas the next morning, but that's another story.)

Anyway, somehow I found my way home from Las Vegas. And Uncle Denny and I texted throughout the season.

I remember him texting me when the Packers beat the Cowboys.

"Romo woulda made it worse."

I remember texting Uncle Denny after we lost to the Lions.

"Has any team ever lost to the Lions and won a Super Bowl?"

It wasn't until the Packers clobbered the Giants 45 to 17 that the texts started getting a bit more serious.

Uncle Denny: *We're gonna be rich. Don't lose that ticket!!!*

And then after the Packers gloriously beat the Bears in the NFC Championship . . .

Uncle Denny: *You have the ticket somewhere safe, right?*
Charlie: *You bet!!*

Because I did, right! Right? *Right?!?!?* What did I do with that ticket????

I couldn't remember. Retrace your steps. I had it at Caesars. Say a prayer to St. Anthony. And then I got drinks with the Wisconsin guys and then . . . then . . . oh no . . . St. Anthony, anything, guy?!

Ope. Shoot.

The Packers went on to win the Super Bowl that season. Our investment had reached maturity. But the thing about being rich on paper is . . . you gotta have the paper.

Ya know, a funny thing happens when you realize you lost a winning ticket from the Caesars sport book likely worth twenty-six times your current net worth. You learn how to tear out car carpeting real fast.

I never did find that ticket. But I did learn a few lessons:

If you invest $150 in something, don't put it in your pocket and drink with your Wisconsin friends.

Do stupid things. They'll help you fill out pages in your book one day.

And most important, *always* bet on the Green Bay Packers. 🐟

Tailgating: Party in the Trunk

Vehicles are a marvelous invention, but vehicles stuffed with precooked meat and twenty-eight fixings for your Bloody Mary are a work of art.

In 1896, Henry Ford rolled out his first automobile for sale, the Quadricycle runabout, and made $200. That same weekend, several Michiganders gathered around the new car to drink beer and eat brats and potato salad. There may or may not have been a sporting event somewhere nearby. Midwesterners are always looking for a reason to tailgate, and they're everywhere: NFL games, NCAA rivalries, high school football, Halloween, backyard lawn darts, Target, traffic jams, a couple of kids playing hopscotch, you name it. Drop that tailgate or pop up that trunk to unleash all the magic waiting within. The foldout tents and tables. The Frito pie stations and bread bowls filled with chili. The flights of mezcal and craft beer carefully arranged . . . just kidding. The Igloo coolers full of Hamm's, MGD, Busch, and Miller High Life (the Champagne of Beers), if you're classy.

The key to tailgating is the groundwork. You've got to plan ahead. All the chopping for fixings is done the day before. Skewer and marinate those kebabs. Make Jell-O shots in your team's colors. Label your coolers. Fill your Craftsman portable toolbox with whisks and wooden spoons, peelers, toothpicks, muddlers, basting brushes, and fish turners. The invasion of Normandy took less preparation.

As with most things Midwest, the next ingredient you'll need is community—and the food and drinking that comes with, but mostly community. Family and friends will drive six-plus hours to get to a ~~game~~ tailgate. Spots in stadium parking lots are well claimed, acknowledged, and literally passed down to preferred offspring. The average football game is only three hours; tailgating turns this into an eleven-hour event, and that's getting more bang for your buck. (Not joking: polls suggest some 35 percent of tailgaters never actually go into the game.) The key is to meet the folks parked around you and their friends and family. Keep doing this until you have two hundred new friends and are invited to the wedding of some family you met seven seasons ago while playing bags.

Bonfires: Some More S'mores

A million years ago, more or less, we invented the bonfire when a group of friends and family gathered around a pile of burning wood, antlers, dodo feathers, and whatever else they could get their hairy palms on. A night of sharing stories, maybe flirting with someone new, quietly watching the stars, some guy named Oggggkok poorly strumming that tricky F chord . . . and everyone going to bed later with a final comment about the smell of smoke trapped in their hair. Like humanity, the bonfire hasn't evolved all that much in the ensuing millennia. All you need is stuff to burn, one person who knows how to get it started, several others to weigh in on their methodology, and a general commitment to making a night of it. ***Bonfire parties are the best parties*** because you're outside, and we all know that outside rules are different from inside rules. You're in the woods or in a field . . . and there's nothing to ruin or break out here. So, spill that drink, toss some chaw into that lip, sneak off to puke, take that bathroom break—the woods or field will be there long after you are. The cost is almost nothing: just BYOB and find some stuff to burn (sur-

prisingly everywhere: sticks, old furniture, unread textbooks, cardboard, toxic plastics, closet doors, Dutch shoes, toothpaste, drywall, and so on). You won't find a line, cover charge, or $12 beer out here. And no need to get gussied up; layer up in whatever you'd rake leaves or clean the garage in. The more casual you look, the better. Come one, come all—bring your dogs, leave your dignity . . . find pictures of Eddie Vedder and dress exactly like that. Now all you have to do is eat, talk, listen, and stone-cold chill. S'mores are okay, but "a couple" of beers or whatever is currently legal in your state ain't too shabby either. The fresh air, the stars above, the moon, the sounds of large unseen Lovecraftian things moving in the darkness just behind you—so fun! Staring at your cell phone would undermine the whole point of the evening and so, just stare at the fire instead. It's the world's oldest distraction.

When in doubt, toss something on the fire. Anything. (Just make sure Smokey the Bear isn't holding the high sign.) When London burned in 1666, neighboring hamlets gathered at the edges to drink and sing "Wonderwall." The great philosopher Alfred Pennyworth once observed, "Some men just wanna watch the world burn." But we all know by "world" he meant a Milwaukee's Best can.

County and State Fairs

Midwesterners love their county and state fairs. The Minnesota State Fair alone brings in two million visitors a year. Three presidents have visited Wisconsin's State Fair: Abraham Lincoln, Rutherford B. Hayes, and Howard Taft. The latter blamed Wisconsin State Fair cream puffs for his record-breaking bath. But people don't just come to these fairs for cream puffs. They also come for cheese curds, funnel cakes, deep-fried buckeyes, corn dogs, potatoes made of ice cream, pork chops on a stick, bierocks, and beers. They come to hear the greatest cover bands this side of the Miss . . . Dairyland competition. Yes, I'm talking about Billy Goat Joel, Shotguns and Roses, Run-D.M.V., and Hard of Hearing Leopard (who got caught in the bathroom doing a line of Tums). They come to see 4-H carcass judging, goat milking, and the occasional sheep with spray-painted knees. But mostly they come together around a shared love for the place they live. . . . Also, did I mention the cream puffs?

Church Festivals

Part high school reunion, part family reunion, part occasion to safely bring the kids where you can drink all night . . . *that* is the church festival. If you plan ahead, you can hit one pretty much every weekend.

Thou Shalt

I
Play games of chance.

II
Meet old classmates you saw at the last church festival.

III
Lie to yourself about going to church more often, starting . . . soon.

IV
Bid on auction items you will never actually use.

V
Excuse yourself to the port-o-pots to get out of conversation.

Thou Shalt Not

I
Park easily.

II
Leave early.

III
Ever volunteer to run a booth again.

IV
Have a clue where your kids are.

V
Say no to the pastor pushing raffle tickets.

Cornhole

Bags, beanbag toss, tailgate toss, soft horseshoes, baggo, chuck-o, doghouse, dadhole, dummy boards . . . and despite all those names, most people still land on cornhole. This is one of the all-time ultimate Midwestern sports. Notice I didn't say game.

Its origin is ascribed to German immigrants or Kentucky farmers or the Blackfeet tribe of Illinois. At the epicenter of all those options is Cincinnati—which generally gets credit for gifting the rest of the Midwest with its cornhole (seriously, out of all the names). The game has been around for a century, but in recent years, it's spread to coastal bars as something new to try out. If you're in the Midwest for forty-eight hours, believe-you-me you'll be called on to play this great Midwest tradition. No graduation party, family re-union, cookout, funeral, protest, barn raising, outdoor concert, or pontoon can escape cornhole's grasp.

It's a simple game similar to horseshoes in which two teams square off and take turns tossing four bags filled with beans or corn kernels or deer teeth at two angled boards (27 feet from front edge to front edge) with a hole cut in them. Land on the board: 1 point. Land in the hole: 3 points. Play to 21. Repeat.

It is the ultimate Midwest sport for a number of reasons. And, well, here they are:

1. **It's social. Unlike darts or horseshoes, you must play with a partner.** Better still, you split up and play standing next to the *other* team's player. So it's a great opportunity to make a new friend, hear a new story, and/or talk a lot of trash.

2. **It takes just one hand to play.** The other one is usually holding a beer. Or a bratwurst. Or a baby.

3. **It's a bag filled with beans or corn.** Unlike darts or horseshoes or lawn darts, an errant bag throw will not put someone in the hospital. It'll just make everyone laugh.

4. **Variety is the spice of life.** There isn't one way to toss a bag. Some will flick sideways, others go softball-style underhand, wide swing, the football pass, the push. Then there's your feet: knees swaying or lock steady, feet together or one foot back, one foot off the ground or up on the toes. Depends on the player *and* the situation. (Like shuffleboard, you can knock bags off the board.) Also, when the most skilled get tired of putting the bags in the hole every time, you can intentionally create cool designs on the boards with the bags. (The best, and most childish, designs come when the two opposing players work together.)

5. **You play outside.** While folks *do* play inside, Midwesterners are *always* looking for another reason to be outdoors. Most cornhole matches are out in the fresh air behind a bar or some house or campfire.

6. **You can personalize your boards.** Whether you buy the boards in a store or make them yourself, each provides a distinct opportunity to show off your alma mater, favorite pro team, favorite child, a picture of a fish, a Chippendale's dancer, your last will and testament . . . the possibilities are endless!

Hockey

Hockey may still be far behind football, baseball, and auto racing in popularity in the United States, but those other thirty-seven states are wrong. With all the lakes and ice, and located only a slapshot from Canada, the Midwest was bound to become a land of hockey. There are company leagues with coworkers and leagues for five-year-olds. No joke: the Midwest has *more hockey rinks than Russia*. Your goal is to watch some matches (outside rinks are ideal), maybe even play a bit, and learn enough about back-checking, the five hole, and the grinder to not giggle about it.

HOCKEY STAR

Before I wanted to be an archaeologist, because I saw *Jurassic Park* and thought paleontologists were archaeologists, I wanted to be a hockey player. Why a hockey player? I found my dad's old hockey helmet in the basement. It was a sign from God. The black helmet was dented and scuffed like a gladiator who'd survived the Coliseum. It also *smelled* like a gladiator who didn't survive the Colosseum. But I suffered through the smell, because that helmet fit me like a glove . . . on a twig.

Noticing how much I loved the helmet, my parents got me hockey gloves for my birthday and my dad sawed his old hockey stick in half so it would fit me. Then during the day I would play in the basement. But my other brothers didn't like hockey as much, so I played with my best friend Jim in the basement.

My mom would always watch us. It was just foot hockey with a tennis ball, but that didn't mean it was a leisurely game. You see, Jim was a dirty player and almost twice my size. He would often check me into the wall or slash me when mom wasn't looking.

Jim watched a lot of hockey on TV. He liked how they fought.

I remember the first time Jim threw off his gloves. I didn't know what to do, so I cried to my mom for help.

But Mom didn't come to my rescue. She just said, "Honey, life is full of Jims. If I step in now, you'll never know how to fight the next one."

That was a tough thing for a five-year-old to hear. But I knew what I had to do. I threw off my gloves and threw up my dukes. Jim threw a right hook and I ducked. He threw a left and it knocked me on the ground. Damn near knocked me out. I cried again for my mom, but she wouldn't help me up. "If I save you now, how will you ever save yourself?" she shouted.

It was up to me. So with every bit of strength I had, I rose to my feet. I says to Jim, "Is that all you got?" Jim wound up and sent over another left hook. This time I ducked and countered. BANG. Connected to Jim's jaw. He was knocked unconscious. Mom smiled with pride. And that's when I knew how much she loved me. Because Jim was imaginary. ><>

The College Life

The American heartland has a collegiate cornucopia of good schools to choose from if you or your kids are looking for another piece of paper. University of Wisconsin, the University of Chicago, Notre Dame, Northwestern, Washington University, Ohio State, DePaul, Purdue, and all the great little colleges and big state universities in between. No wrong answers here; *every one* gets an A.

Choosing Your Ivory Tower . . . in the Land of Velvet Antlers

For homegrown scholars or those coming from outside the region, no matter which school you choose, you can count on a couple of things:

It's Inexpensive*: Like everything else in the Midwest (houses, gasoline, beer, firewood, chislic), you'll get your education at a discount. When compared to the rest of the country, there's also more money to be saved. Getting an apartment off campus is cheaper. Coffee at the local shop is cheaper. Tuition is lower. Heck, if you flip through your secondhand textbooks, there's a good chance you'll find some unexpired beer coupons that doubled as last semester's bookmarks. All the more reason to come here.

Spring Semester: Coming out of a rough winter that starts sometime in early September, the arrival of spring is celebrated on Midwest campuses like some pagan fertility ritual. At the very first hint of springtide, the legs, miniskirts, and tank tops all come out—and those are just the frat bros. Every lawn sprouts cornhole boards, bottomless kegs, and the chance to show off the biceps you could have worked harder on all winter. The stark juxtaposition (a fancy college word you now know!) between winter and spring is an existential awakening students in other states will never experience the way you have. It's the ranch to winter's pickles and brings a joy you'll never find in any textbook.

"Nice" Classmates and Teachers: Again, we admit there are nice people everywhere. (And jerks, also.) But in poll after poll, the American heartland is still champ for producing "nice people" and "happy people." If that sounds like the kind of person you'd like to sit next to for four years, room with, learn from, maybe even fall in love with, then a Midwest school is for you. Most college students have nightmare stories about their first freshman-year roommate. Here are some true roommate stories from the Midwest:

---

* Well, to be clear on "inexpensive," that's compared to buying a home or a heart transplant or a hundred acres in the UP or a top-of-the-line jet pack or getting a ticket on Jeff Bezos's bratwurst-shaped spaceship . . . or to other schools around the country.

- *"He said, 'Cool story, bro.' And meant it."* —Moose, Kent State University
- *"Asked if I wanted any chips. The bag was still half full."* —Abbie, Valparaiso University
- *"Heard me puking all night. She never once brought it up the rest of our lives."* —Lisa, Presentation College
- *"Two slices of pizza left, and he took the smaller one."* —Kyle, Creighton University
- *"I slipped on ice. He caught me before I went 'ass over teakettle.'"* —Dominic, University of Wisconsin-Milwaukee

Hirability: The job market is tight and any step up on the competition is a plus. Companies (for internships and real paying jobs) know all about that Midwest work ethic (to be covered in the next chapter). Midwesterners show up on time, stay late, and put up with a lot more crap at work without complaint than folks from other regions. That's just a fact. Our great-grandparents (or parents) were working the fields or factory floor like their lives depended on it—because they did. That same work ethic has been passed down to the generations who followed. Are there some slackers here? Sure. But companies know that the chances of nabbing a grade-A employee are pretty strong when hiring from the heartland. Even if you go to Harvard or Cambridge, make sure where you grew up ends up on your résumé somehow. Or just spill some ranch on it—they'll get the idea.

The Five Best (Meaning Most-Midwest) Midwest Colleges

Take this one with a grain of Thirsty Thursday margarita salt. Feel free to cross out the ones you disagree with and write in your own. But here are five representatives who capture life in the Midwest.

University of Wisconsin–Madison (Wisconsin) Okay, I'm biased. UW is my alma mater. But I think I have some solid ground to stand on. . . . As long as it's not between the third and fourth quarters during the Badgers game. That's when Camp Randall explodes into the "Jump Around," causing seismic activity that's been registered on the Richter scale at the UW Geology Department nearly two miles away. UW Madison knows how to party. Just ask anyone who lived on Mifflin St. Actually, never mind, they won't remember. Okay, so then ask the police who arrested them. But it's not just sports and parties. A diploma from UW is one of the most respected in the nation (especially if I'm one of the people judging diplomas). Then, there's the city of Madison itself, which is nestled on an isthmus. (I'll spare you the time of googling that definition: *Isthmus, n, a narrow strip of land with sea on either side, forming a link between two larger areas of land.* [*Oxford*].) In this case the "sea" is two lakes: Mendota and Monona. And they're a source of unlimited recreation. Boating, skiing, ice fishing, regular fishing, lounging, tanning (in my case, burning), and of course swimming. Lake Mendota is home to the Memorial Union Terrace. It's an outdoor café/bar/restaurant that students go to to study or drink or both. If I have three drinks left in this world, two of them would be on the Terrace. (See also: UW–La Crosse, University of Minnesota, Michigan State, Indiana University–Bloomington.)

Ohio University (Ohio) OU, Ohhhhhh Yeah! Not to be confused in *any* way with Ohio State in Columbus (Ohio State's lawyers required me to say this), Ohio University is in lovely Athens, Ohio—which is more than an hour from . . . *everything*. The next closest town of note is some forty miles and, um, in the hills of West Virginia. What's that tell you? And what do thirty thousand college students with nothing to do all day and night do? Well, not since Lot's wife turned into salt has that answer played out more thoroughly. Whatever your Hollywood notions of a "wild college party" are—double them. Number Fest and Caligula may be things of the past, but their spirit lives in Athens forever. OU also offers uncredited PhDs in cornhole (*not* what you think; see page 149), partying, and getting degrees in . . . I don't know; marketing, I guess. (See also: Illinois at Urbana–Champaign, Millikin, Wheaton College, and the University of Dayton.)

University of Notre Dame (Indiana) There are a lot of Catholics in the heartland, and every one of them still has the dream that one of their kids will have the smarts or sports skills to get into the "Best Catholic University" on the planet. Where else can you find a world-class education and a 134-foot mural of the Savior signaling another touchdown? (See also: Loyola University Chicago, Saint Louis University, Xavier University.)

Carleton College (Minnesota) The Midwest is most known for its huge state universities, but it also has enough small, and venerated, private colleges to keep things interesting. Carleton (just two thousand students) consistently appears near the top of *any* college list. The college graduated its first class in 1874, two Minnesotans, James Dow and Myra Brown, who married each other on Christmas Day later that same year. Isn't that sweet? The school now has thirty-three different majors and thirty-one minors to choose from. (See also: Grinnell College, Macalester College, Wheaton College, Denison "University.")

Hamburger University (Illinois) More selective than Harvard (yeah, no, seriously), HU provides various degrees and curricula in restaurant management for those seeking managerial duties within the McDonald's Corporation. The school has more than 275,000 graduates who took more than two thousand hours of classes, which are transferable and about halfway to an AS degree. (See also: Alverno College and the University of Phoenix.)

The College Care Package

Few moments capture love in the same corporeal reality as a box of stuff carefully selected, packaged, and shipped for $80 to a homesick college student. Care packages say, "Yes, we're still thinking of you and are so proud. And you shouldn't worry about the fact that Mom and Dad have turned your bedroom into a place to store yard-sale finds, fishing poles, and extra blankets (because you *never* know). Also, we found where you hid our brandy."

For Midwestern Students Attending College Far Away

- dehydrated cheese curds
- mystery jerky from some meat raffle (aged anywhere from two months to two years)
- microwavable casserole
- cargo shorts for winter
- camo Crocs to attract mates
- pretzel maker
- six different mustards
- local chips: Mikesell's, Sterzing's, Better Made, Gold'n Krisp (insert your favorite here)
- a sugar cream pie
- a coleslaw recipe
- alarm clock from the garage
- bobbers
- a box opener from the junk drawer
- a bag of slush to think of home
- sunscreen
- a pheasant

For Nonmidwestern Students Attending a Midwestern College

- a small fan for August; their dorm room (surprise!) has no AC
- another coat for September; the temperature (surprise!) is now 35°F
- cold medicine
- a mirror, for them to practice saying hello to other people without panic
- pepper and/or bear spray
- UV phototherapy light
- more socks
- a 24-pack of lip balm
- vitamin D3 pills
- a copy of *Football for Dummies*
- insect repellent
- a bag of coal
- a stack of Scoopie tokens
- a buck call, to attract friends

Major Majors

Just about anyone can be a sports marketing or engineering major, and there are enough of those enrolled in schools these days to last us six or seven generations. For a résumé-up on the competition for future employment, you might want to cultivate your area of study and check out these unique—and *very* real—majors offered at Midwest colleges.

Major	College/University	Perfect for students who . . .
Bakery science	Kansas State University	Like to eat coffee cake, hoppel poppel, kolache, and kringle
Comic art	Minneapolis College of Art and Design	Dream of a Batman/Snoopy crossover; we're counting on you
Costume technology	DePaul University (IN)	Want to dress superheroes
Blacksmithing	Southern Illinois University	Would like to be of actual value when the world ends
Popular culture	Bowling Green State University (OH)	Enjoy binge-watching shows, listening to music, and reading about what YouTuber is trying to be a boxer
Boilermaking	Ivy Tech Community College-Southwest (IN)	Recognize the best-heated houses in the world are those that still use steam or hot water
Ethical hacking	Dakota State University (SD)	Recognize *unethical* hacking has room for improvement
Medicinal plant chemistry	Northern Michigan University	~~Love getting high.~~ Envision lots of fun experiments
Decision sciences	Indiana University	Can't decide on a major?
Bowling industry management	Vincennes University (IN)	Abide

Midwest Drinking Games

One of college's highest traditions is the art and rapture of "drinking games"—contests of chance or skill that encourage camaraderie, merriment, and, well, drinking. When Midwest college students reach the age of twenty-one, they are now responsibly able to responsibly take part in these responsibly bildungsromany rituals built upon responsibly played games of chance and skill. First game: Spell *bildungsromany* backwards.

While euchre and bags are two mainstays in college social gatherings, drinking is not a central part of either game, only a pleasant addendum. Here are the other most popular drinking games you may—when you are twenty-one and not a moment before—encounter:

Beersbee/Frisbeener: The name changes depending *where* in the Midwest you are (the closer to Canada you are, the more you'll hear "beersbee"). Teams of two stand at least forty feet away from the other team and toss a Frisbee at a beer can or bottle that has been balanced atop a ski pole speared into the ground in front of each team. Your snow-crusted ancestors would be so proud! There are points for catching the Frisbee and/or bottle/can if/when knocked off. You *must* play with one hand holding an adult beverage. (This is only *optional* in cornhole, horseshoes, and similar games.) There are kits and plastic bottles to replace the ski poles and glass, but what would your ancestors think?

Sinkers: Bouncing a quarter into a shot glass is so 1990. Try bouncing a sinker into a . . . shot glass. Okay, so the end part isn't that creative, but that's all right because bouncing lead is a lot harder than it looks. Don't do this on glass or your game will be cut short . . . also your finger.

King's Cup: A delightful getting-to-know-you game using any old deck of cards and simple (yet difficult to keep track of after a few drinks) rules connected to each card. The rules may change depending on your school, sorority/fraternity, or astrological sign, but here is the basic Midwest version:

Ace	Waterfall	Everyone at the table drinks.
Two	You	You get to choose anyone to drink. Feel free to choose yourself.
Three	Me	Bottom's up, you're drinking to you.
Four	War	Grab half the cards on the table. Shuffle, cut, and choose someone to play a game of war. Loser drinks. (Yes, four is sometimes called something else but it's not nice and kids could read this. It's bad enough they're learning king's cup.)

Five	Never have I ever	You say an action of some kind. Anyone who's ever done that action drinks. This game gets weird quick.
Six	Ticks	Everyone checks themselves for ticks. Anyone who finds one drinks.
Seven	Heaven	Raise hands to the heavens. Last person to do it drinks and has to confess to Father Tom on Sunday.
Eight	Mate	Pick someone to drink with you. Choose wisely; what goes around comes around. If you can't choose, choose *everyone*.
Nine	Rhyme	Go around the table and come up with words that rhyme with Lambeau, Ditka, Nitschke, Butkus, Ewbank, Halas, Lombardi, LaFleur, Holmgren, Fontes, Lambeau, Dungy, or—for beginners—Grant. Wait, did I just say Lambeau twice? Drink!
Ten	Categories	Come up with a category (duck calls, ingredients to add to basic puppy chow, Packers on the 96/97 Super Bowl team, and so on). First person who can't come up with an answer drinks.
Jack	Rule	Invent a rule and those who break it must drink. Elbows on the table, drink! Someone says *Ope!*, drink! If you look at someone, drink!
Queen	Mean	Pretend to be mean until someone else draws a queen, then it's their turn to try out how the rest of the country lives without excessive thanks, unwarranted apologies, or somberly putting others' needs above your own.
King	Pour into center cup	First three kings dump booze into center cup. Last king drawn drinks the now-filled cup.

Flip Cup: A team-based relay game in which players must, in turn, first drain an adult beverage and then "flip" a cup of ranch dressing so that it lands facedown on the table. When they've successfully landed a flip, the teammate to their left may now go. Advanced players may also do this with ranch bottles.

Titanic: In honor of the Chippewa Falls Dawson family, watch the film *Titanic* and drink every time someone says "Rose" or "Jack." Those counting on their honed and trusted Power Hour skills have been known to tap out before Jack tells Rose about ice fishing in Lake Wissota (which wasn't even around then).

The Art of ~~War~~ Euchre

While many first pick up this game as a Midwestern child, you are guaranteed to acquire the full art and philosophy of euchre if you go to college. Let those other twentysomethings play Texas Hold'em and crazy eights; the game of euchre is both recognized and celebrated by the heartland's youth as something sacred and traditional and regional.

Originally brought to the Midwest by German immigrants, the game is now played fanatically from Cleveland to Waterloo (and up into Canada). It's a trick-taking card game in the spades, whist, contract bridge, and pinochle family that features trump suits, atypical attention on the jacks, and four players split evenly into two teams. It has also directly led to fistfights, marriages, divorces, in-laws not speaking for a decade, and hearing Nana use the F-bomb as she walks away from the table.

It often appears during family reunions, while drinking with coworkers after work, after Sunday dinner, on a rainy weekend, when stuck in an airport, and whenever a new boyfriend/girlfriend is brought around the family. It is often used as a passive-aggressive test of mettle. Playing well—in front of bosses, future mothers-in-law, and parish priests—is important enough to change the course of your whole life.

The actual rules of euchre, you can find online. These here are the unwritten rules as captured perfectly in Sun Tzu's *The Art of War*.

1. **"The supreme art of war is to subdue the enemy without fighting."** Most of your energy and brainpower and time and words and expressions should be spent antagonizing the other team. The actual game itself is easy enough, so you will have time to primarily focus on this most critical part of the contest. This game is never about the cards—those are random; it's about getting under the skin of your opponents so they make dumb mistakes. If a slow deal or childish shuffle or dealing out the cards in odd patterns bothers your uncle, you do this *every* single time. If your friend likes to be that gal who looks at her dealt cards last, you don't look at yours; sit there for forty-five minutes if you have to. And look at her the way Ivan Drago looked at Apollo while you do it. She'll eventually crack and pick up her cards first. The game is already won.

2. **"If you know the enemy and you know yourself, you need not fear the result of a hundred battles."** The more personal you can get with your "passing comments" or "asides," the better. Casually bring up the jobs they've lost, who their ex is currently sleeping with, or that time their brakes gave out backing the boat into the lake. If they were once up 9-0 on your team three years ago, and you came back to win—bring it up now! Their memories, personal baggage, and heartache are an infinite gold mine for getting your opponents to think about anything but the actual cards in their hands. When you become a true master, you will be able to bring up a topic or recollection that has them *fighting with each other*. "Remember that time you two . . ."

3. **"In the midst of chaos, there is also opportunity."** Steal the deal. Every hand, you try to steal the deal. Even if you just dealt, simply nonchalantly collect the cards and start shuffling. Start talking about religion or sex or money or the last deer you ran into. If someone gets up for another drink, or tells a joke, or drops a card on the floor, collect the cards and start shuffling. If *you* get up for another drink, or tell a joke, or purposely drop a card on the floor, collect the cards and start shuffling. There *is* a slight advantage to having the deal, but the main objective is to humiliate your opponents. For the rest of the game, you and your partner can start giggling about how your team stole the deal, and while your opponents play it off—try and steal the deal again. Even when you get caught, that's now all they're thinking about.

4. ***"All warfare is based on deception."*** Got a lay-down loner in hearts? Then pretend to think about calling up that club as trump and see if it comes around. Got three high clubs and some aces? Pass, and see if the dealer picks up that jack. Got nothing in a stick-the-dealer situation? Call for a loner just to see the fear in their eyes. . . . None of this may get you a single point, and may even cost you a few, but you're not playing for points—you're playing for permanent real estate in your opponents' minds.

5. ***"Quickness is the essence of the war."*** If you have both jacks and an ace, drop all three on the table at the same time. If the last two rounds are 100 percent yours, just toss both your cards out into the middle of the table. This will infuriate and/or confuse one or both of your opponents. Good. There's nothing illegal about it. It's just infuriating and confusing. "Can't we just play it out?" someone will plead. "I'm still trying to learn." No. If your ten-year-old niece can't keep up, she never should have sat down at the table. Buck up, kiddo!

6. ***"A kingdom that has once been destroyed can never come again into being."*** When you win, be obnoxious about it. The "barn" (the moment at the end of the game when a team has nine points and is only one from winning) is not about this match—it's about the next one hundred matches. The cards jammed behind your ears, the crudely suggestive "churning of the butter" and "feeding of the chickens," the getting on your partner's back and riding around the table like he's a bull or Ned Beatty in *Deliverance* . . . these are images that will be burned into your opponents' eyes forever. Whenever they play you, they will think about that "stupid laugh" of yours or you playing "We Are the Champions" at full blast, or that routine where your partner milks your thumbs . . . and they will do *anything* to never see/hear/taste any of that again; they are no longer thinking about a simple card game.

7. ***"Who wishes to fight must first count the cost."*** Be *very* careful when your opponents' team includes spouses, siblings you like, mothers-in-law, mothers, or bosses. Winning a card game is fun for about ten minutes but *can* lead to ruinous ramifications. When putting teams together, make sure you've chosen wisely. Worst case, just pull back on your bag of tricks for the night. Euchre is a card game; always play the long game.

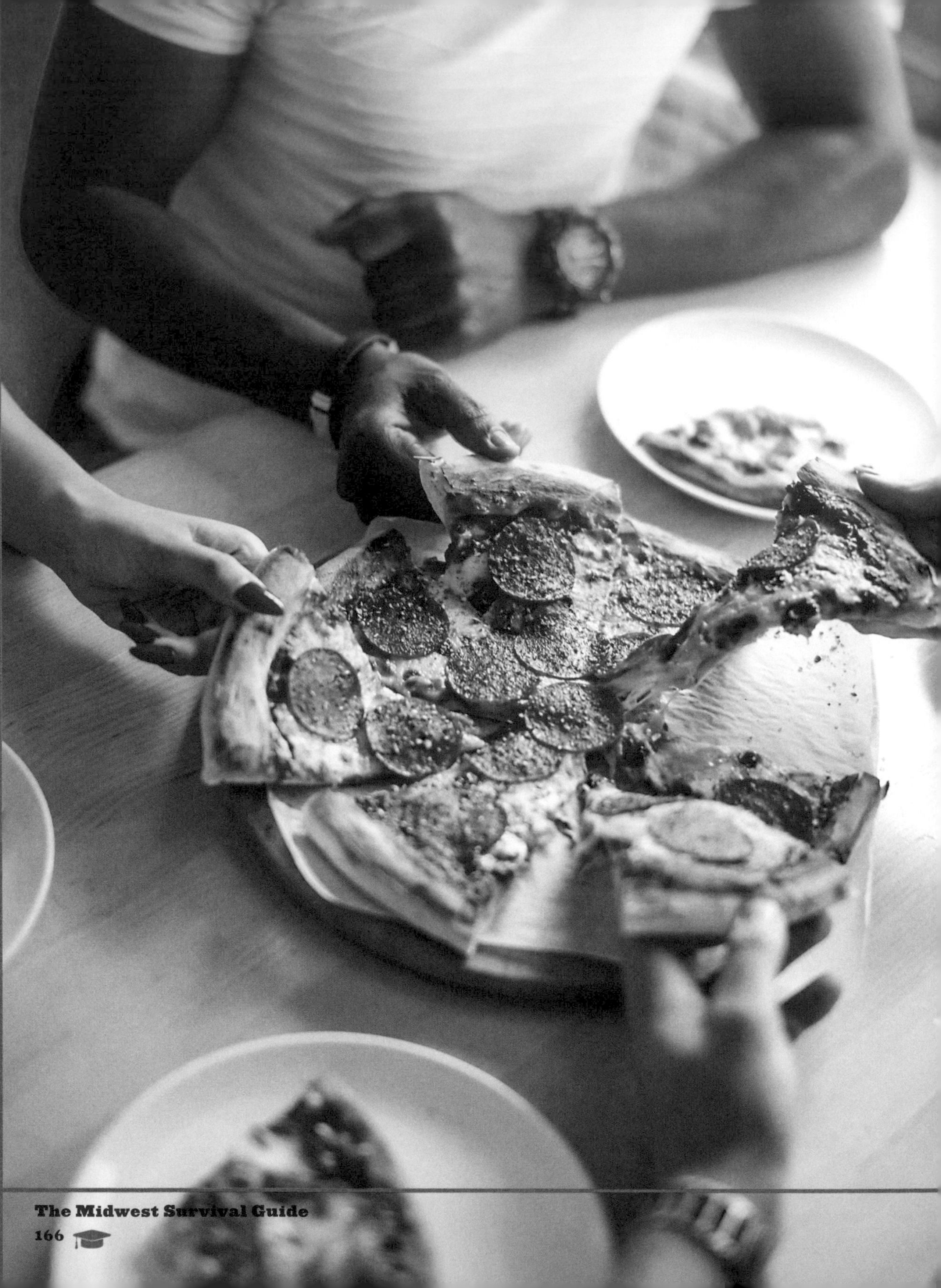

The Weekend Back Home . . .

Here's a nice easy chart for where you'll be eating the weekend your Midwest child comes home for a weekend visit. This information will also be announced by the student the week before arrival, in texts the day before, and when they first enter the house before or after the return-home hug. There's a very good chance you will be asked to eat here *again* on their way home on Sunday.

Illinois	Harold's Chicken Shack or Portillo's
Indiana	Schoop's Hamburgers
Iowa	Happy Joe's
Kansas	Freddy's Frozen Custard & Steakburgers
Michigan	Big John's Steak & Onion
Minnesota	MyBurger
Missouri	Winstead's
Nebraska	Runza or Taco John's
North Dakota	Kroll's
Ohio	Skyline Chili
South Dakota	Harrisburgers
Wisconsin	Culver's

Being There

Y ou're out of school . . . now what? Well, get ready: it's the rest of your life. Career, marriage, kids, installing a new sump pump, choosing a president for the rest of the country, retirement. There's a lot of toil and struggle left. Time to grab a rake or shovel, strap in, quit your griping, and get to work. That little plastic car's not gonna fill itself with pink and blue pegs all on its own. So, spin that multicolored wheel and start your life's journey to Countryside Acres. Even if you don't hit the big time, you never really wanted to anyway. You just wanted a "nice" life, and there's no better place in the world for that than here.

Get a Job!

Manufacturing, marketing, farming, DNR, mining, social work, transportation, finance, tech, education, construction, the arts . . . jobs and careers are plentiful in the Midwest. Major companies are drawn by inexpensive land and dependable labor. Here are some tips for the interview, and—if you follow the directions perfectly—what to do after they offer you the job.

At the Job Interview

Into one of your answers, work in where you went to high school. It builds camaraderie. There's a good chance the interviewer knows someone who knows someone and/or has good feelings about your high school even if you were archrivals back in the day.

Mention multiple times that you grew up in the Midwest and, if true, how your parents grew up in the Midwest. The interviewer(s) will know you'll continue to work hard for years even after you hate your job, and them.

When asked to describe yourself in three words, say, "I'll bring in butterscotch pies." (They won't mind or notice the extra words.)

If there's an eight-pointer hanging in the office, say "nice 12-pointer." They won't correct you. They've told strangers it's a 12-pointer, too.

Show some confidence. But not too much. Yes, you want to show up wearing something nice. And yes, you will get complimented on it. But don't take the bait. Tell them you bought it with a coupon or Kohl's Cash. Maybe even go the extra mile and offer to send them that coupon as a follow-up.

The best way of getting a Midwest job is to not stand out. Appear as "normal" and "generic" as you can. (This should be easy if you grew up in the Midwest; if not, fake it until you make it.) Don't let your weirdness shine through—yet. That will reveal itself gradually over time. By then, you'll have told too many people about the boss's 12-pointer to be fired.

When negotiating a salary, don't. It'll be too awkward for both sides. Regardless of what you read online or saw in some movie once, everyone knows you don't *actually* care about money all that much, so why go through the awkward dance. You were going to work anyway; the money's just icing. If you absolutely can't help yourself: whatever they offer, ask for 5 percent more. It'll be terrifying for both sides. Yes, more terrifying than haggling over a vacuum at a garage sale. But just like the vacuum, you'll brag about the whole experience once it's done.

FiRST JOB

When I was ten or eleven, I started working at this place called the Yarn House. It was exactly what it sounds like: a house with a bunch of yarn in it. It was a building from the 1800s that stuck out from the rest of its suburban surroundings. My job was to cut the grass, clean brush, paint, and of course sort yarn.

The woman who owned the Yarn House was named Shirley Grade. She was as unique as the business she started. Shirley grew up during the Great Depression, which means *if* she ever threw anything out, I wasn't there to witness it. Shirley was unconventional to say the least. She was a Catholic woman with the kids to prove it. She had twelve, ten of whom survived childhood, and her husband passed away in the 1980s. I always knew her as a strong, independent woman who had lived through tragedy but never let it dominate her disposition.

Shirley had a true lust for the simplest things in life, but what I admired most is she didn't care what anyone thought about her. She did things her way. And people admired her for her unique approach to business and life.

Here's a quick example: One summer Shirley had a bunch of dandelions in her yard. Now, most people in the suburbs see dandelions and they call someone up to spray their lawn with pesticides to kill 'em. Not Shirley. She just called me up to pick all the dandelions.

So I did it and came into the house with hundreds of dandelions and yellow-stained hands. I said, *So what are we doing?* Shirley said, *Well, we're making wine . . .*

Of course we are.

We put these dandelions in this big jug in her basement and made dandelion wine. It was a pretty cool job for an eleven-year-old . . . but honestly I didn't appreciate it at the time.

I hated picking dandelions. They stained my hands and made them smell. Some had thorny leaves that pricked my hands and forced four-letter words from my mouth. I got real depressed watching them turn white, which meant they were seeding, which meant more work was just a breeze away.

It wasn't until years later that I'd learn the lesson Shirley was teaching me. When life gives you weeds, make dandelion wine. ♥

Climbing the Corporate Corn Silo . . .

To succeed at work and continue your ascension to management and/or being completely left alone by your coworkers, here are a few tips that work for any career or industry:

Arrive early: Plan ahead and get to work before everyone else. This is a great time to organize your whole day and get things done without interruption. Back in the day, some neighborly hog-caller might wake you predawn from afar to help start your day, but we're not back in the day: *Set an alarm.* Now, what precisely to set that alarm *to* gets somewhat trickier. There are thirteen US states with more than one time zone. The Midwest counts for more than half of them: Nebraska, Kansas, both Dakotas, Michigan, and Indiana. Meaning, if you drive five miles one way or the other, you might lose or gain an hour. In the Upper Peninsula, there's a time vortex near Paulding where you drive straight *east* to pass from Central Time into Eastern and then *back into Central Time*! Your cell phone's battery will always be at 30 percent as it tries to keep up with the latest time jump. And once daylight savings rolls around, you might as well tell time with the number of raccoons still in your garbage can. In short, it's best to set your alarm for 4:00 A.M. No matter the daylight savings whatnot or time zone you're driving into later or how much bacon you eat first or how many orange construction barrels you'll have to dodge on the way, you'll get to work an hour early. Which *is* late, but six hours better than that dude they hired out of Fresno.

Leave late: Yes, technically work may end at 5:30, but you shouldn't even know that. You just keep going. Five thirty is for starting that special project you set aside early to make sure you have something to do until 6:45-ish. Look, you can leave work on time, but the traffic is slow because of the snow, construction, and/or cows. You're looking at ninety minutes at best. But if you leave an hour later, the traffic will settle. You'll look like a hero to your coworkers and kids and God, and be home just forty minutes after the last cow is corralled. It's not even debatable. Speaking of God, that day of rest didn't happen *because* it was Sunday . . . Sunday happened because the good Lord was done with what needed gettin' done. Think about it.

Work, work, work: Okay, you're arriving early and leaving late; let's put all that time between to use. The first five days after the weekend are always the hardest, but just keep grinding and you'll make it through. You're like a postage stamp; stick to it until you get it there. It's okay if you don't like where you're going, because you're already on your way. Always remember that the reward for good work is more work. (*Or, just say to hell with it and go fish.*)

Don't stand out: You see what happens to the biggest cow or turkey? No one's shooting at the two-point buck. *Something about tall poppies . . .* Basically, no fad haircuts. Or unusual piercings. Or tattoos you want to explain. No loud noises. No sudden movements. No quirks. Approach the boardroom and/or your coworkers as if you were approaching a wounded bear. Reserved. Calm. Polite. If someone infuriates you at some meeting, keep quiet and complain later when you get home. Better yet, hold it in and use it to keep warm when you go on a long walk after dinner. Will this bowling ball of suppressed energy one day launch from your body and knock down the carefully placed pins of your loved ones' emotional well-being? Yes, but only if you don't go bowling three times a week. *Find your league!*

Dress for the job you want, not the job you have: (This is why you shouldn't feel bad showing up to work in a Packers jersey.) Good news—you probably won't have to change your clothes at all. The CEO and new kid in customer service are not from central casting. They're from Milwaukee or Scottsbluff and probably shop at the same stores.

Don't gossip or complain: No one likes a gossip or a complainer. Okay, *everyone* likes a gossip or a complainer, but don't *be* the gossip or complainer. For you, it's only outward smiles and inward screams. If you have to get something nasty off your chest, you know the rules—tell it to the next fish you catch.

Don't get caught sleeping: If you do, tell them you were up late getting Miss Johnson's truck out of the ditch. Everyone knows a Miss Johnson, and everyone knows she has a truck.

....

Make small gestures: The Midwest's "love language"—as we will explore in an upcoming section on dating—is Acts of Service; all the rest is window dressing. Use this at work. Offer to grab coffee or lunch for someone if you're grabbing one for yourself, or bring in doughnuts or a Bloody Mary bar for everyone. Come in on the weekend and sweep the warehouse. When there's freezing rain in the forecast, make sure everyone's windshield wipers are standing up. Hide cash in the Caymans for your CFO. You get the idea.

....

Leave it at work: The reason you work so hard and so long is because when you leave work, you leave work. This nonsense does not follow you home. Home is for family time and yard work, fried fish, watching football, and breaking the TV because your team lost and you just threw the clicker at it. Work hard, play hard. Mingling work and home is a bad idea for everyone involved. Become a sociopath who is able to separate these two worlds into two realities completely separate from each other. In fact, when you're at home, pretend you don't even *have* a job. When at work, pretend you don't have a family or friends. There's no way this could backfire.

....

MY SHARP IDEA

This is the story of a $60 pocketknife. It wasn't just any pocketknife; it was the Leatherman Super Tool. And I wanted it. Yes, I already had a pocketknife. But for a thousand reasons that I still remember and will spare you, twelve-year-old me *needed* the Leatherman Super Tool. Now, the Tenth Commandment explicitly states, Thou shall not covet anything that belongs to thy neighbor. Luckily my neighbor didn't own this knife. My dad did. And it's a good thing, because it would've really sucked to break the Tenth Commandment every single day.

Anyway, I decided I was going to buy a Leatherman Super Tool of my own. The only problem was that my family had its own commandments. One was: Thou shall spend only 10 percent of the money you earn. Thou rest must go in thou stupid bank.

But, as a young landscaper with an underdeveloped client base, that meant I wasn't going to be purchasing my Leatherman until the end of the summer! And everyone knows summer is the best time to have a pocketknife. (You can use it for fishing and hunting and dissecting dead frogs found at the park. But frogs disappear in the winter. I had to get that knife ASAP.) So I tried appealing the 10 percent ruling to the high court of Mom.

Unfortunately, she had two kids in diapers and five others running around somewhere and didn't have time for this nonsense. She kicked the case to the lower court of Dad.

Dad heard my contention and immediately struck it down. In my father's decision, he cited his own childhood. You see, Dad was a worm man. He sold night crawlers on the side of Winnebago Drive for 25 cents a dozen. He even made a sign that the *Fond du Lac Reporter* published back in the seventies. It read: Nightcrawl .25. (Apparently he didn't leave much room in the marketing budget.) But what my dad lacked in brand development he made up for in predatory employment practices. He paid his siblings, ages five to eleven, a penny per worm. For my dad, the sound of rain was the sound of money. Because as any good worm man (or robin) knows, worms always surface when it rains. And let me assure you, there were a lot of thin robins in Fond du Lac back in the seventies, because my dad and his siblings sold enough worms to stuff a coffee tin full of cash.

Dad's family didn't have a lot of money while he was growing up. He didn't even have a winter coat. So one day, while Dad was at school, Grandma Sue took $40 of hard-earned worm money and purchased my dad a brand-

new coat. Dad was pissed. Years later, this 10 percent childhood trauma was now playing out on me "for my own good."

Fast-forward to the Fourth of July and Dad is trying to fix the rubber hose on a keg of beer. Dad asks, "Charlie, you have a knife on you?" Did I ever. I'd been waiting for this moment. Because if there's anything people who carry pocketknives know, it's that reasons to actually use your pocketknife don't come around as often as you would think. So when someone asks do you have a knife on you, you have to do everything in your being to maintain your composure. Sometimes you can lose track of time, other times you can lose track of what things may get you grounded. This was the latter. I handed my dad the brand-new $60 Leatherman Super Tool.

"Is this my knife?" he asked. Oh, sh*t.

"Yes," I replied. Broke two commandments in one with that word. There's no way to honor thy father while bearing false witness. Dad replied, "No, it's not. Mine's rusted." Busted. "I meant, yes, it's mine," I amended, breaking two commandments yet again (but at least I used more words this time).

He asked how much it cost. "Sixty dollars." I woulda lied again but I knew my dad already knew. He also knew I hadn't earned $600 yet, which is what I would have needed to afford a $60 knife following the 10 percent rule. I'd just planned on making the $600 by the time he knew about the knife.

"Guess what you're doing with this knife on Monday," he said.

"Dissecting frogs?"

"You're returning it to the hardware store, or I'll dissect you."

And that was my first time getting audited. ♥

The Big Bratwurst: Your Midwest Boss

Treat your boss as good as you treat a bratwurst and you'll be fine. Marinate them with compliments and batter them with beer. If they fall on the sidewalk, tell them they'll still be good. *Never* poke them with a fork. You get the idea.

Of course, a large part of your career advancement will be directly linked to your relationship with the boss. The Top Dog holds both your keys to the executive suite and final say on maybe taking off early on that one Friday for an "emergency root canal," which even your boss knows is code for "perch are biting." Here are some considerations to keep in mind the next time you and they cross paths.

- They probably started in the milking parlor, mailroom, or customer service and worked their way up the ladder. This is, ultimately, a good thing. They *do* know what you're now dealing with. Be extra wary of those bosses for whom this is not the case.

- It's not about the money or the power for these people, those just came with doing good work. Most Midwest managers don't even want to be managers. They were just too nice to decline the extra work. One day they looked at their paycheck and realized they got a raise. The good cubicle by the bubbler came next. They apologized to corporate for having to pay them more, and now they're your boss.

- They *will* drink with you after work but have 0.00 problem chewing you out—or even firing you—the next day. Work and after-work are two entirely separate universes. Your boss will never confuse them; neither should you. All that said, the best form of job security is knowing—and *sharing*—a good walleye spot. It's your get out of unemployment free card.

- They never get sick and will drive through six feet of snow to get to work on time. Just something to keep in mind if you decide to get lazy sometime between September and April.

Love in the Time of Cheese Curds: Coupling in the Midwest

If you grow up in the Midwest, there's a good chance you'll have met your spouse by the tenth grade, but for those of you from other states who've just moved here, passing ranch packets during AP Bio is no longer an option. Have no fear. The other ways people meet that special someone are well covered here: Through friends. At the cookout. At work. At church. At the game. But mostly at bars.

Some special wrinkles to keep in mind:

- Most of the men you meet are already married. Their biological clocks—wanting their own yard to mow and being a Pop Warner assistant football coach—start ticking around fourteen years old.

- You might have heard about this "love language" thing—how people like to give or receive love via Acts of Service, or physical touch, some other crap we forget. Midwesterners give and receive love via Acts of Service. Period. There is nothing sexier than when your new guy scrapes the ice off your windshield or that special gal reshingles your roof.

- No one's breaking up or calling a lawyer when they're focused on being passive-aggressive. Midwesterners often give the silent treatment for a couple months, until we forget about the argument altogether. For the more serious squabbles, we'll merely hold a grudge for eight years and get in a well-timed dig now and again. Do that enough times, and a golden fiftieth is still a possibility.

- Midwesterners, as we've previously established, put others first—usually even ahead of our own happiness and longings. And if that ain't a motto for being a couple, what is? When both of you put the other person "first," everyone ends up number one. (Or two, depending on how you look at it.)

- If a Midwesterner takes you on a walk through the woods or a cornfield and calls it a date . . . they're not "being cheap." They genuinely thought scouting new hunting land was the most fun thing you could do together. Well, second most. Also, I lied. They're being cheap.

- Getting "dressed up" usually just means putting on the "nice jeans and flannel." For us, there's nothing sexier than a walking picnic table.

- There are *many* ways to say "I love you" without saying "I love you." Just trot one of these long-standing love gems out: Watch out for deer; I shoveled your drive . . . salted it, too; I brought you a casserole; Can I get you anything at St. Vinny's?; I got some extra rhubarb in the garden with your name on it; I got a bag of perch in the freezer with your name on it; How's about you let me can your tomatoes; Let me untangle your pole; I'm getting gas. . . . Can I bring you some doughnuts?

- Disagreements, busy schedules, pulling a hundred-pound sturgeon out of an ice hole . . . Whatever the challenge, a Midwesterner simply takes a deep breath or two and gets back to work. If that doesn't work, they go for a long drive and count the potholes. Eventually they'll be more mad their tax dollars have been going to waste and forget those other challenges ever existed.

What About Online Dating?

Now, dating apps have quickly taken the number five spot on where paramours meet, and that number will only rise as we move forward. To help you navigate these sites and read between the lines, here are a couple profiles to start practicing your online selection skills. For each, just peruse (real meaning) the profiles below and pick the best person for you or someone you care about. (You'll find the recommended answers below each chart.)

	A	**B**	**C**

	A	**B**	**C**
Ideal Saturday night?	Some popcorn and a good scary movie	Dinner and then a little hike around the lake	Admiring self in mirror, window, or fresh coat of paint
Still on the bucket list?	To yell at someone angrily	To travel on an airplane	Laser hair removal
Best scar story?	I freed a coyote that was stuck in a fence.	My sister hit me with an ice scraper.	I beat up six dudes (i.e., I walked into a door when it was dark).
Any special skills?	I can make a mean perch fry.	I can field-dress a buck with a butter knife.	Nunchuk and computer hacking. Also, sex stuff.
What are you looking for?	Someone who can string a fishing lure in the dark	Someone like my mom, but younger	A new reflective surface
Your signature drink?	Beer	Beer	Vodka/Red Bull or Jägerbombs
Best meal ever	Fish fry in Fond du Lac	Culver's	Someplace in Mykonos
First date ever	Fish fry in Fond du Lac	Culver's	No dates. Let's get to it.
Most valuable possession	The golf clubs Grandpa gave me. I hate golf, but . . . you know.	Does my dog count?	Mirror
Currently reading	*The Book of Perch*	*The Midwest Survival Guide*	*I Hope They Serve Beer in Hell*
Most embarrassing moment	Got bit by a coyote stuck in a fence	Forgot to bring a sixer to the potluck	I punched some guy in the face and *he* apologized. I was so confused.
Most interesting job	Built a house with my two uncles	Culver's	Digital platform consultant making bank

Either A or B is the best answer.

Dating Site Picks #1

	A	**B**	**C**

	A	**B**	**C**
Your big passion	Education. Travel. And my family.	Experiencing life to the fullest	God. Helping others. And my family.
Favorite film	*Escanaba in da Moonlight*	The book was better.	*Hoosiers*
A special place you like to visit	Lake Winnebago	Morris & Sons	My grandparents' house
The perfect burger topping	Bacon. Mild Cheddar. Sharp Cheddar. Onion. Ranch dressing. And half a slice of Swiss.	I'm vegan and you should be also.	Walleye
What gets you out of bed?	Early bird gets the worm.	To check my cell phone	The neighbor's rooster
Your biggest role model	My grandmother	Cleopatra	Vince Lombardi
Life motto	Keep 'er movin'.	Live today as if it were your last.	Watch out for deer.
Go-to drink on a night out	Beer	Armand de Brignac Champagne	Old-fashioned
First concert	Farm Aid	NSYNC	Rock on the Range
First memory	Playing hockey with my brothers	The table of gifts all for me at my fourth birthday party	Petting a deer in the backyard and Mom yelling about Lyme disease
Accomplishment you're most proud of	Hiking the Maah Daah Hey Trail in the Badlands	50K followers on TikTok	Launching a local nonprofit for teens experiencing homelessness
What reality show would you most likely be on?	*Naked and Afraid*	*The Bachelorette*	*The Real Housewives of Bloomington*

Either A or C is the best answer.

Dating Site Picks #2

Raising Chickens

With big yards and rural neighbors, you may eventually decide that raising chickens in your own backyard seems like an eggsellent idea. One hen can make three hundred fresh eggs a year, produce fertilizer, teach responsibility, and, per studies, therapeutically help with issues ranging from depression and anxiety to dementia. But producing your own eggs isn't always what it's cracked up to be. Before you start, here's the inside coop:

- Chickens poop constantly and it gets everywhere. It's fowl. (*There's one more pun for Dad's birthday.*)

- Your chicken coop should have two doors; four doors is a chicken sedan. (*Sorry, that's a terrible yolk.*)

- Chickens live for eight to ten years and make eggs for only four. So make your omelets while you can. After that, make sure there are cards in the chicken coop. For the rest of their stay, they're either gonna play bridge or chicken.

- Be prepared to harass family, friends, neighbors, and co-workers to "just take some eggs." Remember how one hen makes three hundred eggs a year? You have six hens. If you weren't good at math before, you are now.

- Chickens roost anywhere and everywhere. They love to play hide and scream. They hide, you scream.

FARM LIFE

The Midwest is home to more than 127 million acres of agricultural land. From the cornfields of Iowa to the fruit belt of Michigan, from the dairy cows of Wisconsin to the soybeans of Indiana. It's been an honor to have several farmers on my *CripesCast* podcast, and, in addition to growing our food, they've also harvested some incredible insight on everything from politics to kindness. Enjoy these quick bits:

"Many hands make light work. If we work together, we can get through this heavy stuff. We can figure it out. We just all have to do our part. And stop and watch the cows chew their cud and take a breather and think about things before you just go off half-cocked on someone on a Twitter rant. It's okay to slow down sometimes and just be okay with what you got."

—Carrie Mess (aka Dairy Carrie)

"If farmers were politicians it'd be different. I'd pick on you for having John Deere and you'd pick on me for having Case IH. But when your John Deere broke down you know darn good and well you wouldn't have to call me. I'd be pulling in there and I'd be frickin' helping you get your crops out. And when you got your machine fixed, you'd be coming over. That's what we need to get back to in the political arena. That's what we need to get back to in the United States."

—Jeff Ditzenberger (aka Ditz)

"Sometimes the only person a farmer will see is the UPS, FedEx guys, maybe a bull stud guy coming out to breed cows, maybe the milk man. What I tell those people is 'Listen, I know you've got a job to do. I know you're on the clock. Slow down. Slow down.' If he has a thermos and wants to pour you a cup of coffee, slow down for God's sakes. There's a reason. He's got things to do too. There's a reason. If he wants to show you something for just a quick second, slow down. . . . If you wait, and you talk, and you go about your day after that, and six months later they come up to you and tell you that was their lowest day. Think about that. The non-farm people that only drive past, ya know, get a bunch of cookies and put a note in that just says, 'We're glad you're here.' It is the simple human connection that sometimes farmers really lack because they're so isolated. That can make a world of difference. . . . It's not just farmers. . . . I think we've all found that the human element can get pretty frail in these situations. Slow down and think a little bit how your simple gesture can make a world of difference in somebody's life."

—Pam Jahnke (aka Fabulous Farm Babe)

Raising Children: Tailgaters in Training

It's never been easy fostering offspring and with the speed of social changes and technology these days, it's only getting trickier. To keep things simple, here's a checklist you can follow to make sure you're producing the proper Midwest child.

✔	Age	Developmental Milestones
	1 to 3 months	Shows interest in faces, makes eye contact, can hold head at 90-degree angle, uses arms to prop, can visually track through midline, coos like a duck, can recognize distress in others
	3 to 5 months	Can roll over, notices toys that make sounds, shows interest in ranch dressing, reaches for objects and can transfer them from hand to hand, plays with feet and genitals (ideally, not at same time), babbles and imitates deer sounds (ditto), begins to eat cereals and pureed foods (such as rhubarb, pumpkin, squash, apple, venison)
	5 to 7 months	Sits in tripod, "rakes" with hands, distinguishes between parents and all those aunts and uncles, sits without support, picks up fishing poles and beef jerky, recognizes sound of their name, starts rooting for local NFL or D1 college team, shows emotive facial expressions
	8 to 11 months	Learns to hide emotive facial expressions, crawls, pulls to standing, shows interest in colors and patterns, points to pictures in books in response to verbal cue, says Ma or Da, solitary play, plays solitaire
	1 year	Starts walking, says *Ope!*, practices all known social roles, holds doors open for others, claps hands, enjoys music, walks independently, follows simple directions (this will continue for rest of life), responds to yes/no questions with head nod or shake and then says "or no"
	2 years	Climbs up stairs, learns to apologize, shovels driveway, understands guilt, uses simple pronouns, knows difference among dem/deese/dose, begins to run, enjoys listening to stories at bonfires
	3 years	Cuts with scissors, can draw a cartoon deer, ties clinch and palomar knots (see page 132), potty trained, understands right and wrong, strict adherence to rules (this will continue for rest of life)
	4 to 5 years	Gets first job, can field-dress a deer, counts tree or more objects, recognizes most letters and possibly writes their name, learns to make friends

✔	Age	Developmental Milestones
	6 to 10 years	Asks about birds and bees, learns euchre, throws a football, can tell time, can read some books, learns to keep friends by showing up to every playdate with a sixer of root beer
	11 to 13 years	Cares about how they look/dress, identifies with peer group, exploratory mating behavior like telling romantic interests to watch for deer, drags feet, engages in activities for intense emotional experience, risky behavior, blatant rejections of parental standards, learns to work microwave and shotgun
	14 to 16 years	Stops caring about how they look/dress, identifies with grandparents, learns to work oven, uses basic punctuation and can write own name in cursive, learns to work turkey fryer
	17 to 19 years	Mostly canoodling and illegally drinking
	20 to 25 years	Understands multifarious concepts of space and time, says yes to offers of overtime, holds head steady (unsupported)
	> 25 years	Nope, not your problem; all they're supposed to do now is work and make grandkids: neither of these has anything to do with you

"On Lake Erie, As It Is in Heaven . . ." Religion in the Midwest

The Midwest is still mostly an assortment of Christian types (everything from "cafeteria Catholics" to fundamentalists), but you'll also find many mosques, synagogues, Hindu temples, Buddhist monasteries, Sikh gurdwaras, and places to meet other Taoists, Shintoists, Zoroastrians, Wiccans, or whatever else you may believe.

All that said, based on attendance at religious services, the Midwest is neither in the top (can we get an "Amen!," South?) *or* bottom (hi, New England . . . your ancestors would be *sooooo* proud) on the list of "most religious" states. Each of the twelve Midwest states is somewhere smack-dab in the middle of the other fifty.

From the small one-room church that seats thirty in a rural seven-church town to one of those nondenominational megachurches in an old shopping mall that plays Rush and Duran Duran between sermons, you'll find that spiritual life cuts a wide swath through the Midwest. This includes everything from the devoutly regular church attendees with Mary, Joseph, or St. Francis in the yard to the spiritually middling who accept Pascal's wager, go to service every now and then, and watch their language (just in case). But again, Christianity is just part of the Midwest religious landscape. Minnesota and Illinois are both in the top five states in Muslim population, and Illinois is currently first in the nation percentage-wise.

While people may disagree on the details of religious observance, we can all find common ground in the traditions. And by traditions we mean church festivals, Bingo night, fish fries, church-sponsored pub crawls, basketball leagues, and any excuse to drink in the name of raising money for a good cause. Unless of course your religion prohibits the latter, in which case don't worry, we won't tell.

Speaking of Religion...

You're probably now wondering which apostle matches up best with each Midwest state. No? Well, it's too late now...

Illinois	Judas Iscariot	The one state the other eleven eye suspiciously...
Indiana	James ("The Lesser")	James is often referred to as "the little" or "the lesser" to differentiate him from the other James; Indiana is the smallest Midwest state.
Iowa	Bartholomew	The Hawkeye State is the nation's top pork and corn producer; Bartholomew is the patron saint of farmers and butchers.
Kansas	Andrew	Breadbasket of the world; Andrew was wingman on the "five loaves" miracle.
Michigan	Simon the Zealot	Only a zealot would lay claim to the Upper Peninsula when it clearly should be part of Wisconsin.
Missouri	Thomas	The Show-Me State; the Show-Me Saint.
Minnesota	Matthew	Preconversion, Matthew was a tax collector. The Gopher State has the highest taxes in the Midwest.
Nebraska	Jude (nicknamed Thaddeus)	Saint of lost causes; state of getting lost in a cornfield.
North Dakota	James (John's brother)	Inseparable brothers.
South Dakota	John (James's brother)	Inseparable brothers.
Ohio	Phillip	Phillip loved the Greeks; Ohio loves Greek chili.
Wisconsin	Peter	Peter was a God-fearing fisherman capable of cutting off a high priest's ear. If that doesn't scream Wisconsin, I don't know what does.

ANOTHER THURIBLE STORY

I'm one of twelve kids. I was mass-produced. That's Andy, Charlie, Billy, Betsy, Maggie, Addie, Mary Kate, John, Emily, Nora, Bridget, Ellie, and Frank. Twelve kids is so many kids I just listed thirteen names and you didn't know the difference. There's no Frank. Not yet, anyway. When you're one of twelve, people have questions. Are you Catholic? Are you Mormon? Are you homeschooled? The answer is yes. All of the above. (Kidding. I wasn't homeschooled.) Actually, I was born Catholic, but I was raised guilty. And that was okay, because Catholics have a tool for combating our self-imposed guilt: the confessional!

The confessional is amazing. You go into this little wooden box, tell a priest your sins, the priest gives you a penance, and boom. Your soul is clean as a whistle. The confessional is the Kwik Trip car wash for your soul.

I've been going to confession ever since I was in second grade. The penances were always the wild card. Sometimes they were a walk in the park. (Father tells you to say a decade of the rosary or read a passage in the Bible.) Other times they had real-life consequences . . . like making amends with the person you hurt.

By the time I got to the fifth grade, word was getting around that Father Jack (don't worry, this isn't going where you think it's going . . . but I've still changed some names) was going light on the penances: two Our Fathers and three Hail Marys. Didn't matter the sin! Of course, Father Jack became a rock star almost overnight. Everyone wanted a chance to get in his confessional. You should have seen the line. It was like a liquidation sale at Fleet Farm on Black Friday. My buddy Joe Dorsey got in there the night before and set up a tent.

I got in that line one day because I had a real humdinger to confess. "Bless me, Father, for I have sinned. My last confession was about a month ago. If you remember, I confessed to smoking the used cigarette butts Mrs. Hoff left outside the adoration chapel. Anyway, I got an airsoft gun and I accidentally—okay, purposely—shot my brother Andy . . . in the nipple."

"In the nipple, you say?" Father reiterated for clarity.

FIRST COMMUNION WITH BETSY
FROM NEXT DOOR

I nodded. I was shaking. What if this didn't wor—

"Two Our Fathers and three Hail Marys. Go in peace, child."

HAAALELLUJAH, HALLLELUJAH! I sang it in my head. I was so excited I forgot to say the third Hail Mary. I got home and found my brother Billy. I told him: "Billy, Father Jack's going light on the penances." Just like that, I'd become a TED Talk motivational speaker for the devil. "Start living your best life today. See that bottle? Throw it through a window. Wait, it's Red Dog. . . . Drink it first, then throw it through the window!" Billy cried. I was getting cocky. And that turned out to be my downfall.

At this same time, I was also an altar boy (also not going where you think it's going). But I wasn't just any altar boy. I was the incense altar boy. Why? Probably because I

liked matches the most. (A lot of people don't understand why Catholics use incense. But I think the answer is pretty clear. It's to remind asthmatics why they still need Jesus Christ in their lives.) Now, typically an altar boy will add two charcoals to the thurible . . . if they're an amateur. But I liked to roll five charcoals deep at a minimum. I also liked to add a little more incense when nobody was looking.

So anyway, it came time for Good Friday. Now, Good Friday Mass is like the Super Bowl Sunday for incense. And I wanted to make it special, so I went eight charcoals deep. There was so much charcoal in there, Father gave me a weird look when he went to put the incense in. I knew I'd done the job right when the cantor was coughing. "Were you there when they c— (*cough*)." Mission accomplished. We proceeded down the aisle. My thoughts are the worst in moments like these. But that's okay, I'll just confess them later. *"Were you there when they crucified my Lord?"* No?! That was two thousand years ago, were you there? Does this guy think we're vampires? *"Were you there when the sun refused to shine?"* Well, yeah, this was Wisconsin, that was every day for the past three weeks.

By the time we got to the altar, the church looked like a Pink Floyd concert. I could barely see Father Jack on the other side of the altar telling me to get the incense outta here. "Sorry, I did my job too good." I said that in my head. (Another one for the confessional.) So,

I took the incense to the sacristy, where we'd just gotten beautiful new carpeting. It was whiter than Burning Man. Father Tom usually had funny homilies, so I didn't want to miss it. But I turned too quickly and accidentally kicked over the thurible, dumping out two coals. Ope!

Now, this wasn't a sin; this was an accident.

Here's where the sin came in. I carefully added six more coals to make a "smiley" face. In my defense, smiles are contagious. I covered up my new smiley face with a plant and figured nobody would ever notice. Plus I could just confess it if I ever felt guilty. Well, I did. But luckily for me, it would just take two Our Fathers and three Hail Marys to clear this up. Enter confessional. "Bless me, Father, for I have sinned. My last confession was one month ago. Andy's nipple has since healed. I accidentally—well, purposely—made a smiley face out of the charcoal I spilled in the recto—"

"That was you?!" Father interjected. Uff da, I might be in trouble . . .

CHARLIE: Yes.

FATHER: Two Our Fathers. Three Hail Marys.

CHARLIE: Thank you, Father.

FATHER: I'm not finished yet.

Shoot.

FATHER: And I want you to tell your parents what you did.

CHARLIE: NOOOOOO. Father, please.

FATHER: Go in peace, child.

I was beside myself. So I got out of the confessional and I appealed directly to God. I got down on my knees in the pew and said, "God, I know I don't often hear your voice but I could sure use it right now."

GOD: Yes, Charlie.

CHARLIE: Oh, hey der God. How's it going?

GOD: Going great. The Packers are looking good this year.

CHARLIE: That's right, you're a Packers fan; how could I forget? So, God . . . I was just in the confessional with Father Jack—

GOD: I know. I was there.

CHARLIE: That's right, you're everywhere. So, well, what should I do?

GOD: Charlie, priests are a lot like doctors. You could always use a second opinion. Father Romantu is right across the hall—

CHARLIE: Thank you, Lord. Amen.

Moments later, I was saying "Bless me, Father Romantu, for I have sinned. My last confession was forty-eight seconds ago. I accidentally made a smiley face out of the charcoal in the sacristy. I'm so sorry."

Father Romantu laughed. "That was you? You got me off the hook for spilling wine on the new carpeting. Say a decade of the rosary and go in peace, child."

HAAAH—AHH—AHH—LEEE—UU—AHH!!!

And this is why I love the confessional. ♥

Midwest Politics: Purple All Over . . .

Now that the tough discussion of religion has transpired, here's another taboo subject: politics. Every four years, the rest of the country turns its attention to the Midwest to see who the next president will be. Sorry, this wasn't our idea. New York, California, New England, the South . . . We're not even sure why you vote; just give the points and move on. Meanwhile, politicians from across the country stop flying over the flyover states. Minnesota, Ohio, Michigan, Wisconsin, Iowa . . . no real clue who these swing states will swing toward. Combined with Florida, Arizona, and Pennsylvania, these battleground lands will be deciding who you detest for the next four years or longer.

Why is this so? Why can't we make up our minds on a political identity? Because, despite what many might believe, we're not just sixty-eight million of the exact same person. The Midwest is still a part of the world that breeds self-reliance . . . but the idea of helping our neighbors is just as important. What role government should play in that mix is where things get complicated and interesting. The combination of rural areas and cities small and large, mixed with suburbs that are a house-to-house (often room-to-room) blend of leanings, makes it tough to determine which way the Electoral wind will blow.

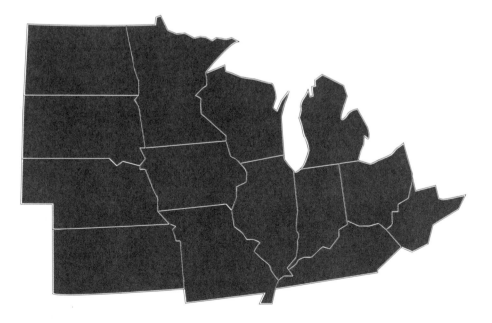

ROCKING THE VOTE

A quick story that could help you understand Midwest politics a little bit better. Back in 2008 I was reporting on the election for MTV News and was in St. Paul, Minnesota, covering the protests during the Republican National Convention. After nearly twelve hours of demonstrations, police surrounded the protesters, journalists, pedestrians, and even a taxi driver who was just trying to cross the blocked-off bridge. Didn't matter who you were, anyone on that road was going to the slammer. After we all got prints taken and a fun pic for the public record, we were escorted into giant chain-link enclosures. And because the police didn't take much time sorting out pedestrian from protester, this makeshift cell was now filled with philosophies from every end of the political spectrum.

At first it was pretty tense. The protesters started doing their chants and were halfway through their greatest hits collection when the taxi driver sitting beside me asked them politely to quiet down. Others not involved in the protest applauded his plea. The protesters kept going. The back-and-forth lasted a couple hours. But then people got tired. People got quiet. And as boredom took hold, people started talking. Even people on opposite sides

of the 2008 American political divide. And then they even started saying nice things to each other. One guy even complimented another fella's Detroit Lions socks. In Minnesota. The police then came and gave us all peanut butter and jelly sandwiches. I'll tell ya what, weird things happen when you spend the night in a big chicken coop. I gave the taxi driver half of my PB&J because he asked, and a few hours later, he returned the favor with a free ride home. He also gave a protester a ride home. But before he dropped us off, we all stopped for breakfast in Dinkytown. What a long way we've come since 2008. Social media changed America's political arithmetic. But I think this may be a more productive equation: PB&J + Nowhere to go = Can't be worse than Twitter.

Retirement: When You Quit Working Just Before Your Heart Does . . .

Congratulations, you've made it to your golden years, and it's time for the world's longest coffee break. No pressure, no stress, no heartache . . . unless you still fish or hunt or own a boat or root for the Lions. In any case, now what do you do?

There are as many ways to retire in the Midwest as there are types of fish in Lake Superior. Here are the ones most people manage with some success.

Cabin Up Nort'

When it's time to vacation, Midwest people often head up nort' to the family cabin. That cabin is likely owned by a very generous retiree. (Better bring them a six-pack, and don't drink them all the first night.) Results from a Pew research poll conducted while bored in church one time show that most parishioners had dreamed of buying their own cabin before the homily. (But, before you think that's disrespectful, it's not, because all cabins are located in God's country.) Endless fishing, hunting, boating, skiing, sleeping, and watching the water move has driven many to look out their cubicle, daydream, and scroll Zillow prices in sweet anticipation of retiring in a place with terrible email access.

Farm Life

Whether you're a real farmer looking for better land or a hobby farmer looking to take advantage of lax tax codes, buying a farm after you cash in those decades of Roth IRA contributions isn't a bad way to go. Beware, however, if you fall into the latter category. Don't ever *pretend* you're a real farmer. The real farmers will know, and you don't want to annoy your new neighbors. Farming is a tough business, and while you may share in your mutual love of the countryside, their way of life is tethered to a complicated set of laws and economics that don't always scream R&R. If you go this route, take your new neighbors some beer and jerky; you'll need help when you get your ATV stuck in the river.

Snowbird Retirement

Whether it's Florida, Arizona, or maybe the Boundary Island in China, there's no shortage of snowbird escapes that could make the perfect winter getaway. Many people keep dual residences: the Midwest for the summer ('cause ya can't beat a Midwest summer) and anywhere else but here for winter because . . . well, Midwest winters. Here are the most popular choices:

- **Florida:** East Coasters stay on the Atlantic and flock to southeast Florida; Midwesterners head to south*west* Florida and the Gulf of Mexico. Anything from Venice to Marco Island will do nicely (Cape Coral, Fort Myers, Naples, Punta Gorda, Port Charlotte). Some people complain these towns are "boring, flat, featureless land, with endless developments and big box stores," but Midwesterners just see it as a warmer version of home.
- **Arizona:** Places like Sun City West near Phoenix are quite common destinations for heartland retirees, and, since it's mostly Midwest people there, it's just like the popular Villages in Florida, but without all the venereal disease.

Retirement Job

So you've worked your entire adult life imagining how much better things will be when you retire. And then you retire. You spend the first few days fly-fishing and catching trees, and before you know it, you're watching *Days of Our Lives* at two P.M. on a Wednesday, drying your tears on Fleet Farm receipts. Maybe work wasn't so bad after all. Time to get a retirement job. Odds are you'll want a job where you can talk to people to take some pressure off your significant other. Bait shop cashier, Uber driver, Fleet Farm, the help desk at the airport, ticket person in the state park, or even the highly coveted "key guy" at the hardware store. Unlock your retirement job today.

Highway Cabin

What if you've spent your *entire* life in one location and have a lot of traveling to do while your body still allows it? Maybe an RV is the way to go. You can live your retirement years the way Willie Nelson does, on a tour bus. Just make sure to hide your psychedelics better than he did. Or just go the speed limit when you're driving through Texas.

Food & Drink

From fish boils and brat fries to fish fries and brat boils, Midwest cuisine is among the most eclectic in the world, as our palates extend far beyond sausage and perch. We also love catfish and walleye! Midwest culinary traditions are rooted in Indigenous and European culture, and more recently, immigrants from Somalia, the Middle East, and China have expanded the region's better-known dishes. From Wisconsin's dairy breakfasts to traditional Indigenous cuisine, from Hmong kitchens in Minneapolis to Chicago's deep-dish dinners, and all the German beer hall pretzels, soul food specials, tacos al pastor, and buffalo stew in between, the Midwest has something for everyone . . . as long as everyone remembers the Tums.

Ranch Dressing

The Midwest's love for ranch dressing is legendary.

And though it's the number one salad dressing in America (three times more popular than the next closest, Caesar or Italian, depending on the year), this has little to do with salad and croutons.

Midwesterners dump ranch on *everything*: pizza, chicken nuggets, French fries, tots, cauliflower and broccoli, fry bread, potato skins, chicken wings, jalapeño poppers, hamburgers, playful spouses, hot dogs, fried mushrooms, fried zucchini, fried pickles, unfried pickles, fried onion rings, fried hush puppies, tacos, pretzels, casserole, popcorn, mac 'n' cheese, nachos, tuna, grilled cheese, coleslaw, muffins, potato salad, jerky, nuts, Chex mix, mashed potatoes, and more. None of that is a joke; ranch dressing soda is made, sold, and consumed. When that's not on hand, people *will* drink it straight from the bottle.

The ambrosia of Aurora. The nectar of Nebraska. The manna of Milwaukee. The lembas of Lansing. (We could do this all day. . . .) The point is, when you're in the Midwest, ranch dressing will be found everywhere and on everything. If you had a special *CSI* blue light that just picked up ranch, everything would be blue. Or white. You understand. Anyhoo, here's the rundown on the keystone of your Midwest diet.

What Is It?

A sauce made from buttermilk, mayonnaise, and various herbs. There *are*, technically, other brands of ranch dressing, but Hidden Valley Ranch is the most popular. Why? Probably because they were the first to make it. Does anyone have a strong brand loyalty to Hidden Valley Ranch? Doubt it. Ranch is ranch. It's like butter or pizza or brandy. Purists will argue over which is the best, but at the end of the day, the worst still gets the job done. So no need to get pretentious about it. Over the years, Hidden Valley has produced seventy different varieties, but nobody cares about those flavors. Original remains the best and most accepted style.

Where Did It Come From?

A Nebraskan named Kenneth Steve Henson moved to Alaska in 1949 with his wife, Gayle, to work as a plumbing contractor. The job included cooking for his coworkers, and he eventually messed around with the recipe for the buttermilk dressing they used each night. Five years later, Steve and Gayle opened a 120-acre dude ranch near Santa Barbara, where he served his Alaskan concoction to guests. They called it Hidden Valley Ranch. When the dude ranch failed, the Hensons sold half the acreage and focused on his "ranch dressing"—which had been far more popular with guests than the dude stuff. Steve and Gayle Henson eventually created a dry-packaged mix to sell. Customers anywhere could

now add the mix to some buttermilk and mayo and it sold like crazy. They eventually sold the product to Clorox (which apparently makes more than bleach) for $8 million in 1972 (that's $50 million by today's numbers . . . soon to be $90 million).

Why Does Everyone in the Midwest Eat It?

First, because the packets of herbs were easy to ship inland. Midwest restaurants and busy Midwest parents could easily dump a packet into some buttermilk and mayo and have a quick, simple, and cheap meal that featured seasonings from somewhere warmer and more exciting.

Second, for decades, major food companies would test new products in one of two cities: Indianapolis and Columbus. Well, what do you know? In the mid-eighties, Clorox figured out how to make a bottle of ranch shelf-stable up to 150 days. Two factories produced the stuff: one in Los Angeles and the other in Wheeling, Illinois. *Every* Midwest grocery shelf was packed with the bottles by 1983. Ditto Cool Ranch Doritos, also first tested in the Midwest in the early eighties.

Third, around this time, Ypsilanti-based Domino's and Detroit-based Little Caesars were first exploding across the Midwest. The companies were always looking to one-up the other on dipping options—garlic butter and "Crazy Sauce" were *sooooo* 1980—and here came ranch.

Fourth, because it's friggin' delicious.

Anything Else I Need to Know?

Hidden Valley Ranch sells half a billion dollars' worth of salad dressing a year. In St. Louis, you'll find the Twisted Ranch restaurant, where every item on the menu (from appetizers to dessert pudding) contains one of their thirty-plus house-made ranch dressings. Also, Steve Henson was a point guard at McPherson High School in Kansas and then Kansas State, was drafted by the Milwaukee Bucks, and later played for the La Crosse Catbirds, Rapid City Thrillers, Fargo-Moorhead Fever, Grand Rapids Hoops, *and* the Detroit Pistons. He is *not*, apparently, related to the Steve Henson who invented ranch dressing. But he's so dang Midwest, had to work him in somehow.

Now, get dippin', people.

Meet Your Meat

There are a lot of different weenies out there, each with its own shape, size, and flavor. Picking the right one for you may take some time and experimentation. But don't feel pressured to commit to just one, as you'll find a wide assortment of forcemeats to try out at the next barbecue, picnic, tailgate, office party, bonfire, or prom.

Brats, chorizo, Italian sausage, Polish sausage, hot dogs . . . and those are just the ones that race around Miller Park during Brewers games. Adding to the fun, any and all of these can be stuffed with cheese, peppers, bacon, jalapeños, potato, apple, even asparagus, and can be sautéed, broiled, boiled, or grilled (always the best choice! Don't kill the messenger.).

To outsiders, it's all just hot dogs. To a Midwesterner, every sausage, wiener, and frank is a canvas waiting to be turned into a unique piece of art at the condiments stand. But before we get to the art, let's define the canvases. (Frank-ly, the topic of sausages could fill an entire book. This list is not meant to be exhaustive; it's just enough to get you by at most taverns, cookouts, and street meat vendors you may encounter.)

Weenie Type		Distinguishing Features
Brat		Pronounced "brot" and made with pork and veal and sometimes also beef, coarsely ground and seasoned with caraway seeds, coriander, ginger, or nutmeg. Visit Madison, Wisconsin, on Memorial Day weekend for Brat Fest.
Mett		A strongly flavored German sausage made from raw minced pork preserved by curing and smoking, often with garlic.
Knackwurst/ Knockwurst		Ground pork, veal, occasionally beef, and garlic, aged for a few days and smoked over oak wood.
Bockwurst		Veal and pork flavored with white pepper and paprika and sometimes marjoram, chives, and parsley. Typically smoked.
Italian sausage		Coarsely ground fresh pork flavored with garlic and fennel seed. The hot version includes red pepper flakes.
Weisswurst		Made from minced veal and pork back bacon and usually flavored with parsley, lemon, mace, onions, ginger, and cardamom.
Currywurst		Steamed, *then* fried, pork sausage typically cut into bite-size chunks and seasoned with curry ketchup—spiced ketchup topped with curry powder.
Chorizo		A Spanish or Mexican sausage with large pieces of fatty pork, chili pepper, and paprika.
Hungarian sausage		Coarsely ground and salted pork mixed with spices and a slurry of garlic.
Andouille		A smoked French sausage made with pork intestines, pepper, onions, wine, and seasonings.

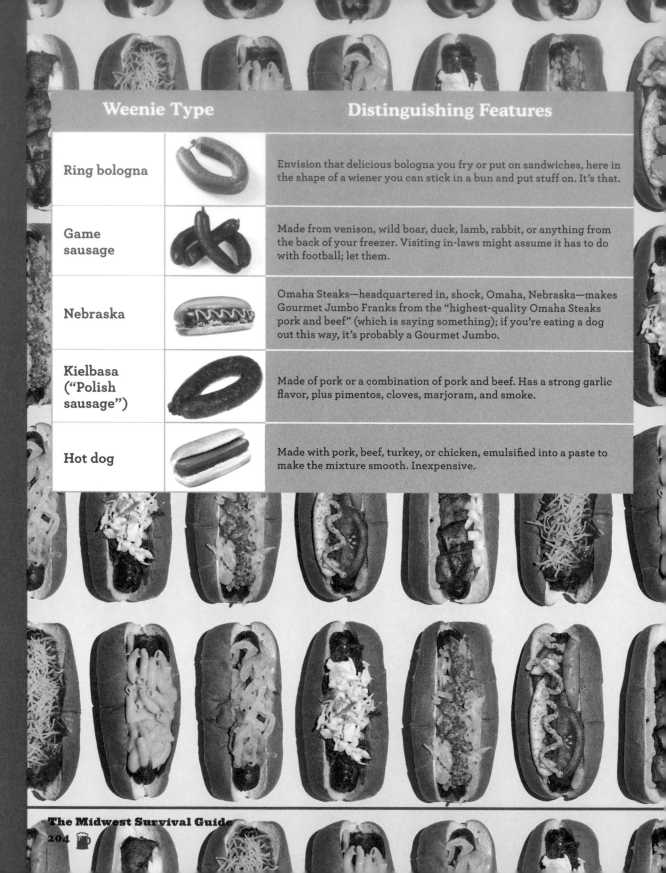

Weenie Type		Distinguishing Features
Ring bologna		Envision that delicious bologna you fry or put on sandwiches, here in the shape of a wiener you can stick in a bun and put stuff on. It's that.
Game sausage		Made from venison, wild boar, duck, lamb, rabbit, or anything from the back of your freezer. Visiting in-laws might assume it has to do with football; let them.
Nebraska		Omaha Steaks—headquartered in, shock, Omaha, Nebraska—makes Gourmet Jumbo Franks from the "highest-quality Omaha Steaks pork and beef" (which is saying something); if you're eating a dog out this way, it's probably a Gourmet Jumbo.
Kielbasa ("Polish sausage")		Made of pork or a combination of pork and beef. Has a strong garlic flavor, plus pimentos, cloves, marjoram, and smoke.
Hot dog		Made with pork, beef, turkey, or chicken, emulsified into a paste to make the mixture smooth. Inexpensive.

Sausage Condiments

Now that we've got the sausages pretty well defined, it's time to dive into the topping options, perfect for lunch, dinner, and especially breakfast. Here are the more popular styles you'll encounter:

Chicago style: The world-famous beef frankfurter placed on a poppy seed bun and loaded with mustard, pickle spears, chopped onions, relish, tomato, pickled peppers, and celery salt. No ketchup, thanks.

Cincinnati chili dog style: Cincinnati chili, diced onion, and shredded cheddar cheese (see the dip version of this on page 222).

Kansas City style: Pork sausage in a sesame seed bun topped with brown mustard, sauerkraut, and melted Swiss cheese. It's as if a Reuben and a hot dog met on Tinder. Thousand Island dressing also a possibility.

Gas station style: The tragically overlooked gas station sausage, remarkable in its elegance and simplicity. Always go with the cementlike mustard packets. The more adventurous should apply one of every packet—whatever it is—that sits to the right of the rotating wieners.

Michigan style ("Coney Island"): A beef or beef and pork European-style Vienna sausage topped with a spiced sauce made from ground beef heart, one or two stripes of yellow mustard, and diced or chopped white onion. There are three variations: Jackson style (ground beef sauce); Detroit style (a soupier beef-heart-based sauce); and Flint style (a thicker, meatier sauce that's more like a goulash).

St. Louis style: Wrap bacon around a hot dog and grill and steam the bun. Baked beans go on the bun first, *then* the hot dog.

Tailgate style: You'll be served any number of wiener condiments at a tailgate. For toppings, my best recommendation is to start with everything. Whatever they got out: various mustards, sauerkraut, diced avocado, bacon, chili, coleslaw, baked beans, relish, more bacon, chips, gravy, fries, pickles, chopped tomato, chopped onion, Buffalo sauce, blue cheese, chopped jalapeño, peanut butter, ranch dressing, popcorn, mac 'n' cheese, pepperoni, sardines, Pop Rocks, even ketchup! You get the idea. If something doesn't hit you right, feel free to remove the next round. But keep in mind that each ingredient heals a different part of your soul, so—subtract wisely.

Midwest Pizza

Okay, the East Coast probably wins the "best pizza" challenge, but it's not as clear-sliced as you might think. From Chicago's world-famous deep dish to those regional concoctions that have only spread a state or two (yet), you'll find that Midwest pizza comes in all shapes and sizes, and that America's official "favorite food" is alive and well in the American heartland. The styles to twig and taste:

Chicago style: Legendary thick crust. Every tourist's first meal in the Windy City.

St. Louis style: Cracker-thin crust.

Detroit style: Square, with burned cheese on the crust.

Illinois stuffed style: Essentially a stuffed calzone with *another* whole pizza cooked on top.

Ohio Valley style: Toppings (cheese, meat, and so on) are put on *after* the sauced pizza comes out of the oven.

Quad Cities style: The dough is drenched in brewer's malt and the pizza is topped with lean pork sausage and cut into strips with giant scissors. Quad Cities = Rock Island, Moline, and East Moline, Illinois, and Bettendorf and Davenport, Iowa. Worth noting: Davenport, Rock Island, and Moline began as the "Tri-Cities." It's only a matter of time before the *entire* Midwest is cutting its pizza with giant scissors.

Brier Hill style: Pan cooked and topped with bell peppers and Romano cheese instead of mozzarella, this pizza was invented in Youngstown, Ohio.

***Slaughterhouse-Five* style:** A meat-buried pie named for the celebrated Indianapolis author; found in Indianapolis.

Casey's style: A thin-crust delicacy acquired at local gas station.

Omaha style: Has a flaky crust that's more like a biscuit; the bottom of each pizza is grilled in a special rotating-deck oven to give it a bakery-style crust. Typically topped with a thick yummy blanket of ground beef and a sprinkle of onions or mushrooms.

East Coast style: Thin and relatively oily, with big black bubbles in the coal-fired crust; can be found if you're a transplant jonesin' for a taste of home. (For Maryland people, we also have Pizza Huts.)

The Right Brew for You?

Now that you're twenty-one, it's time to start drinking beer. (*My first beer was a Red Dog. Me and my cousin Tom snuck them into the basement when we were nine. Tom got caught and didn't rat me out. I still owe him a Red Dog for that.*)

Sometimes, it's tough being a beer drinker in this hard seltzer world. But for most people in the Midwest, there's no better adult beverage than a brewski. There are some beer snobs out here, and while we can appreciate their dedication to the craft, the Midwest is an equal opportunity suds-sumer. Macro, micro, foreign, domestic, home brewed, closet brewed . . . we'll even do bathtub brewed as long as you promise you didn't just give your dogs a bath. (But honestly, if you brewed an IPA, we probably couldn't tell the difference.)

Some of you may not be so adventurous, so here's a good quiz to help you think about what kind of beer may be right for you.

What colors do you like to ingest? _____
amber, red, brown, black, palish yellow (worth 6½ points)

What smells do you like? _____
hoppy, malty, floral, fruity, vinegary (worth 5 points)

What should beer feel like in your mouth? _____
light, full, gravy-like, air, chunky (worth 4¾ points)

How much of your beer should actually be water? _____
99.9%, 95%, 70%, 40% (worth 5 points)

What is the local beer? _____ **(worth 77 points)**

What did/does your dad drink? _____ **(worth 51½ points)**

What do your friends drink? _____ **(worth 185 points)**

Add it all up and order a round for the whole table.

Some "Economical" Heartland Hops

With the perfect combination of lots of fresh water, beer lovers, and folks always looking to buy in bulk, the Midwest has no shortage of reasonably priced (okay, cheap) beer choices. If you want to spend $12 on a beer, knock yourself out, but if you're out with pals or picking up a few six-packs for the next bonfire or Mother's Day brunch, you might want to order up these time-tested local winners:

- PBR (Pabst Blue Ribbon)
- Stroh's
- Miller Lite
- Miller High Life Light
- Stone (Keystone Light)
- Grain Belt (the "friendly beer")
- Natty Ice (Natural Ice)
- Natty Light (Natural Light)
- Hamm's
- The Beast (Milwaukee's Best Premium)
- EGL (Extra Gold Lager)
- Red Dog

- Old Milwaukee
- Leinenkugel's
- Keep 'er Movin' by Ale Asylum
- Blatz Light
- Hudy Delight (Hudephol)
- Burger Beer
- Little Kings
- Old Style
- Schlitz
- Name Tag
- Simpler Times
- Buschhhhhh (Busch Light)

Classic Midwest Recipes

Whether you're homesick for the heartland or new to the region or just wanna try the cuisine before wrapping all your plates and moving to Cedar Rapids, here's a collection of classic Midwest recipes for you to prepare and enjoy. While there are, of course, any number of variations to such things, you'll find a nice sample of everything from appetizers to adult beverages and a main course for one hundred of your closest pals. Time to drag out your garlic press, tongs, graters, and old takeout condiment containers turned measuring cups. You'll find there's something for everyone on the Midwest Menu.

Deviled Eggs

MAKES TWICE AS MANY AS YOU HAVE EGGS

1. Place 6 to 666 eggs in a saucepan and cover them with water by one and a half inches. Heat on high until the water boils, then cover the pot, turn the heat to low, and cook another minute.

2. Remove from the heat and leave covered for 14 minutes. Rinse the eggs under cold water for a full minute.

3. Peel the eggs under cool running water and slice them in half lengthwise. Remove the yolks to a bowl and set the whites on a platter. Mash the yolks using a fork or empty beer bottle. Add mayonnaise (¼ cup for every 6 eggs), mustard (enough to taste), apple cider vinegar (some), salt and pepper to taste, garlic powder (if you dare), chives (if you'll notice), crumbled cooked bacon (if you wish), and so on. Mix well.

4. Stuff the waiting egg-white halves with the yolk mixture. Sprinkle with paprika or whatever and serve.

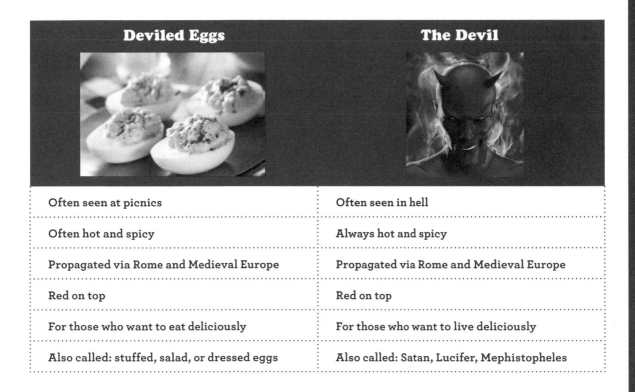

Deviled Eggs	The Devil
Often seen at picnics	Often seen in hell
Often hot and spicy	Always hot and spicy
Propagated via Rome and Medieval Europe	Propagated via Rome and Medieval Europe
Red on top	Red on top
For those who want to eat deliciously	For those who want to live deliciously
Also called: stuffed, salad, or dressed eggs	Also called: Satan, Lucifer, Mephistopheles

Kringle

You'll find plenty of recipes for Kringle online, and—if you're a serious baker—by all means, go for it. But for the mere mortals among us, perhaps use the powers of the internet to order directly from folks who truly know what they're doing. Here are four Wisconsin-based options: ohdanishbakery.com, kringle.com, lehmannsbakery.com, and larsenskringle.com. Perhaps buy some kringle from each for whatever the next holiday is—there's an unwritten rule that kringle can only be eaten on holidays, but anything from Palm Sunday or Mischief Night to Go Fishing Day (June 18!) will do—and have a family/friends taste-off.

See also: **Fish Fry French Toast**

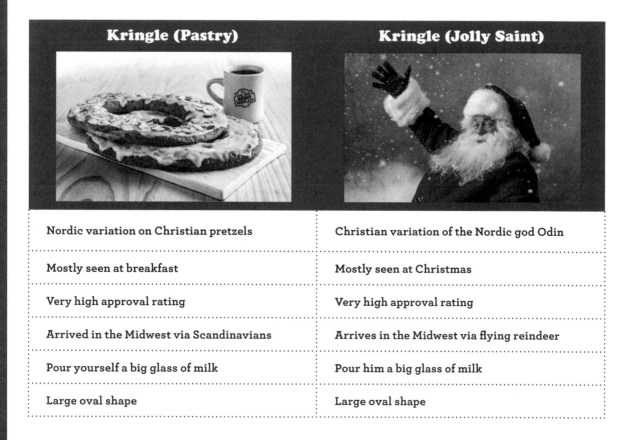

Kringle (Pastry)	Kringle (Jolly Saint)
Nordic variation on Christian pretzels	Christian variation of the Nordic god Odin
Mostly seen at breakfast	Mostly seen at Christmas
Very high approval rating	Very high approval rating
Arrived in the Midwest via Scandinavians	Arrives in the Midwest via flying reindeer
Pour yourself a big glass of milk	Pour him a big glass of milk
Large oval shape	Large oval shape

Fish Fry French Toast

MAKES 4 SLICES (SERVES 2, AT BEST . . .)

Go to a local fish fry on a Friday night. Enjoy the meal and good company but remember to set aside four slices of the rye bread that comes with the meal. A purse or the kangaroo pocket of your hoodie will do nicely. When you get home, put the rye bread in a paper bag.

Two mornings later, get up and whisk 1 egg, 1 teaspoon vanilla (or bourbon or other flavoring of choice), and ½ teaspoon ground cinnamon in a shallow dish. Stir in ¼ cup milk. Dip the slightly stale bread in the mixture, coating both sides evenly. Lightly grease a nonstick griddle or skillet and heat over medium heat. Cook the French toast until browned on both sides, one minute or so per side. Serve warm with the syrup of your choice.

Lefse

MAKES A LOT

10 pounds russet potatoes

½ cup (1 stick) butter

½ cup heavy cream

1 tablespoon table salt

1 tablespoon sugar

2½ cups all-purpose flour, more for rolling out the dough

1. Peel the potatoes, cut them into large chunks, and cook in boiling water until tender. Run the still-hot potatoes through a potato ricer and place in a large bowl. Add the butter, cream, salt, and sugar and gently mix until combined. Let cool to room temperature, then stir in the flour.

2. Preheat a large griddle (or borrow a lefse pan from your aunt).

3. Make golf ball–size balls from the dough (keep them covered as you go) and roll them out on a lightly floured surface to ⅛-inch thickness. This is a good process to do with friends.

4. Cook the lefse on the griddle until bubbles form on the bottom and brown, then flip and cook the other side. This will happen quickly! Place the lefse on a damp towel to cool slightly, then cover with *another* damp towel until ready to serve.

5. Serve with brown or white sugar and butter, or however your family does it. Lefse can be refrigerated (covered) for several days or frozen for longer.

See also: **Grandpa Bob's Potato Pancakes**

Lefse	Jay-Z
Soft flatbread made from potato and flour	Rapper and entertainment mogul
From Norway/Midwest	From Brooklyn
Will attend your next party for $5+	Will attend your next party for $1 million+
Great with butter, brown sugar, or jelly	Great with Beyonce, Yeezy, or Linkin Park
Pronounced LEF-suh	Pronounced Jay-ZEE
Also called tynnlefse, lompe	Also called Hova, Jazzy, Lucky Lefty, S-dot

Grandpa Bob's Potato Pancakes

MAKES 5 PANCAKES

Grandpa Bob always decided halfway through this recipe that he didn't need recipes. His seven kids disagreed. "When he made these, it took an Act of Congress to get anyone to eat them," Dad said. These were always served with fish fries and occasionally dunked in apple sauce to disguise the taste.

2 large potatoes, peeled and grated
(*make the kids do it; that's why ya had 'em*)

1 tablespoon lemon juice
(*really, anything citrus lying around: OJ, lime, lime Bud Light*)

¼ cup (½ stick) butter, melted
(*the real stuff; we're in the kitchen, not the Norda Trek or however ya say it*)

2 tablespoons flour
(*ask your smartest kid to get flour, otherwise they'll bring ya dandelions*)

FOR FRYING, PER BATCH
1 tablespoon cooking oil
(*the best is leftover grease from Friday's fish fry*)

⅓ cup finely chopped yellow onion
(*use your sharpest buck knife*)

1 large egg, whisked (*not stirred*)

¼ teaspoon salt
(*if you shoot it in with one of them Bug Assault guns, even more fun*)

¼ teaspoon ground black pepper
(*you can shoot this in, too*)

¼ teaspoon baking powder (*and this*)

Applesauce, to serve

1 tablespoon butter
(*again, you use that Can't Believe It's Not Butter stuff, we got problems*)

1. In a large bowl, combine the potatoes and lemon juice. Let stand 5 minutes. Drain well. Add the melted butter, flour, onion, egg, salt, pepper, and baking powder. Mix well.

2. Heat 1 tablespoon each of oil and butter in large skillet over medium-high heat. Working in batches of three or four pancakes, place heaping tablespoonfuls of the potato mixture in the skillet. Flatten with a fork and cook 3 to 4 minutes on each side, until golden brown and cooked through. Add more butter and oil as needed. Drain on paper towels.

3. Serve with applesauce. Kids will love these. If they don't, they're grounded.

Cannibal Sandwich

Okay, so maybe many Midwesterners grew up eating this and still do . . . but raw meat *is* super dangerous, so we're going to do the responsible thing and skip the actual recipe. Not that it would take a genius to figure it out. But, legally speaking, we have *not* told you how to make it.

Cannibal Sandwich	Cannibal
Scary and gross	Scary and gross
Rye bread topped with raw beef and onion	Topped with fava beans and a nice Chianti
An acquired taste	An acquired taste
Mostly served at Christmastime	Mostly avoided via special headgear and walls
Legal, ethical, abhorrent	Illegal, unethical, abhorrent
USDA trying to stop	FBI trying to stop

Fish Boil

There's nothing quite like a traditional Wisconsin fish boil. It's something Door County (Wisconsin's thumb) has spent a century perfecting. Imagine a huge pot of potatoes, onions, and Lake Michigan whitefish boiled over an open flame. Now imagine that flame shooting fifteen feet in the sky because some fella fed it a truck mug full of diesel fuel. That's called the boil over. It's intentional. It's also the reason I'm not including a how-to in this book. Because that's how-to get sued. All it takes is one Todd to boil his fish underneath a wood deck, or a Larry to mistake his diesel for an old-fashioned (Larry uses a truck mug for both), and I'm on thinner ice than Green Bay ice fishers on daylight savings. But what I can give you is a few places that know what they're doing when it comes to a fish boil—and they've even got the eyebrows to prove it.

Old Post Office Restaurant, Ephraim

Pelletier's Restaurant & Fish Boil, Fish Creek

Rowleys Bay Restaurant, Ellison Bay

Viking Grill and Lounge, Ellison Bay

White Gull Inn, Fish Creek

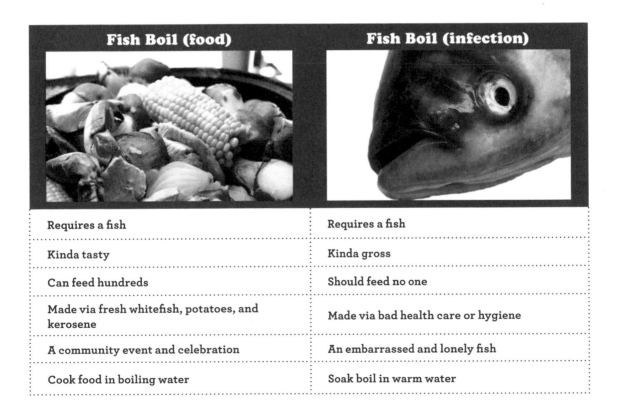

Fish Boil (food)	Fish Boil (infection)
Requires a fish	Requires a fish
Kinda tasty	Kinda gross
Can feed hundreds	Should feed no one
Made via fresh whitefish, potatoes, and kerosene	Made via bad health care or hygiene
A community event and celebration	An embarrassed and lonely fish
Cook food in boiling water	Soak boil in warm water

Watergate Salad

MAKES 12 TO 20 SERVINGS

One 4-ounce package instant pistachio pudding mix

One 20-ounce can crushed pineapple with juice, <u>undrained</u>

1 cup mini marshmallows

½ cup chopped nuts
(such as walnuts or pistachios)

1¾ cups nondairy whipped topping
(Cool Whip)

1. Combine all the ingredients in a large bowl and stir.

2. Refrigerate for at least 1 hour. Scoop and serve.

See also: **Grandma Sue's Brandied Cranberry Sauce**

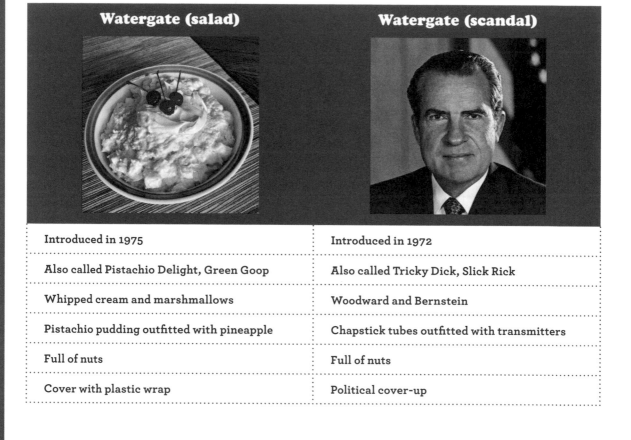

Watergate (salad)	Watergate (scandal)
Introduced in 1975	Introduced in 1972
Also called Pistachio Delight, Green Goop	Also called Tricky Dick, Slick Rick
Whipped cream and marshmallows	Woodward and Bernstein
Pistachio pudding outfitted with pineapple	Chapstick tubes outfitted with transmitters
Full of nuts	Full of nuts
Cover with plastic wrap	Political cover-up

Grandma Sue's Brandied Cranberry Sauce

MAKES 12 SERVINGS

Tastes like some good Wisconsin cranberries grown in a marsh of brandy.

1 pound fresh or frozen Wisconsin cranberries

½ cup orange juice

½ cup brandy

¾ cup sugar

Pinch of table salt

1. In a large saucepan, combine all the ingredients and ½ cup water. Mix to combine. Bring the mixture to a boil over medium-high heat. Lower the heat to a simmer and cook, stirring often, till you hear dem berries pop!

2. Refrigerate in an old Cool Whip container until texture firms.

Note: If you run out of water, use brandy.

Corn Soup

MAKES 10 SERVINGS

This recipe is compliments of Josie Lee, director of Ho-Chunk Museum and Cultural Center. Instructions follow for making it in an Instant Pot or slow cooker.

Dried corn

Meat (venison, chicken, pork—your choice)

Water (or broth if you have it—beef broth for venison, chicken broth for pork or chicken)

Salt and pepper

Cowboy bread, for serving

1. Fill a large pot with enough corn so that you can't see the bottom—more or less, depending on your preference.

2. Cut the meat into bite-size pieces and add it to the pot. Add enough water or broth to cover the meat. Add salt and pepper to taste.

3. If you're using an Instant Pot, turn on the "soup" pressure setting and cook for about 1 hour, until the corn is soft enough to chew. If you're using a slow cooker or Crock-Pot, cook on low for 6 to 8 hours.

4. Season to taste with more salt and pepper.

5. Enjoy with cowboy bread!

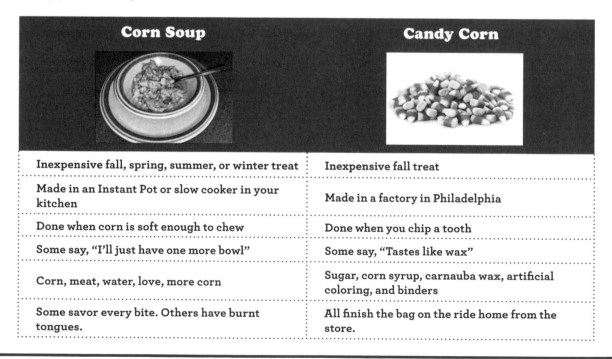

Corn Soup	Candy Corn
Inexpensive fall, spring, summer, or winter treat	Inexpensive fall treat
Made in an Instant Pot or slow cooker in your kitchen	Made in a factory in Philadelphia
Done when corn is soft enough to chew	Done when you chip a tooth
Some say, "I'll just have one more bowl"	Some say, "Tastes like wax"
Corn, meat, water, love, more corn	Sugar, corn syrup, carnauba wax, artificial coloring, and binders
Some savor every bite. Others have burnt tongues.	All finish the bag on the ride home from the store.

Pasties

More complicated than you'd think; check the web for the recipe if you *really* wanna go for it. Honestly, your best bet is to order these online from the pros—check out dobberspasties.com, lawryspasties.com, thepastyguy.com, lehtospasties.com, pastys.com—and have this delectableness simply arrive at your doorstep. Or you can always drive to Michigan.

Michigan Pasties	Las Vegas Pasties
Always edible	Sometimes edible
Pasty (singular) = rhymes with *nasty*	Pasties (plural). Singular illegal in many counties.
Delicious covering	Barely covering
First popular with miners and sailors	Popular with miners and sailors
Appear in medieval Arthurian ballads	Appear in the film *Showgirls*
Can have them flown to you for a modest fee	Can fly to Vegas for $25 to $125

Skyline Chili Dip

MAKES 1 TO 10 SERVINGS, DEPENDING ON HOW YOUR WEEK IS GOING

The Official Skyline-blessed Recipe, courtesy of Skyline Chili (www.skylinechili.com)

> 12 ounces cream cheese
>
> 13 to 15 ounces Skyline Chili
>
> 12 ounces Skyline shredded cheddar cheese

1. Preheat the oven to 375°F.
2. Spread the cream cheese evenly in a 9 x 13–inch pan.
3. Heat the chili through in the microwave or on the stove. Pour it evenly over the cream cheese layer.
4. Bake for 10 minutes.
5. Sprinkle the cheese evenly on top.
6. Let stand for 5 minutes to melt the cheese, then enjoy!

Unofficial add-ons: sour cream, minced onion, diced jalapeños (canned or fresh), diced green chiles or black olives, red-hot sauce of choice (Skyline brand for the real deal!)

Chili Dip (appetizer)	**Chile (country)**
Found at *every* party	Found in South America
"The surefire go-to appetizer"	"The country of poets"
Only salsa consumes more tortilla chips	Only the Germans consume more bread
Usually shallow and round	Mostly very long and narrow
Greeks immigrated to Cincy in the 1900s; opened Skyline	Incas invaded in the 1400s; Spaniards in the 1500s

Stir-Fried Instant Ramen

MAKES 1 LARGE OR 2 SMALL SERVINGS

This recipe is compliments of Chef Yia Vang (owner of the restaurant Vinai in Minneapolis). See his immigration story on page 254.

1 packet instant ramen (save the seasoning and chile packets)

¼ cup canola oil

½ cup chopped onion

½ cup chopped red bell pepper

2 teaspoons chopped garlic

2 teaspoons chopped ginger

2 teaspoons chopped lemongrass

2 teaspoons chopped shallot

2 green onions, sliced

4 to 6 ounces ground pork (or chicken or beef)

1 tablespoon fish sauce

2 tablespoons oyster sauce

1 egg

¼ cup chopped cilantro

1. Cook the noodles according to the package instructions. Drain the noodles, rinse them with cold water, and set aside.

2. In a large frying pan (nonstick preferred) over high heat, heat 2 to 3 tablespoons of the oil. Add the onion, pepper, garlic, ginger, lemongrass, and shallots and sauté until tender, about 5 minutes. Remove the vegetables to a plate and set aside.

3. Add the meat, fish sauce, oyster sauce, and ramen packet seasonings to the pan and sauté for 7 to 9 minutes, until the meat is cooked through.

4. Return the veggies to the pan and add the ramen. Stir to combine, then add another 1 to 2 tablespoons of oil if the noodles are looking dry. Add the egg and cook until the egg is scrambled, stirring often.

5. Toss into a bowl, sprinkle with cilantro, and chow down!

Stir-Fried Instant Ramen	Pool/Lake Noodles
Cook in oil	Floats in water
An easy meal in twenty minutes, tops	Easily lost and replaced
Perfect for soaking up sins still sitting in your stomach after bar time	Perfect for striking siblings and making obscene gestures, often at the same time
Many flavors for your tongue to sort out	Many colors to choose from
Tender and delicious	Kinda chewy and bland
Undo your top pants button to make room for ~~seconds~~ thirds	Squeeze three between your legs to make a comfy water chair

Charlie's (Mom's) Casserole Hot Dish

MAKES 6 TO 12 SERVINGS

1 pound ground beef
(or venison or whatever's in the unmarked bag you won at the meat raffle), "unthawed" (translation: thawed)

½ yellow onion, diced

½ teaspoon garlic powder

½ teaspoon salt

½ teaspoon ground black pepper

2 tablespoons Worcestershire

⅓ cup sour cream

One 10.5-ounce can cream of cheddar cheese soup

3 cups grated cheddar (divided)

One 15.2-ounce can corn, drained

One 14.5-ounce can green beans, drained

Tater tots, to cover the top
(about half of a 32-ounce bag)

1. Preheat the oven to 350°F. Grease a 9 x 13–inch pan. Crack a beer.

2. In a large skillet, brown the ground beef with the onion, garlic powder, salt, pepper, and Worcestershire sauce until the meat is no longer pink. Drain the grease if necessary.

3. In a large bowl, combine the beef mixture, sour cream, cheddar cheese soup, 1 cup of the cheddar, the corn, and the green beans. (You can say something about not putting in the green beans, but don't even think about putting in peas instead.)

4. Spread the meat mixture in the prepared pan, sprinkle with 1 cup of cheddar, and arrange the tater tots all over the top.

5. Bake for 50 minutes, until the tots are browned and crispy and the casserole is bubbling.

6. Top the casserole with the remaining shredded cheese and bake for 5 minutes, until the cheese is melted.

Note: My mother is trying to poison you with those green beans. Place them in a tomato gun and shoot them at the nearest nonliving target that won't get you a felony. Or just donate them.

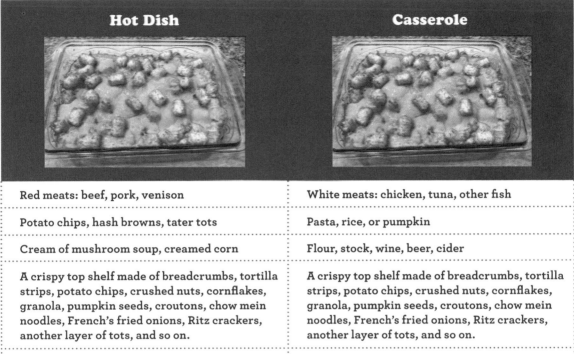

Hot Dish	Casserole
Red meats: beef, pork, venison	White meats: chicken, tuna, other fish
Potato chips, hash browns, tater tots	Pasta, rice, or pumpkin
Cream of mushroom soup, creamed corn	Flour, stock, wine, beer, cider
A crispy top shelf made of breadcrumbs, tortilla strips, potato chips, crushed nuts, cornflakes, granola, pumpkin seeds, croutons, chow mein noodles, French's fried onions, Ritz crackers, another layer of tots, and so on.	A crispy top shelf made of breadcrumbs, tortilla strips, potato chips, crushed nuts, cornflakes, granola, pumpkin seeds, croutons, chow mein noodles, French's fried onions, Ritz crackers, another layer of tots, and so on.
Often called a casserole; can swap in casserole ingredients without any issue	Often called a hot dish; can swap in hot dish ingredients without any issue

"Just Like Oma's!" Knoephla

MAKES 6 TO 10 SERVINGS

1½ cups all-purpose flour

2 cups plus 5 tablespoons milk

½ teaspoon salt

1 egg

2 tablespoons butter

3 russet potatoes, peeled and cut into 1-inch chunks

1 yellow onion, cut into ½-inch dice

1 carrot, peeled and thinly sliced

1 celery stalk, thinly sliced

1½ teaspoons ground black pepper

One 14.5-ounce can chicken broth and 2 chicken bouillon cubes

¼ cup chopped parsley, to serve

1. To make the dumplings, in a medium bowl, combine the flour, the 5 tablespoons of milk, the salt, and the egg. Mix into a stiff dough and set aside.

2. Melt the butter in large skillet over medium heat. Add the potatoes and onion and cook for 15 minutes, stirring often. Add the carrot, celery, pepper, and 2 cups milk and heat until the milk is warm.

3. In stockpot or large Dutch oven, bring the chicken broth, bouillon, and 6 cups water to a boil over medium-high heat. Add the ingredients from the skillet.

4. Dumpling time! Drop rounded tablespoons of the dough into the soup. Return the soup to a boil, then lower the heat to a simmer and cook, uncovered, for 10 to 15 minutes, until the dumplings are floating on top and fluffy (run a toothpick through one; when it comes out clean, they're ready).

5. Ladle into bowls, sprinkle with parsley, and serve.

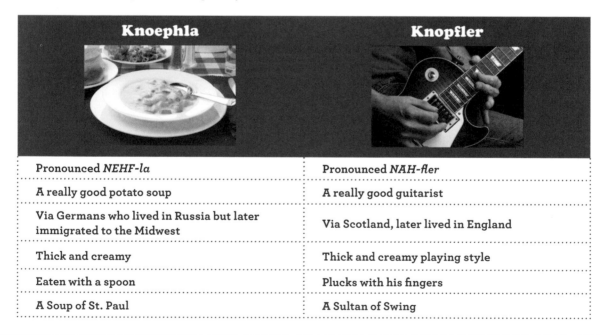

Knoephla	Knopfler
Pronounced *NEHF-la*	Pronounced *NAH-fler*
A really good potato soup	A really good guitarist
Via Germans who lived in Russia but later immigrated to the Midwest	Via Scotland, later lived in England
Thick and creamy	Thick and creamy playing style
Eaten with a spoon	Plucks with his fingers
A Soup of St. Paul	A Sultan of Swing

Buckeyes

MAKES ABOUT 14 DOZEN

PEANUT BUTTER FILLING

1 pound margarine, at room temperature

3 pounds confectioner's sugar

2 pounds crunchy peanut butter

3 tablespoons vanilla

CHOCOLATE COATING

¼ bar/1 ounce Parowax ("paraffin"*), grated to help it melt more quickly

One 12-ounce milk chocolate Hershey bar

6 ounces semisweet chocolate bits

2 ounces baking chocolate

1. In a large bowl, cream the margarine, then add the confectioner's sugar, peanut butter, and vanilla. Mix with clean hands and shape into balls the size of a 1-inch fishing bobber. In other words, shape into 1-inch balls. Chill overnight.

2. To make the coating, melt the wax in a double boiler. Add the other ingredients and mix until fully melted.

3. Using a toothpick or the tip of a kid's fishing pole, dip the balls into the chocolate, but not all the way; you want a circle of peanut butter to show to mimic supertoxic seeds.

4. Place the balls on waxed paper to set.

5. Store buckeyes in a closed container in a cool garage or front porch or in the refrigerator. Gain six pounds with only a tinge of regret.

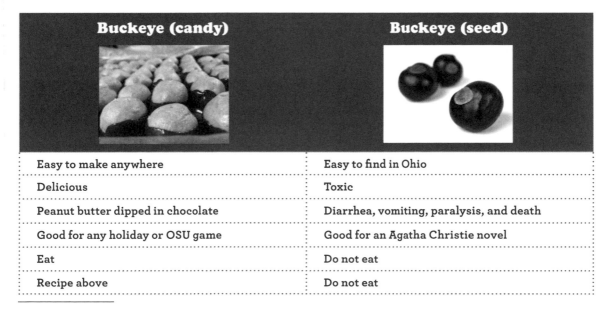

Buckeye (candy)	Buckeye (seed)
Easy to make anywhere	Easy to find in Ohio
Delicious	Toxic
Peanut butter dipped in chocolate	Diarrhea, vomiting, paralysis, and death
Good for any holiday or OSU game	Good for an Agatha Christie novel
Eat	Do not eat
Recipe above	Do not eat

* Also commonly used to grease bicycle chains and make kitchen drawers run smoother. Seriously.

LeRoy's Leap Parmesan Chicken

MAKES 2 SERVINGS

LeRoy Butler is the inventor of the Lambeau Leap and the only chef ever to receive a lateral from Reggie White.

Olive oil, for the pan

2 boneless skinless chicken breasts

½ cup buttermilk

½ cup breadcrumbs

½ cup shredded Parmesan cheese

3 tablespoons chopped fresh parsley

3 sweet bell peppers
(red, orange, and green), sliced

1 lemon

Cooked pasta or rice, for serving

1. Preheat the oven to 350°F. Oil a small baking pan with olive oil.

2. In a medium bowl, combine the buttermilk, breadcrumbs, Parmesan, and parsley. Submerge the chicken in the mixture for 30 to 60 seconds. Remove it from the mixture and let the excess coating drip off. Place the chicken in the pan. Spread the peppers over the chicken and squeeze lemon juice all over the top.

3. Bake for 45 minutes to 1 hour, until golden brown and cooked through.

4. Serve over a bed of rice or your favorite pasta.

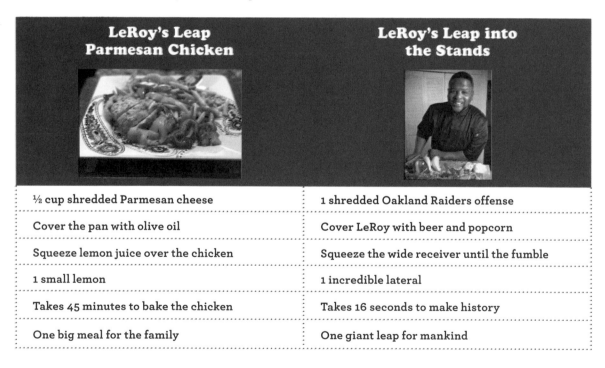

LeRoy's Leap Parmesan Chicken	LeRoy's Leap into the Stands
½ cup shredded Parmesan cheese	1 shredded Oakland Raiders offense
Cover the pan with olive oil	Cover LeRoy with beer and popcorn
Squeeze lemon juice over the chicken	Squeeze the wide receiver until the fumble
1 small lemon	1 incredible lateral
Takes 45 minutes to bake the chicken	Takes 16 seconds to make history
One big meal for the family	One giant leap for mankind

Bloody Mary

MAKES 1 BLOODY MARY

2 ounces vodka

4 ounces tomato juice

1 teaspoon Worcestershire

2 to 10 shakes Tabasco or Frank's Redhot Sauce

½ teaspoon prepared horseradish

Salt and ground black pepper to taste

1 lime wedge

For garnish/serving: crisp bacon strip, celery, olives, pickles, cheese cubes, celery stalk, beef sticks, venison jerky, mini-cheeseburgers, cold cooked shrimp, pickled jalapeño, and don't forget your beer back (aka a chaser, which usually comes in a three-ounce pour)

1. Fill a tall glass with ice cubes. Add the vodka and tomato juice.

2. Spice it up! Add the Worcestershire sauce, hot sauce, horseradish, and salt and pepper to taste. Mix well with a spoon.

3. Squeeze in a lime wedge and drop it in the drink.

4. Add any combo of the garnish and serving items and serve.

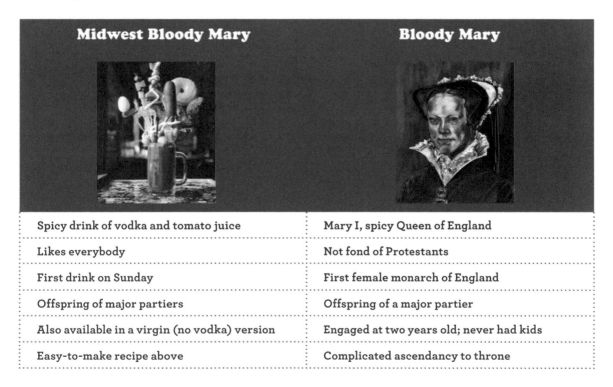

Midwest Bloody Mary	Bloody Mary
Spicy drink of vodka and tomato juice	Mary I, spicy Queen of England
Likes everybody	Not fond of Protestants
First drink on Sunday	First female monarch of England
Offspring of major partiers	Offspring of a major partier
Also available in a virgin (no vodka) version	Engaged at two years old; never had kids
Easy-to-make recipe above	Complicated ascendancy to throne

Grandpa TG's Tom & Jerry

MAKES A BASE MIXTURE FOR 12 DRINKS

Note: You're gonna screw this up. There are too many ingredients not to. Just remember that brandy is like makeup. Hides all imperfections.

More serious note: If you shouldn't be eating raw eggs, you shouldn't be drinking this drink.

6 eggs, whites and yolks separated

2 cups granulated sugar

2 cups powdered sugar

½ shot brandy per drink

½ shot rum per drink

Hot water (or hot milk)

Ground nutmeg, for garnish

1. In a medium bowl, using an electric mixer, beat the whites until very stiff. Add the granulated sugar and beat until combined.

2. In a large bowl, beat the egg yolks until thick. Add the powdered sugar and beat until combined.

3. Gently fold the egg white mixture into the egg yolk mixture.

4. To make one drink, fill a mug about one-third full of the whipped mixture. Add a half shot of your favorite brandy and a half shot of your favorite rum. Fill the rest of the cup with hot water (or hot milk for a creamier drink) and stir well to combine.

5. Sprinkle with nutmeg and serve.

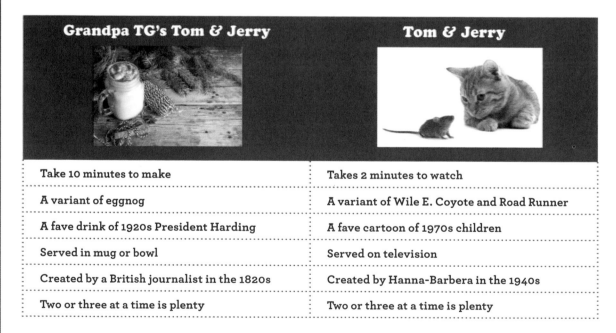

Grandpa TG's Tom & Jerry	Tom & Jerry
Take 10 minutes to make	Takes 2 minutes to watch
A variant of eggnog	A variant of Wile E. Coyote and Road Runner
A fave drink of 1920s President Harding	A fave cartoon of 1970s children
Served in mug or bowl	Served on television
Created by a British journalist in the 1820s	Created by Hanna-Barbera in the 1940s
Two or three at a time is plenty	Two or three at a time is plenty

Brandy Old-Fashioned

MAKES 1 DRINK

1 orange slice

1 teaspoon cherry juice

1 maraschino cherry

1 sugar cube

Couple two tree dashes Angostura bitters

1½ ounces brandy (or 3 fingers high, whichever comes second)

Soda of your choice: lemon-lime, grapefruit, seltzer, Jolly Good, Sprite, Baja Blast, Mountain Dew . . . get nuts

Garnish of your choice: more cherries and/or an orange slice, olives, pickled mushrooms

1. In an "old fashioned" glass (short, a little thick at the bottom), combine the orange slice, cherry juice, cherry, sugar cube, and bitters. Muddle/mash them together gently and take your time; only an animal would muddle the rind.

2. Add the brandy, fill the glass with ice, and top with your favorite floater.

3. Add your favorite garnish.

4. Keep making these until you can't figure out Step 1. Spend the night.

Brandy Old-Fashioned	Old Fashion
Great ideas always last	Great ideas always last
Assembling the drink is half the fun	Assembling the outfit is half the fun
A proper nod to those who came before us	A proper nod to those who came before us
Garnish is essential	Garish is essential
Takes a lot of attitude to pull off	Takes a little attitude to pull off
Never muddle the rinds	Never toss old clothes; fashion *always* returns

Scotcheroos

MAKES ONE 9 X 13-INCH PAN

1 cup white Karo syrup (corn syrup)

1 cup sugar

1 cup peanut butter

6 cups Rice Krispies

1 cup butterscotch chips

1 cup chocolate chips

1. In a large saucepan, mix the Karo syrup and sugar. Bring to a boil over medium heat, then stir in the peanut butter until melted. Stir in the Rice Krispies.

2. Press the concoction into a 9 x 13-inch baking pan (as you would *regular* Rice Krispies treats).

3. In a small saucepan over low heat or in a bowl in the microwave, melt the butterscotch and chocolate chips. Spread them evenly on top.

4. Cut when still warm; eat now or later.

See also: **Nana Fehr's Dream Bars**

Scotcheroos (cookies)	Scotch (drink)
Made into bars	Sold in bars
Delicious	Delicious
For everyone	For refined adults
Rice Krispies, butterscotch, 15 to 20 minutes	Malted barley, yeast, 10 to 50 years
No baking required	Pretty well baked after a few
Bite, take your time	Sip, take your time

Nana Fehr's Dream Bars

MAKES ONE 9 X 13-INCH PAN

I used to bribe, steal, and kick to get seconds on these. One time I was left home alone with a cookie jar of Nana's dream bars. I ate the entire jarful, and my dream turned into a sugar coma. Luckily there was a dog to blame.

CRUST
1 cup flour

½ cup brown sugar, packed

½ cup (1 stick) butter, at room temperature

TOPPING
1 cup brown sugar, packed

2 tablespoons flour

½ teaspoon baking powder

¼ teaspoon salt

12 ounces chocolate chips

2 eggs, lightly whisked

1 teaspoon vanilla extract

1. Preheat the oven to 350°F. Call Grandma if you can and say hello.
2. To make the crust, in a large bowl, combine the flour, brown sugar, and butter. Cut the butter into the flour and brown sugar until crumbly. Pat in the bottom of a 9 x 13–inch pan. Bake for 12 minutes, until golden brown.
3. While the crust is baking, make the topping. In the same bowl, mix the brown sugar, flour, baking powder, salt, chocolate chips, eggs, and vanilla. Spread the mixture over the hot baked crust.
4. Bake 20 to 25 minutes, until golden brown.
5. Let cool, then cut into bars. Enjoy!

Puppy Chow

MAKES ABOUT 8 CUPS

1 cup semisweet chocolate morsels

½ cup peanut butter

1 stick margarine

7 cups Rice Chex cereal

2 cups confectioner's sugar

1. In a medium bowl in the microwave, melt the chocolate morsels, peanut butter, and margarine. Stir until smooth.
2. Place the Rice Chex in a large bowl. Stir in the chocolate mixture until the cereal is coated.
3. Chill in the fridge or garage until at or below room temperature.
4. Place the powdered sugar in a sealable bag. Add the chilled funkified Chex mix and shake until fully coated.
5. Dump into a bowl or munch right out of the sugar-filled bag.

Puppy Chow	Purina Puppy Chow ®
For people	For dogs
Delicious	Delicious
Chex cereal, chocolate chips, confectioner's sugar	Corn, chicken by-products, beef fat
Served in bowls and bags	Served in bowls and bags
Perfect snack for morning/noon/night	Perfect snack for morning/noon/night
Recipe above	Local grocery store

Chippers

MAKES HALF A BAG'S WORTH OF "CHOCOLATE CHIPS"

1 cup milk chocolate chips or one 12-ounce package light or dark chocolate almond bark

5 ounces (half a bag) wavy potato chips (the waves hold max chocolate)

1. In a bowl in the microwave or in a small saucepan over low heat, melt the chocolate.
2. Dip a potato chip most of the way into the chocolate, then tap gently to remove excess chocolate. Lay the chip on a parchment-lined baking sheet to let it cool.
3. Repeat to dip the rest of the chips. Store in a cool place.

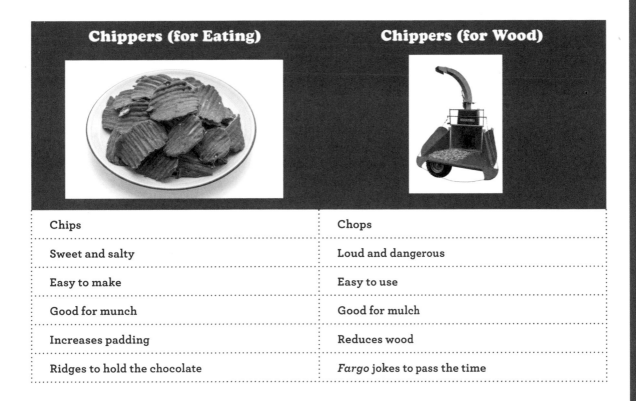

Chippers (for Eating)	Chippers (for Wood)
Chips	Chops
Sweet and salty	Loud and dangerous
Easy to make	Easy to use
Good for munch	Good for mulch
Increases padding	Reduces wood
Ridges to hold the chocolate	*Fargo* jokes to pass the time

Mistake Cake

MAKES TWO 9-INCH PIES

This recipe makes its own "crust" . . . it's easy as pie! Special thanks to Cindy, owner of It's Easy As Pie in the St. Louis area. Since 2012, they've been shipping sweet and savory pies nationwide (www.itseasyaspie.com). In the spirit of Midwestern pie, bake two, one for you and one to share the love with someone.

8 ounces cream cheese, at room temperature

8 tablespoons (1 stick) butter

1½ cups granulated sugar

1 teaspoon vanilla

2 whole eggs plus 2 egg yolks

2¼ cups flour

2 teaspoons baking powder

½ teaspoon salt

⅔ cup powdered sugar

Optional garnishes: Caramel sauce drizzle, dark chocolate drizzle, toasted slivered almonds

1. Preheat the oven to 350°F.
2. Combine the cream cheese and butter in a large bowl and beat until fluffy, 1 minute. Add the granulated sugar, vanilla, eggs, and egg yolks and mix until light and fluffy.
3. In a medium bowl, sift together the flour, baking powder, and salt. Incorporate into the cream cheese mixture using a wooden spoon until thoroughly mixed. Cover the bowl with plastic wrap and chill 30 minutes.
4. Using a spoon and scraper, divide the mixture between two 9-inch pie pans, leaving the top unsmoothed. Sift the powdered sugar over the pies and bake for 20 minutes, until lightly browned. Set aside to cool for 25 minutes.
5. Garnish with the desired toppings and serve.

See also: **Nana Fehr's Rhubarb Cake**

Mistake Cake	Mistake by the Lake
A buttery cake cut into blocks	A city in northern Ohio
Emerged as yummy dessert in 1900s	Emerged as manufacturing center in the 1900s
Also called Ooey Gooey Butter Cake	Also called C-town, Forest City, Sixth City
Typically dusted in powdered sugar	Typically dusted in snow
Don't let the name fool you—great dessert!	Don't let the name fool you—great town!

Nana Fehr's Rhubarb Cake

MAKES ONE 8 X 12–INCH PAN

Rhubarb is like an O-negative blood type. It's the universal vegetable that works equally great in muffins, pies, cakes, omelets, casseroles, Bloody Marys, vaccines, and more.

CRUST
1 cup all-purpose flour

5 tablespoons powdered sugar

½ cup (1 stick) butter, at room temperature

FILLING
1½ cups sugar

¼ cup all-purpose flour

¼ teaspoon ground nutmeg

¾ teaspoon baking powder

2 eggs

2 cups 1-inch-cut rhubarb

Ice cream for serving, if desired

1. Preheat the oven to 350°F.
2. To make the crust, in a medium bowl, combine the flour, powdered sugar, and butter. Mix until crumbly and pat into the bottom of an 8 x 12–inch pan. Bake 15 minutes, until golden brown.
3. To make the filling, in a large bowl, combine the sugar, flour, nutmeg, baking powder, and eggs. Use an electric mixer to mix until smooth, then mix in the rhubarb by hand.
4. Pour the rhubarb filling over the crust and bake for 40 to 45 minutes, until golden brown. Serve with ice cream if desired.

The Junk Drawer

Every Midwest home has a "junk drawer"—an overstuffed kitchen catchall that barely opens anymore and has become an oasis for every wandering (inanimate) soul dwelling in your humble abode. Everything from hammers and fishing line to closed combination locks ("Just in case someone remembers"), half-used tubes of liquid cement, Band-Aids, old ID cards, love letters from the IRS, and keys to only-God-knows-what. Keeping in that spirit, and as we begin to wrap things up, here's a chapter with a little bit of everything. But just like a junk drawer, there's nothing in here you don't need. Especially the deflated tennis ball.

Hall of Fame

Just like the Rock & Roll Hall of Fame (Cleveland, OH), the Pro Football Hall of Fame (Canton, OH), Mt. Rushmore (Rapid City, SD), the RV/Moto-home Hall of Fame (Elkhart, IN), and the National Mascot Hall of Game (Whiting, IN), every couple of years, representatives from cornhole and bowling leagues across the Midwest gather in Knob Noster, Missouri, and select three to five homegrown honorees to enter the Official Midwest Hall of Fame. Congratulations to our latest selected representatives: enduring embodiments of what makes the Midwest so dang great!

Previous Honorees

- **Betty White**, Illinois-born actress and comedian for nine decades and counting
- **John Legend**, from Springfield, Ohio, the first Black man and youngest person to win an EGOT
- **Warren Buffet**, normal-guy trillionaire from Omaha, sold gum door-to-door at seven
- **Mark Twain**, Missouri-born writer of all things Midwest
- **Georgia O'Keeffe**, feminist icon artist born on a farm near Sun Prairie, Wisconsin
- **David Letterman**, gap-toothed Hoosier and American television host, comedian, writer, and producer
- **Susan La Flesche Picotte**, Omaha, first Native American woman to receive a medical degree in the United States, graduating from the Woman's Medical College of Pennsylvania in 1889
- **Gloria Steinem**, Ohioan activist who helped advance the notion that "a woman without a man is like an Arctic char without a snowmobile"
- **Judy Garland**, born in Grand Rapids, Minnesota, tornado survivor
- **Frank Lloyd Wright**, Wisconsin architect of "organic architecture"—in which buildings harmonize with their inhabitants and environment
- **Miles Davis**, Illinoian trumpeter and composer who hauled jazz into a whole other place
- **Charles M. Schulz**, Minnesotan cartoonist of Midwest kids and their dog

- **Bob Dylan**, Minnesotan troubadour
- **Charlie Parker**, generally considered the greatest jazz saxophonist and cocreator of bop/bebop, from Kansas City, Missour
- **Malcolm X**, Nebraskan who, no surprise, believed in "any means necessary" to get the job done
- **Bob Uecker**, Brewers color commentator, often heard emanating from Midwest garages
- **Aldo Leopold**, Iowan father of modern conservation and author of *A Sand County Almanac*
- **Johnny Carson**, born in Iowa but raised in Nebraska, America's bedtime companion for thirty years
- **Standing Bear**, Nebraskan Ponca tribe civil-rights leader
- **Neil Armstrong**, Ohioan, first human to walk on the dang moon
- **Erma Bombeck**, iconic Ohio-born funny mom and writer of all things suburbia
- **Orville** (born in Ohio) and **Wilbur** (born in Indiana) **Wright**, first in flight
- **Harry Houdini**, a Milwaukee paperboy transformed into the most famous magician since Merlin
- **Ray Harroun**, first winner of the Indy 500, invented the rearview mirror
- **Les Paul**, Wisconsin-born guitar deity
- **Annie Oakley**, a Buckeye sharpshooter and entertainer
- **Orson Welles**, Wisconsonite one-hit-wonder director
- **F. Scott Fitzgerald**, a coldly sarcastic brilliant inimitable Minnesotan writer
- **Kurt Vonnegut Jr.**, a coldly sarcastic brilliant inimitable Indianan writer
- **Carrie Chapman Catt,** born in Ripon, Wisconsin, suffragist and peace activist who helped secure the right to vote for American women
- **Michael Jackson**, Indianan, King of Pop
- **Omar Knedlik**, born in Kansas, King of Slushies Pop; invented the ICEE machine
- **Sharice Davids**, **Ho-Chunk**, first openly LGBT Native American elected to the US Congress
- **Richard Pryor**, Peorian who shattered comedy, and race, barriers
- **Ernest Hemingway**, Oak Park, Illinoisan writer who liked to drink and hunt
- **Suni Lee,** Minnesota-born Hmong gymnast and 2020 Olympic all-around champion
- **Winona LaDuke**, environmental activist, founded the White Earth Land Recovery Project in Minnesota
- **Quincy Jones**, Chicago-born mogul/musician
- **Halima Aden**, Somali-American supermodel from St. Cloud, Minnesota
- **Maya Lin**, Ohioan architect and sculptor
- **Langston Hughes**, born in Joplin, Missouri; raised in Kansas, Illinois, and Cleveland; the Michelangelo of the Harlem Renaissance
- **Garrett Morgan**, inventor, businessman, and community leader in Ohio who added yellow to the stop-and-go light
- **Amelia Earhart**, Kansan world traveler
- **Francis Ford Coppola**, celebrated winemaker born in Detroit who had something to do with films once
- **William Harley** and **Arthur Davidson**, grew up in Milwaukee a few houses apart and loved bicycles; one day they decided to add a motor, and the rest is history
- **And last but not least . . . my grandpa Bob**, Wisconsin muskie slayer, walleye king, perch pounder; women (and by women, I mean *woman* and that woman is Grandma Sue) loved him, sheephead feared him

Newest Midwest Hall of Fame Inductees!

Pauline Phillips

You probably know her as "Dear Abby," an advice columnist (born and manner-shaped in Sioux City, Iowa) who imparted Midwest common sense and morality on the rest of the country for thirty years to, at her peak, the tune of 100 *million* readers a day.

Ťhaťháŋka Íyotake (Sitting Bull)

A Hunkpapa Lakota leader during years of Plains Indians resistance to taking of tribal land by white settlers and the US government. Foresaw and led a coalition to defeat Custer.

Curly Lambeau

Green Bay born; Green Bay East High, Notre Dame; Packers player for ten years; Packers coach for thirty; died in Sturgeon Bay at sixty-seven from a heart attack—waiting for his girlfriend to get ready for a date, he collapsed while helping her father cut the grass. How much more Midwest can one be?

Oprah Winfrey

Philanthropist. Mogul. Lady O. Her birthplace of Mississippi may have something to say about this, but the Queen of All Media grew up in Milwaukee and grew her billion-dollar empire out of Chicago, taking a local AM show into the number one show in America and becoming the "most influential woman in the world." Work ethic x 100,000.

Charlie Brown

The Keep 'er Movin' king. No matter how much good grief Charlie took, no matter how many footballs were yanked away, this Midwest blockhead was *always* up to try again. Creator Charles Schulz was a Twin Cities lad himself and was well familiar with the stick-to-itiveness of a heartland hero.

A Boise by Any Other Name . . .

The Midwest is known for unique city, state, and town names. Some of those names are influenced by the Midwest's strong Indigenous heritage. From state names like Illinois and the Dakotas to small cities like Kokomo or Oshkosh, Indigenous names are everywhere. Whether it's Menominee, Wisconsin, named after the Menominee tribe; Neoga, Illinois, which comes from the Kickapoo word for *deer*; or Mankato, Minnesota, a name derived from the Dakota word *Mahkato*, meaning greenish-blue earth (the Dakota definitely named it in the summer), Indigenous influence is omnipresent. And curiosity about those town names can spark a greater connection with Midwest history, environment, and cultural roots.

Then there are other town names like Tightwad, Missouri; Knockemstiff, Ohio; and Intercourse, Illinois, which spark less connection, more confusion. But ya know what they say: You gotta go through Hell (Michigan) to get to Paradise (Michigan). Also if you find yourself in Burnsville (Minnesota) a few hours after Climax (Minnesota), don't worry, you'll be fine. But if you get to Clappers (Minnesota), see a professional.

So how'd they come up with the names? Best guess is booze. Why else would someone name their town Knockemstiff unless they were three Bloody Marys into a bar fight? Let's revisit Climax, Minnesota . . . which may have been named after a chewing tobacco company, but apparently they've used the slogan "More Than Just a Feeling."

The following are some of the weirdest town names in the Midwest.

- Tightwad, Missouri
- What Cheer, Iowa
- Random Lake, Wisconsin . . . *and* North Dakota (great minds think alike)
- French Lick, Indiana
- Buttzville, North Dakota
- Sandwich, Illinois
- Smileyberg, Kansas
- Hazard, Nebraska
- Deadman Crossing, Ohio
- Studley, Kansas
- Dinkytown, Minnesota
- Chicken Bristle, Illinois
- Bean Blossom, Indiana
- Free Soil, Michigan
- Number Eight, Missouri

A simple piece of advice. If you've had a couple and feel like naming something, fulfill that impulse on your cat, your dog—your ferret, for cripes' sake. Swamp Angel: fun name for a ferret. Weird name to see on a speeding ticket in Kansas.

Things That Go Ope! in the Night . . .

There's a lot of really weird and unexplained stuff out in the world. (Like, where do all the Midwest frogs go in the winter? Do they hop on a goose and fly south?) And some of the weirder stuff slithers when it should walk or walks when it should slither. Whether you're visiting the Midwest or staying for a couple generations, here are the cryptids and creatures you should always keep in mind when going down in the basement or out for a walk in the woods. While most haven't yet reached the level of fame as Bigfoot, the Loch Ness Monster, or even the Jersey Devil, these here are the most feared, and most celebrated, creepy-crawlies we got!

Illinois: The Enfield Horror

An alien, demon, or mutation, this human-size creature has grayish slimy skin, reddish eyes, and three legs that end in clawed feet. Multiple witnesses in the 1940s (near Mount Vernon) and 1970s (Enfield). Reported to have hopped more than twenty-five feet in a single bound. *See also: Giant black panthers, the Cole Hollow Road Monster, Big Muddy, and the Wolfman of Chestnut Mountain*

Indiana: Beast of Busco

A gigantic snapping turtle. Five-hundred-plus pounds, first spotted in Churubusco. *See also: The Cable Line Monster, Lake Manitou Sea Monster*

Iowa: Van Meter Visitor

A nine-foot-tall pterodactyl-like creature able to shoot bright light from a horn on its forehead. Unaffected by bullets. First appeared in early 1900s. When eventually hunted, *two* appeared at the same time. *See also: Iowa dragons, the Ventura Marsh Monster, Lockridge Monster*

Kansas: Sinkhole Sam

Prehistoric water sea creature that lives in "Big Sinkhole" near Inman. Pre-1920s, central Kansas had several freshwater lakes that have since become mostly empty and very deep sinkholes where folks still fish. "Sam" is said to mostly live in a dark water-filled cavern miles beneath the Kansas earth. *See also: Beaman, Pterosaur, Bigfoot sightings*

THE MICHIGAN
DOGMAN

Michigan: The Michigan Dogman

Just as the name implies, a werewolfish seven-foot-tall creature that howls in a way that's far too human. Spotted throughout Michigan, but mostly along the Manistee River and within the northwestern Lower Peninsula. *See also: Pressie, Nain Rouge, Ada Witch, and Melon Heads*

Minnesota: Wendigo

Massive man/creature (seven to fifteen feet tall) first recognized by the First Nations Algonquin tribes. Seeks human flesh; possesses humans and turns them cannibal. Half rotted like a zombie, giant fangs, often described as having the head of a deer. They're not limited to Minnesota. Wendigos are found all over the Midwest and can mimic your loved ones' voices. Gray in color. *See also: The Witches of Loon Lake, the Lake Pepin Serpent, and the White Pickup of Grey Cloud Island*

Missouri: Momo (The Missouri Monster)

A Missouri Bigfoot. *See also: The Devil's Chair, the Ozark Howler*

Nebraska: Alkali Lake Monster

An enormous alligator-like thing with a rhino horn on its head, forty to one hundred feet long. Also called the Walgren Lake monster (the lake changed names). Near Hay Springs in northwestern Nebraska. Snatches livestock and tips boats. Dozens of witnesses over centuries. *See also: Radioactive hornets, the Salt Witch*

North Dakota: Thunderbird

Gargantuan bird. Snatches slow pets and children. Pterodactyl-like or dragonlike. Another creature first discovered by Indigenous Peoples. Causes thunder with the flap of its wings, and lightning comes from its eyes. Probably related to the one in Iowa. *See also: Devils Lake Monster, the Miniwashitu*

Ohio: Loveland Frogmen

Living under bridges and along the banks of the Little Miami River are a species of humanoid frogs or froglike humans standing between three and four feet high. Some apparently carry wands and know magic. *See also: Grassman, Minerva Monster, Cedar Bog Monster, Orange Eyes, Charles Mills Lake Monster, Crosswick Monster*

South Dakota: Taku-He

A Bigfoot-like being usually reported to be seen in a coat and top hat. Which sounds sociable enough until you discover that its favorite pastime apparently is tearing the genitals off local cattle. *See also: "Little Devils" of Spirit Mound, Banshee of the Bad Lands*

Wisconsin: The Hodag

Ever since 1893, a reptilian creature with "the head of a frog, the grinning face of a giant elephant, thick short legs set off by huge claws, the back of a dinosaur, and a long tail with spears at the end" has tormented the town of Rhinelander. It was discovered by a part-time timber cruiser and full-time BSer named Gene Shepard. Gene kept the beast in his barn until it escaped to the woods of Rhinelander, where it still lurks today. *See also: The Beast of Bray Road, Rocky, Devil's Lake Monster*

THE LOVELAND
FROGMEN

Paul Bunyan: Midwest Icon

Speaking of legends. . . . Let's talk about Paul Bunyan. He's a Midwest guy who doesn't say too much and represents the tenacity and hard work that defines the Midwest. Legend has it he emerged from the womb dressed in plaid. A colossal blue ox as a sidekick is just the brisket on top. There'd be a small altar dedicated to him in every house, but Father Frank called it sacrilegious. Instead, you'll find massive Paul Bunyan statues throughout Minnesota, Michigan, Indiana, Iowa, and Wisconsin. Given that he was supposedly anywhere from seven to seventy feet tall, at least one of them is probably life-size. The Bible was clear: never worship a golden calf. But the Bible didn't say a peep about a blue ox.

Most folks think of him as a logger from Canada or Maine (Michigan has also "officially" claimed to be his birthplace) who worked his way down into the Dakotas or Michigan or Wisconsin and settled in the Midwest. His supposed grave is marked in Kelliher, Minnesota. Midwesterners in lumber camps were telling tall tales about his exploits by the 1850s. Michigan's *Gladwin County Record* gets credit for first putting his name in print, in 1893, and the first stories about him appeared in the *Duluth News Tribune* a few years later, claiming he cut and saved millions of logs during the winter of the "blue snow," a winter so fiercely cold that the snow fell blue. (Instead of getting frostbite, Paul Bunyan apparently bit the frost.)

There are many legends about the world's most famous lumberjack and true Midwestern son—from how he's responsible for Minnesota's 10,000 lakes (chasing Babe all over the state one day), scooping out Lake Superior, and, um, building Lambeau Field. Here are a few you might not yet know:

- Paul Bunyan caught Covid-19 and Covid-19 was put in quarantine for two weeks.

- Paul Bunyan drowned a fish.

- Paul Bunyan ordered a Big Mac at Culver's and got one.

- Paul Bunyan does push-ups by pushing the Earth down.

- Paul Bunyan once slammed a revolving door.

- Paul Bunyan killed two stones with one bird.

- For many men, one testicle is smaller than the other. For Paul Bunyan, *each* testicle is *larger* than the other.

- Paul Bunyan had the idea to sell his pee as a canned beverage. It's now called Red Bull.

- Paul Bunyan once shot a moose down with his finger by yelling, "Bang!"

- Paul Bunyan played the fiddle using a piano as the bow.

- Paul Bunyan once punched a man in the soul.

- Paul Bunyan dribbled a bowling ball.

- The Great Wall of China was originally built to keep Paul Bunyan out. It didn't work.

- Paul Bunyan beat the sun in a staring contest.

- It is believed that Paul Bunyan's tears cure cancer. But he has never cried.

Midwest Mythbusters

"The Midwest Is Just Cornfields and Suburbs."

False. We also have soybeans. Okay, it's true that we only have four cities in the top twenty-five US cities by population (and just eight in the top fifty). And yes, there are a lot of suburbs. But let's not forget about the hundreds of thousands of acres of state parks. And how 'bout them lakes? When climate change dries up the water in the west, Cleveland's gonna look a lot more appealing to everyone in Santa Monica. But it already should. Cleveland's a great spot. Same with Dayton, Madison, St. Paul, and Scottsbluff, where you'll find live music, great bars, crowds, art shows, street performers, and a traveling Broadway show or original theater production. All while you're within striking distance of a city with one-million-plus.

"Everyone in the Midwest Hunts and Loves Guns."

Nah. Wyoming, Montana, and Idaho all have more. And there's actually a higher percentage of Vermonters who hunt than in most states in the Midwest. Statistical fact. Frankly, most of the Midwesterners you meet have never owned—or even shot—a gun. That said, the rest do have enough stockpiled for everyone . . .

"North Carolina Is 'First in Flight.'"

If you consider two guys born and raised in the Midwest who created special tools in Ohio, raised funds in Ohio, ran early flight tests in Ohio, built a plane in Ohio, and then drove to North Carolina (*soooo* Ohio) to take advantage of some dunes and wind being "first in flight" . . . then sure?

"The Midwest Is Entirely Flat."

Yes, we've made our little jokes in this book, but let's not forget the Ozark Mountains, the Black Hills, or Wisconsin's Driftless area. Missouri's Taum Sauk Mountain is 1,772 feet. South Dakota's Black Elk Peak is 7,244 feet above sea level. And even Nebraska has Panorama Point, which is 5,427 feet above sea level (but appears as flat as a basketball court, so what does that say about "sea level"?). Speaking of basketball, let's not forget Hoosier Hill in Indiana, a whopping 1,257 feet above sea level—which is far more impressive than, say, the Florida Keys. (To be fair, and no joke: researchers at Arizona State and Kansas State ran tests to determine if Kansas was "flatter than a pancake" and, compared to a pancake bought at a local IHOP, proved that it *was*.)

"The Midwest Lacks Diversity."

Untrue. Every Midwest state cracks the top forty-four states with the most diversity. (Okay, there's still a lot of work to do . . .) Not working in our melting pot favor, large percentages of Central and South Americans are not *yet* embracing the promise of 35°F weather that the Norwegians and Germans found so irresistible one hundred years ago. Illinois, Michigan, Ohio, Missouri, and Indiana all make the top half in the country with Black representation. And Ohio, Illinois, and Michigan are top ten for those Americans who identify as Middle Eastern. (Detroit alone is home to more Arab Americans than L.A. or New York.) The Midwest was, of course, also originally home to scores of Indigenous tribes, and 10 percent of South Dakotans identify as Indigenous. While my ability to write on these topics is limited, there's no shortage of books already in publication if you're looking for more. Some recommendations:

- Angeline Boulley, *Firekeeper's Daughter* (New York: Henry Holt and Co, 2021).
- Tom Jones, *People of the Big Voice: Photographs of Ho-Chunk Families by Charles Van Schaick, 1879–1942* (Madison: Wisconsin Historical Society Press, 2011).
- Patty Loew, *Indian Nations of Wisconsin: Histories of Endurance and Renewal*, 2nd edition (Madison: Wisconsin Historical Society Press, 2013).
- Cary Miller, *Ogimaag: Anishinaabeg Leadership, 1760–1845* (Lincoln: University of Nebraska Press, 2016).
- Mai Neng Moua, *Bamboo Among the Oaks: Contemporary Writing by Hmong Americans* (St. Paul: Minnesota Historical Society Press, 2002)
- Jim Terry, *Come Home Indio: A Memoir* (New York: Street Noise Books, 2020).
- Anton Treuer, *Everything You Wanted to Know About Indians but Were Afraid to Ask* (St. Paul: Borealis Books, 2012).
- Isabel Wilkerson, *The Warmth of Other Suns* (New York: Random House, 2010).
- Terrion L. Williamson, *Black in the Middle: An Anthology of the Black Midwest* (Cleveland: Belt Publishing, 2020).
- Fadumo Yusuf, *Ayan of the Lucky* (St. Paul: Beaver's Pond Press, 2020).

The Great Midwest Potluck

Indigenous Peoples inhabited the Midwest for centuries before white settlers arrived. Since then, there's been wave after wave of groups of people coming here. Initially it was the French, Norwegian, Irish, German, and other European people. Then the Great Migration brought many Black Americans from the South. More recently, Hmong, Mexican, and Somali refugees and immigrants have found their way to the Midwest as well.

This convergence of cultures makes the Midwest what it is today: an imperfect potluck. The table is filled with venison casserole, tater tot–topped hot dish, moose burger, walleye tacos, old bottles of whiskey Diane didn't want to roll the dice on but figured someone wouldn't mind, Hungarian brats Tom got from the Brat Stop on his way over. Some might say we didn't need five potato salads and who put the raisins in that one over there; others may say twelve ranch dressings is thirteen too few.

But everyone brought something. And if you just look around long enough to see, you'll find it.

On the *CripesCast* podcast, I was lucky enough to speak with a great Midwesterner, Chef Yia Vang. Chef Vang is the son of Hmong immigrants. During the Vietnam War, many Hmong people risked their lives for the United States. And they were promised a home in this country for their actions.

The following is a story Chef Vang told me on my podcast about what his parents did during the Vietnam War and why he's proud to call the Midwest home (lightly edited for clarity):

It was all-out guerrilla warfare, so they came to the Hmong people and said, "Hey, if you guys help us fight this war, win, lose, or draw, you have free citizenship. You can come to America." So there's a handshake deal that's made with a bunch of Hmong leaders and the US government, and then they sent CIA and Special Forces to come in and train the Hmong people. So my dad, at the age of twelve, with all his brothers, they joined the— basically, it was like the militia. So they joined, and it was, "We're going to give you guns, we're going to give you a uniform, we're going to teach you night mission options. We're going to teach you how to use, you know, bombs, grenades, we're going to teach you how to use everything, you guys, and you guys will be our troops on the ground."

And so one of the main jobs the Hmong people had was when Air America, which was the US Air Force, would do their bombing and if they were shot down over Laos, the Hmong people, their job was to run rescue missions to rescue downed US pilots. So all of that happened and the US pulled out, and when the US pulled out, they said, "Oh shoot, we can't take everyone with us," so all the Hmong people were left behind.

And then the Northern Communist party came through, and if you were Hmong, basically they were saying, "Hey, you, you fought against us." They saw you as the Americans. So then there was a genocide of thousands and thousands of our people. And then they had to escape from the hills of Laos, they had to escape and go down through the jungle, hide in the jungle for two or three months, and then cross the Mekong River in the dead of night to try to make it to Thailand.

And in Thailand, if you were one of the lucky ones, there would be one of the NGO groups which find you and take you to the refugee camp, but if they caught you, they would send you back to internment camps. So my dad and my mom . . . that's what they did. So there's this huge story; my mom tells me even till today, she's like, when she hears fireworks going off, she still freaks out because she has that memory as a girl, like the bombs going off, you know, the gunshots, like when firecrackers go off, it still freaks her out, so she's still jumpy. She's in her sixties.

My dad fought in the war, and after the war was over, they disbanded everything because they said, "Hey, America pulled out, our families are getting slaughtered, we have to leave," and so my dad made sure his boys, like, he was kinda like a middle-management kind of guy in the troops, so he had to make sure they all got home.

My dad tells me a story—he gets back to his village, everybody looks at him, they're like "Help us, how do we escape?" So, he had a compass, and he pointed it south, because he knew that Thailand was south, and they started walking in the jungle. And he said for months they just hid, and they got to the river. And the Mekong River is the ninth largest river in the world, right? So it's like, imagine the Mississippi but worse, a lot harder [to cross].

How do you cross the river? Well, the Hmong people were mountain people, right, so that means that not a lot of us know how to swim. So, we're not the Lowland people, we don't mess with water. So they get to the Mekong River, my dad makes a little raft out of bamboo where he can just hold on to it, kinda like Leonardo DiCaprio, you know, like Jack-style. He said he just threw his body across, you know what I'm saying? And he said all he had was his gun, and he had a plastic bag he put all his clothes in, he had his gun *and he put it on, and basically the people in his village just followed him because they were like, "Hey, you were in the army, you know how to do this." So they followed him, and he would tie himself to people who didn't know how to swim. He had one arm kinda over the raft, and he would paddle with the other arm, and I'm like, "Wait, what happens if the rapids took you one way," and he goes, "You switch arms and paddle again against it." And he got across.*

Now he eventually got into the refugee camp in '77, which, the name of the refugee camp is called Ban Vinai, which is where our restaurant (Vinai) is named after. So the restaurant's name is an homage to the refugee camp. So Ban Vinai, he got there in '77, and he met my mom in '77 or '78, they got married, and I was born in '84. We left the camp in '88, and the camp closed down in '92, and from '75 to '92, it housed 75,000 people. And out of those, 90 percent were Hmong, and out of those, 90 percent ended up in the Midwest. . . .

I love America . . . and I know America's not perfect, but this is what I tell people. My dad fought for America before he even stepped foot in America. My dad, my uncles, my grandfather who died in the war—like many people I know, many of my buddies, their families, their dads fought for America before they even stepped foot in America. My dad fought for America. And fought for the idea of what America could be for his children . . .

I'm not that kid who's like, "Oh, I can't stand America because all these things are wrong." No, I want to fight for the America that my dad fought for, that he sacrificed for, that my grandfather died for. There are these great men and women that have gone before me that sacrificed everything so that I could stand here in this land where I'm free to do what I want. It blows my mind that I wake up every day where my main job is to start a fire and put meat over that fire, grill that meat, have people eat it, and then I get to tell the story of Mom and Dad's legacy.

—Chef Yia Vang

The next time you're in Minneapolis, stop in at Vinai and tell Chef Yia I says hi. Also make sure you look out for the Hmong food at your next neighborhood potluck. Every dish tells a story.

More Games

We live in the age of the smartphone. It's constantly there for us, providing information, work, and amusement. It dings, vibrates, bings, pings, talks, and splashes when it falls to the bottom of the lake. Sorry, did I hit it out of your hand? Welp, now that your traveling coaster is swimming with the walleyes, how are we going to amuse ourselves? No, we're not going snorkeling for it. The ice just melted last week, you'll turn into Jack Dawson. We're playing games, and you're gonna like it! Why? Because nothing says "Midwest family" like cards, dice, and board games. I know they always lead to gambling and punching! That's. What. Makes. Them. Fun.

Sheepshead

If you're shuffling through your relative's junk drawer and stumble across a deck of 32 cards, Uncle Jack didn't lose a game of 52 pickup. He just discarded all the cards not needed for Sheepshead. If you throw this deck out, it may be the *last* thing you throw (Uncle Jack's been known to cut off an arm for less).

Sheepshead is often compared to euchre, but it's most commonly played in Wisconsin. In fact, in 1983, Sheepshead was declared the official card game of Milwaukee, and the largest tournament is held every September in Wisconsin Dells. Sheepshead came to Wisconsin via Bavarian immigrants who played a similar game, called schafkopf. (*Sheepshead* was easier to say.)

While I can't tell you how to play Sheepshead well (that would take an entire book and several bottles of brandy), here are the basics:

- Sheepshead is played with only 7-8-9-10-J-Q-K-A in all suits. The rest of the cards, you can use to start a fire or light your cigar or something still not legalized in Wisconsin; you'll never need them. And for most Sheepshead players, there's no other card game that matters.

- When you play Sheepshead, you want trump cards. There are 14 of them. That's all diamonds, plus queens and jacks. The rest of the 18 cards are fail suit. Your job is to use the trump or highest fail card to get tricks and thereby acquire points. Ace is 11 points, 10 is 10 points, king is 4 points, queen is 3 points, jack is 2 points, and everything else don't count for squat.

- From here, it gets a little complicated. And by that, I mean you always want to get the most points, unless you're playing a leaster hand. You have partners that are determined by calling an ace or whoever has the jack of diamonds. There's mosters, doublers, and schwanzers. There's cracking, blitzing, doubling the bump. You can play four handed, five handed, two handed, eight handed. And don't forget to schmear when your partner has the highest trump . . . from here you're gonna need to come to Wisconsin. We have plenty of brandy, no need to pack your own.

Dice

Five dice. That's all you need to turn a boring night at the bar into a Vegas casino. Or a sidewalk into a craps table. Or a church into something you'll need to confess next week. Whether it's Bar Dice, Cee-lo, Liars Dice, Ship Captain Crew, Street Craps, Klondike, or Tally-hold, no venue is safe from the hours of fun, excitement, and lost watches.

Cribbage

Here's a game of luck, skill, and a long board with lots of holes and pegs that have often been lost and replaced with half-chewed toothpicks. Oh, there's cards, too. Cribbage is traditionally for two players, but different boards can support more players. The goal is to get 121 points (those tiny holes and toothpicks are so you can easily count your score). Consider investing in a cribbage board today. Worst-case scenario, you hate the game and you've still got a charcuterie board for your goat cheese and venison.

Game: Psychological/Personality Test

The word scramble below has been filled out with various words associated with the East Coast, West Coast, South, and Midwest. What are the first three words you see? This will reveal in which of these four regions you should, psychologically speaking, probably live.

D	A	K	O	T	A	S	P	E	M	C	M
B	R	E	T	F	A	V	R	E	I	O	I
Z	Z	A	P	Z	N	T	Z	Q	D	R	N
F	A	R	G	O	P	E	K	D	W	N	N
O	P	E	T	E	D	M	A	E	E	H	E
P	Z	L	Z	Q	R	C	N	E	S	O	S
E	I	E	Z	A	A	U	S	R	T	L	O
W	G	P	W	Z	R	L	A	E	O	E	T
E	P	O	P	E	I	A	S	E	Q	P	A
M	I	C	H	I	G	A	N	D	B	O	E
O	P	E	I	N	D	I	A	N	A	Z	Z
O	H	I	O	Q	M	I	D	W	E	S	T

Are We There Yet?

Whether a Midwesterner your whole life, a recent resident, or just planning on a short visit, there are thousands of sites, museums, landmarks, and attractions to discover and enjoy. With no recompense for endorsement or any promise they're still open, here are a few special ones worth adding to your Midwest Bucket List.

Illinois

The Super Museum (Metropolis): Raised in Smallville, Kansas; created by two guys in Cleveland; it's a bird, it's a plane, it's Superman! And so the world's-largest collection of Superman stuff was (single) bound to land in the Midwest somewhere and Metropolis makes as much sense as anywhere. This museum has a $2.5 *billion*—with a B—collection of Superman memorabilia and hosts a massive annual Superman celebration each June.

Muddy's First House (Chicago): This is the first house purchased by Muddy Waters, the father of Chicago blues. This house became a home away from home for Muddy (originally from Mississippi) and fellow musicians who had jam sessions in the basement.

***Popeye* Character Trail (Chester):** The spinach-loving sailor/boxer came from the mind and pen of Chester native E. C. Segar and was based on a Chester local named Frank "Rocky" Fiegel. Celebrate both men—and Wimpy, Bluto, and Olive Oyl, too—with everything from a trail of statues that runs throughout the entire city to the world's only spinach-cans collectible museum.

The Tower of Baa-Goat (Windsor/Shelbyville): A thirty-foot-plus tower of brick and more than 250 winding steps that is home to thirty-plus goats. How they built it, we have no idea, but if you've ever spent any time with a goat (honorary, conspiratorial, and spiteful souls), it's no real surprise. Visit if you dare.

DuSable Museum of African American History (Chicago): This museum, named after the founder of Chicago, showcases the history of African Americans in the Midwest, and the United States more broadly.

Cahokia Mounds (Collinsville): Mysteriously abandoned one hundred years before Columbus, Cahokia was once a major city in North America (with more than twenty thousand people), and at the time larger than London. There are more than eighty sites remaining to explore to learn about early American history, including a series of Stonehenge-style wooden structures built more than a thousand years ago.

Woodstock Willy (Woodstock): Punxsutawney Phil is, for now, the more famous marmot prognosticator and, yes, the movie *Groundhog Day* is set in Punxsutawney, Pennsylvania . . . but it was filmed almost entirely in Woodstock and starred Illinoian Woodstock Willy in the role of Phil. So be sure to stop by Woodstock for any number of events connected to a rodent weatherperson who's almost as reliable as other Midwestern meteorologists. (After, you can next visit Sun Prairie, Wisconsin—self-proclaimed "Groundhog Capital of the World" and home to Jimmy the Groundhog.)

Indiana

The "Shoe Tree" (Milltown): Want to see hundreds of shoes dangling from a large Sycamore tree? Sure you do. A tradition that goes back generations at the intersection of Devil's Hollow and Knight Road. Larry Bird himself, a Hoosier patron saint, is said to have once tossed his sneakers into the tree. There's one in Albany also, but . . . yeah, head to Milltown. You also get a free pair of shoes when you bring a ladder.

The Eiteljorg Museum of American Indians and Western Art (Indianapolis): Located in downtown Indianapolis, the museum offers a wide-ranging assembly of visual arts by Indigenous Peoples of the Americas. The collection also includes artists such as T. C. Cannon, N. C. Wyeth, Andy Warhol, Georgia O'Keeffe, Allan Houser, Frederic Remington, Charles Russell, and Kay WalkingStick, and its contemporary Native American art collection has been ranked among the best in the world.

City West Ghost Town (Chestertown): City West, Indiana, was once going to rival Chicago (built on a swamp and with subpar football skills) but then, yeah, didn't happen. Not enough folks came to the party and, while swampy Chicago cleaned up and became the country's third-largest city, City West was soon swallowed by Indiana sand dunes, time, and a big fire in 1835. Still, Indiana's got a nice little slice of Lake Michigan shoreline, and walking over what was once City West is the best way to enjoy it.

Bluespring Caverns (Bedford): Beneath Indiana flows the longest underground river in the country, with miles of caverns and a waterway that's home to blind, albino, and/or transparent creatures, bugs, and fish. They had me at blind fish.

Indiana Basketball Hall of Fame Museum (New Castle): This one's for all the Hickory Huskers and Hoosier teams (high school, college, or pro) who ran the ol' picket fence play before or after.

Iowa

Future Birthplace of James T. Kirk (Riverside): Visit the. Birthplace. of. Starfleet Captain. James T. Kirk. Born. Stardate March 22. In a classic cinema scene, Kirk is challenged by a skeptic: "Don't

tell me! You're from outer space," and the *Enterprise* commander responds simply: "No, I'm from Iowa. I only *work* in outer space." One of the most-Midwest explanations ever. A Trek Fest is held every June.

Roller Coaster Road (Waukon): The false notion that the Midwest is entirely flat (a notion promulgated in this book) is challenged by the rolling hills and valleys of Iowa. For further proof, take a drive just outside of Harpers Ferry and down Roller Coaster Road—actual name—a solid one and a half undulating miles of those sudden ups and downs that give you a funny feeling in your "tummy" if you like that sort of thing.

The National Farm Toy Museum (Dyersville): Many grew up collecting Hot Wheels cars, but just as many Midwesterners found Ertl trucks, John Deere tractors, and Case excavators beneath the Christmas tree each year. This museum celebrates thousands of toys connected to agriculture from around the world, including the toy horse-drawn sickle mower first crafted by Fred Ertl Sr. in nearby Dubuque to help make some cash after he was laid off in 1945. The first batch of toys was sold to drugstores and gas stations on the way to a pheasant-hunting trip.

Field of Dreams **Movie Site (Dyersville):** If you film it, they will come. Dubuque County is not usually known as a hot spot for tourism, but for those hoping to catch a glimpse of Moonlight Graham or Shoeless Joe or, say, your late estranged father . . . then you can still, maybe, head to the spot where *Field of Dreams* was filmed and visit the ballfield and museum. No guarantees you'll get any visuals unless you stopped in Illinois or Michigan on your way in to procure some edibles.

Iowa's Largest Frying Pan (Brandon): Okay, so maybe it's not the biggest in the world (that's in Turkey), or the country (looking at you, North Carolina), but it's probably the biggest in the Midwest. So if you ever really catch one of those monster crappies you've been talking about, you now know where to go.

Kansas

Oz Museum (Wamego): Yes, Toto, you'll still be in Kansas. And what's more Kansas than Dorothy, the farm girl who traveled to magical lands and killed the occasional wicked witch with a farmhouse. Be sure to combine this museum with another: Dorothy's House and Land of Oz in Liberal, just five short hours away.

Kansas Barbed Wire Museum (La Crosse): The Devil's Rope has a long and complicated history, as its nickname might suggest. Invented by Lucien B. Smith of Kent, Ohio, and updated for mass production by Joseph F. Glidden of DeKalb, Illinois, it would soon shape the American Midwest and West, for better or worse.

Knute Rockne Memorial (Matfield Green): The Notre Dame coaching legend died in a plane crash in 1931 three miles south of Bazaar Schoolhouse on K-177. The crash-site memorial is on private property and no public access is allowed without special arrangements with the owner. So, get that.

Original Pizza Hut (Wichita): Before the Stuffed Garlic Knots and Cinnamon Sticks, before the Triple Chocolate Brownie and beloved Meat Lover's, there was a small brick building in Wichita the size of a . . . hut.

Boot Hill and Museum (Dodge City): All the lore and history of the Wild West frontier town, re-enactments, museums, and more. There are dozens of attractions in Dodge to celebrate gamblers, gunslingers, and cows.

Michigan

National Trout Memorial (Kalkaska): Also known as the Fisherman's Shrine, an eighteen-foot beauty that requires no tricky camera angles to impress. It springs majestically before the Kalkaska Historical Museum, which also has some other stuff to look at. Kalkaska hosts the annual National Trout Festival.

Da Yoopers Tourist Trap (Ishpeming): An Upper Peninsula shop that wants your money—as long as you promise to leave the Upper Peninsula soon after. The brainchild of a Michigan comedy troupe, it features row upon row of fun Midwest keepsakes, and the chance to see the world's-largest working chain saw and "Christine on Steroids," a 1957 Buick with a snowplow.

Great Lakes Shipwreck Museum (Paradise): Another in the UP, on Whitefish Point, dedicated to Great Lakes maritime life and, more specifically, the six-thousand-plus shipwrecks that have claimed as many as thirty thousand (!) lives over the years. And you thought losing that fishing pole in Lake Nebagamon was rough.

Ziibiwing Center of Anishinabe Culture and Life Ways (Mount Pleasant): A museum and cultural center built to share the history of the Saginaw Chippewa Indian Tribe of Michigan.

World's Largest Cherry Pie Pan (Traverse City): Sorry, neighboring Charlevoix—the bigger pan is in Traverse City now. Charlevoix opened with a pie weighing 17,000 pounds plus, but Traverse City responded with a 28,350-pound pastry. Only the pans now remain. Take a pic! It'll be worth its weight in gol—er, tin.

World's Largest Tire (Allen Park): What's Michigan without the invention of the automobile? About the same as automobiles without tires. The biggest tire in the world weighs twelve tons, stands eighty feet tall, and can be passed on the Detroit Industrial Expressway east of Detroit Metro Airport. Go give it a kick.

Minnesota

SPAM Museum (Austin): Remember those fried-SPAM sandwiches Dad used to make you for dinner when Mom was out? Or maybe the one you just fried up last week? Eight billion cans of SPAM have been sold since Minnesota's Hormel Foods started filling tins with meat stuff in 1937. And, while six billion of those tins remain tucked on shelves in a zombie apocalypse bunker somewhere, those others proved mostly quite delicious.

Mary Tyler Moore Statue (Minneapolis): A bronze statue honoring a hat-flipping Minnesotan TV character, celebrated for being one of the first to show an unmarried woman with a cool job just, you know, being a woman. This was revolutionary in 1970.

Northwest Angle (Angle Inlet): The Treaty of Paris ended the American Revolution in 1783, and turns out they had some bad maps while sorting things out. Ben Franklin—yes, *that* Ben Franklin—ended up claiming a chunk of mainland Canada that is now still part of Minnesota. The few US citizens who live on a peninsula can only be reached, or visited by you, via boat across a lake or an hour-long drive through Canada.

Mille Lacs Indian Museum and Trading Post (Vineland): This museum is the product of a partnership between the Minnesota Historical Society and the Mille Lacs Band of Ojibwe and designed to conserve precious artifacts and incorporate the beauty of its setting to tell the band's history.

Willie the Walleye (Baudette): This forty-foot-long, two-ton fish is the largest walleye statue on Earth and pretty hard to miss when you drive into the self-proclaimed walleye capital of the world. Bonus points if you see Willie the Walleye and the World's Largest Frying Pan in the same day.

Jolly Green Giant Statue (Blue Earth): Ho, ho, whoa . . . a fifty-five-foot-tall jolly green giant in a toga! With no underwear??!! The Minnesota Valley Canning Company was founded in 1903 in Le Sueur, and the giant mascot was added in 1928. The "Valley of the Jolly Green Giant" refers to the Minnesota River valley. The big guy attracts more than ten thousand visitors a year. Look up at your own risk.

The Somali Museum of Minnesota (Minneapolis): Home to more than 700 pieces of traditional Somali art and culture. This museum dives into the rich history of Somali folks in a region that hosts the largest concentration of Somali-born people in the United States.

World's Largest Boot (Red Wing): Sized 638½D, these boots are even too big for that big green fella. They're more than twenty feet tall and required the hides of eighty cows.

Missouri

Jesse James Home Museum (St. Joseph): Missourian bad boy Jesse James was born in Kearney and died thirty-four years later in St. Joseph in the house that's now a museum to his infamous life. One of the most notorious criminals in United States history, James was known as a good father and husband. Still, there remains a bullet hole in the wall from the shooting.

Missouri Meerschaum Corn Cob Pipe Museum (Washington): Just what you'd expect. This attraction is beloved by humans and snowmen alike.

Chuck Berry's House (St. Louis): The small redbrick house where a major father of rock 'n' roll penned such classics as "Roll Over Beethoven," "Sweet Little Sixteen," and "Johnny B. Goode."

SubTropolis (Kansas City): Visit the "World's Largest Underground Business Complex," buried 160 feet underground; a 55,000,000-square-foot city with more than eight miles of illumined roadway. All sorts of businesses store things here, including millions of USPS postal stamps and the original film reels of *Gone With the Wind*.

The Pony Express National Historic Trail and Museum (St. Joseph): Before fax machines and AOL, we had the Pony Express. This modern eighteen-hundred-mile trail captures *most* of what once connected the Midwest to the Westwest.

Precious Moments Chapel and Gardens (Carthage): Yes, those little figurines of kids all over your aunt's house or Christmas tree. Every year they sell about $200 million of those little suckers, and one of yours may be worth more than a thousand bucks on eBay. One more reason to be nice to your aunts.

Whiteman Minuteman Missile Site (Knob Noster): For thirty-plus years, Missouri was home to 150 Minuteman II missile sites and enough warheads to take out Russia, or whoever, several times over. When the Cold War "ended," the silos were almost all destroyed. One, at the Whiteman Air Force Base, was left open as a museum. It's good to know conflicts with Russia are a thing of the past.

Nebraska

America's smallest town (Monowi): With just one citizen, this is officially the smallest town in the United States. Elsie Eiler—the town's mayor, librarian, and bartender—is just one minister's license away from providing everything a good Midwest town might need.

The Villagers (Taylor): As too many Taylor folks began moving away, the town started putting up plywood cutouts of people to replace them. There are now more than one hundred of the plywood citizens standing about town. It's a cool spot even if everyone looks board.

Angel DeCora Memorial Museum and Research Center (Winnebago): The Museum has strived to protect, preserve, and educate both Tribe and public on the history and culture of the Hōcąk Nįšoc Haci (Winnebago Tribe of Nebraska).

Willa Cather Prairie (Red Cloud): More than six hundred acres of open grassland in honor of an Easter gal whose most famous novels were about life in Nebraska and the Great Plains. The Pulitzer Prize–winning author captured frontier life in classics such as *O Pioneers!*, *The Song of the Lark*, and *My Ántonia*.

Klown Doll Museum (Plainview): If you don't suffer from coulrophobia, you might enjoy this museum of more than seven thousand clown dolls. While on the topic, James Bailey (of Barnum & Bailey) was from Michigan and the Ringling brothers were from Wisconsin.

North Dakota

Fargo **Wood Chipper (Fargo):** *Oh geez* . . . Sophisticated movie memorabilia and a great selfie op can be found at the Fargo-Moorhead Visitors Center.

Oldest Mosque in the United States (Ross): Yup, in a remote prairie in North Dakota. Immigrant farmers from present-day Syria and Lebanon built the original in 1929. There were mosques in the United States before this, but those ones are no longer around.

Earth Lodge Village and Three Affiliated Tribes Museum (New Town): The MHA Nation (Mandan, Hidatsa, and Arikara) invite all to the shores of Lake Sakakawea to walk in the steps of Indigenous Peoples at the Earth Lodge Village and visit a full museum of artwork, crafts, artifacts, and historical pieces.

The Medora Musical (Medora): Since 1965 an "ode to patriotism, Theodore Roosevelt, and the Great American West!" is performed each summer in the Burning Hills Amphitheater. Attendance tops one hundred thousand per year.

International Peace Garden (Dunseith): The US invaded Canada multiple times during the War of 1812, but—despite constant verbal jabs across the border—we've gotten along pretty well ever since. To honor that, explore twenty-three hundred acres of trails and gardens split evenly between Canada and North Dakota.

Ohio

Field of Corn (Dublin): Giant fields of corn may be common here, but how 'bout a field of giant corn? We're talking six-foot-high shucked ears made of concrete. You'd need a pretty big bun to butter these bad boys. More than a hundred are positioned in long rows. ~~Ancient astronaut theorists speculate that~~ It's an early 1990s art piece commissioned by the Dublin Arts Council, and it's open twenty-four hours a day.

Amish Country Ohio (Holmes County): Forty percent of Holmes County is Amish folks. Come learn about the traditions and history of the Amish and Mennonite peoples—and buy some cool wooden furniture while you're at it.

Hot Dog Bun Museum (Toledo): Speaking of buns, how about a chance to see more than fifteen hundred hot dog buns signed by famous people? American patriot John Hancock would have needed a brat bun.

A Christmas Story House (Cleveland): The now-classic *A Christmas Story*—yes, the one about the glasses kid and the BB gun—is set in Indiana, based on the writer's memories of growing up in Illinois, and was filmed in Ohio. Join more than one hundred thousand who've toured the house used in the film. It's even been refurbished to capture every detail from this classic. Commemorative leg lamps run from $15 to $200, depending on how commemorative you're feeling. Just be careful when you're watering plants.

Museum of Divine Statues (Lakewood): Speaking of Christmas, stop by the Sanctuary Museum (formally the Museum of Divine Statues) to see more than two hundred pieces of ecclesiastical art conserved and restored from churches around the world. BYO fish fry and beer if looking for an authentic spiritual experience.

National Underground Railroad Freedom Center (Cincinnati): This museum showcases the history of the Underground Railroad and highlights the role some Midwestern states played.

South Dakota

The Corn Palace (Mitchell): Iowa grows more corn than anyone, but a town in southeast South Dakota claims to be Corn Capital of the World. Their main arena/theater, which hosts everything from polka festivals to college basketball games, is constructed of concrete but almost completely covered in murals and trimmings crafted from corn and other grains.

The National Music Museum (Vermillion): Exactly where you'd expect to find a fifteen-thousand-piece collection of centuries-old instruments. Called a "musical Smithsonian" by the *New York Times*, the museum was founded in 1973 on the campus of the University of South Dakota and includes a five-hundred-year-old harpsichord for the kids to bang on. (Joking; touch with your ears.)

Art Alley (Rapid City): Along a brick-paved alley that runs from Sixth to Seventh between Main and St. Joseph, you'll find an organic and ever-changing community art gallery featuring the work of pros and amateurs painted right on the walls.

Porter Sculpture Park (Montrose): If Salvador Dalí and Beetlejuice moved to South Dakota together and started making oversize art out of iron, this is what that would look like.

Racing Magpie (Rapid City): Positive community change through consulting and creative space via exhibitions of native art, wellness workshops, and classes.

Wisconsin

Ho-Chunk Nation Museum and Cultural Center (Tomah): There's no better way to discover the Midwest than by exploring its rich Indigenous culture. While there are twelve tribes in Wisconsin and this museum mainly focuses on the Ho-Chunk, it's a great place to start. In this rapidly changing world, there's much to learn from those who were here first.

Crash site of Korabl-Sputnik 1 (Manitowoc): On September 5, 1962, a piece from Russia's Sputnik IV hit North Eighth Street in front of the Rahr-West Art Museum in Manitowoc. No other pieces were found. Every year, folks in Manitowoc dress up in their best alien attire to celebrate Sputnik Fest. You can also visit the precise strike location. Just look both ways first.

National Mustard Museum (Middleton): What's a brat without mustard? Celebrating more than five thousand mustards from around the world.

World's Largest Six-Pack: (La Crosse): Six fifty-four-foot-tall storage tanks turned into giant beer cans, capable of holding seven million regular beer cans. That's enough to drink a six-pack a day for tree thousand years. Started as Old Style, later became La Crosse.

A World of Accordions Museum (Superior): No state still (ever) loves its polka like Wisconsin, and there's no polka without a good accordion or six going. There're thirteen hundred accordions in the museum's collection.

Gary Gygax Memorial (Lake Geneva): Who is Gary Gygax, you say? -3 Wisdom points for you, brave knight. This Wisconsinite invented Dungeons & Dragons and, so, pretty much *World of Warcraft* and most all role-playing. D&D players believe rolling your twenty-sided die on his memorial will bring good luck on later adventures.

Wisconsin Dells: If you're anywhere within fifty miles of Wisconsin Dells, the billboards will tell you all about it. Miles of water slides, Ho-Chunk Casino, magic shows, music, Tommy Bartlett's Water Ski Sky and Stage Show (RIP), Duck Boat tours, Upside-down White House, even a Trojan horse go-kart course. It's one part Vegas, one part Pleasure Island, two parts Lincoln Logs. But if you come for any of the madness, make sure you stay for the serenity. The best part of the Dells is the surrounding parks, trails, rivers, and lakes. Within minutes of the strip you can be overcome by the sounds of birds, the wind, and a fast-moving river—*ahhhhhh*. Oh, don't mind that. It's just some kid's first time dropping down the Scorpion's tail at Noah's Ark Waterpark.

Shrine to Anglers (Hayward): Right outside the National Freshwater Hall of Fame, a 143-foot muskie, four and a half stories tall, soars majestically into the Wisconsin sky, with an open mouth that can hold twenty people and is used as a wedding venue. The muskie's innards include a museum with hundreds of historical outboard motor models and more than four hundred mounted fish that didn't get away.

Laws of the Land . . .

Turns out, saying "I didn't know that was illegal" doesn't somehow make it legal; you can still face judicial consequences. Whether antiquated or just plain quirky, here are some likely unfamiliar laws to keep in mind for each Midwest state. Whether anyone would actually cite you for breaking them might depend on which judge is in session.

Illinois

- If you are physically carrying less than $1, you can be arrested for vagrancy.

- You can't fish in pajamas or fly a kite in Chicago.

- You can't drive a car without a steering wheel in Decatur. Okay . . .

- It's illegal to hang "obstructions" from a car's rearview mirror, including air fresheners, graduation tassels, or pandemic masks.

- If your wheelbarrow has a FOR SALE sign, it may not be chained to a tree in Des Plaines.

- It's illegal to urinate on street signs in Normal.

- Throwing a snowball in Mount Pulaski is, erm, only illegal for girls.

- Ice-skating during June and August is prohibited in Moline. The fact that there's a law about this should tell you plenty about the weather in Moline.

Indiana

- It's illegal for men to stand in a bar. *How do they play cornhole?*
- Anyone over the age of fourteen who "profanely curses, damns, or swears" can be fined for each curse, and up to a total of $10 a day for it.
- It's illegal to make a monkey smoke a cigarette. Noted.
- You may not catch a fish with your bare hands.
- It's illegal to have a mustache for those with the "tendency to kiss other humans." First, the "humans" specification is a bit unsettling. Second, what about the mustache-and-beard combo?
- It's illegal to enter a movie house or public streetcar within four hours of eating garlic.

Iowa

- It's illegal for a kiss to last longer than five minutes.
- One-armed piano players must perform for free.
- It's illegal to do palm readings in Cedar Rapids.
- Horses are forbidden to eat fire hydrants in Marshalltown. Kinda makes you wonder what hydrants and horses are made of in Marshalltown.
- It's illegal to pick a flower from a city park.

Kansas

- Snowball fights are illegal in Topeka.
- Restaurants may not sell cherry pie à la mode on Sundays.
- It's illegal to use mules to hunt ducks.
- You may not screech your tires. (Keep 'em properly inflated like Mom taught ya.)
- It's illegal to hit or shake a Derby vending machine that just stole your money.

Michigan

- A woman can't cut her hair without her husband's permission.
- Cars can't be sold on Sunday.
- Deliberately destroying your radio is illegal in Detroit.
- Deliberately scowling at your wife on Sunday is illegal in Detroit.
- It's illegal to kill a dog using a decompression chamber. *Oh geez!*
- It's illegal to paint sparrows in an attempt to sell them as parakeets in Harper Woods.
- It's against the law to serenade your paramour in Kalamazoo.

Minnesota

- Men driving motorcycles must have a shirt on. Women, unregulated in this same regard.
- However, women can be arrested for impersonating Santa Claus.
- It's illegal to tease skunks.
- It's illegal to sleep naked.

Missouri

- It's illegal to honk the horn of someone else's car.
- It's illegal to have a garage sale last four or more days in Jefferson City.
- It's illegal to drink beer from a bucket *while* sitting on a curb in St. Louis. There goes my Friday night.
- It's illegal for a firefighter to rescue a woman wearing a nightgown. However you take this sentence will suffice.
- Frightening a baby is illegal in Mole.
- Dancing is banned in Purdy. Yup, just like in that Kevin Bacon movie with the giant flesh-eating worms.

Nebraska

- You can be arrested if your child burps in church.
- Men may not run about shirtless *with* a shaved chest in Omaha.
- It is illegal to wear false teeth constructed from leather.
- You may not purchase a cocktail that mixes liquor *and* beer. Buying one of each apparently not an issue.

North Dakota

- It's illegal to lie down and fall asleep with your shoes on.
- You can get tossed in the slammer for wearing a hat while dancing.
- Beer and pretzels can't be served together at any bar or restaurant. This law should be illegal.

Ohio

- It is illegal to fish for whales on Sunday. (And not possible Monday through Saturday.)
- It is illegal to throw a snake at someone.
- Getting a fish drunk is illegal. (But sturgeons can handle a couple old-fashioneds.)
- You may not participate in a duel.
- You may not run out of gas in Youngstown.

South Dakota

- It's illegal to "disturb" a mink den.
- It's not allowed to fall asleep in a cheese factory.
- Hotel rooms are required to have two twin beds kept at least two feet apart. What happens in the space between is none of our business.

Wisconsin

- It's illegal to sprinkle your property in any manner "to the distress or annoyance of others."
- All AA-rated cheddar must be "highly pleasing."
- "Whenever two trains meet at an intersection of said tracks, neither shall proceed until the other has." This is a classic Ope-off.
- It's illegal *not* to give livestock the right of way.

A Midwest Bucket List . . .

_____ Ride a roller coaster at Cedar Point

_____ Catch a walleye

_____ Play a lay-down loner in euchre

_____ Visit Detroit

_____ Boat in the Ozarks

_____ Eat a three-way in Ohio

_____ Visit Brainerd Lakes

_____ Visit Branson

_____ Stare helplessly as a deer runs into your car

_____ Chop wood

_____ Eat barbecue in Kansas City

_____ See a game at Lambeau

_____ Purify yourself in Lake Minnetonka

_____ See a game at Soldier Field

_____ Order a deep-dish pizza in Chicago

_____ Attend the Indy 500

_____ Complete a Milwaukee beer tour

_____ Visit the Crazy Horse Memorial

_____ Tweezer a tick off your privates

_____ Get married

_____ Hike the Maah Daah Hey Trail

_____ Ice-fish

_____ Visit Brown County, Indiana

_____ Visit Sleeping Bear Dunes

_____ Find something Frank Lloyd Wright built

_____ Travel down Route 66

_____ Visit the Iowa State Fair

_____ Visit the Ohio State Fair

_____ Visit the Indiana State Fair

_____ Visit the Minnesota State Fair

_____ Visit the Wisconsin State Fair

_____ Get laid in Put-In-Bay (or try)

_____ Mow your neighbor's lawn

_____ Get lost in a cornfield

_____ Attend a Big 10 rivalry game

_____ Attend the Sturgis Motorcycle Rally

_____ Attend Schmeckfest in Freeman, SD

_____ Consider buying a lake house

_____ Chicken dance at a wedding or fair

_____ Shovel your roof

_____ Eat fried and cold cheese curds

_____ Wear shorts in below 30°F weather

_____ Order a Juicy Lucy

_____ See Charlie Berens perform live

_____ See a black squirrel

_____ Visit the Football Hall of Fame in Canton

_____ Skydeck Chicago

_____ Spend two-plus hours in a Costco or Target

_____ Try apple pie topped with cheese

_____ Buy from the Amish

_____ Dip your pizza or cereal in ranch

_____ Visit the Apostle Islands

Make Your Own Midwest List Below!

_____

_____

_____

_____

_____

_____

_____

_____

_____

_____

_____

_____

_____

_____

_____

_____

_____

_____

_____

Final Exam:
How Well Do You Know the Midwest?

Welp, I s'pose it's about that time . . . I hope I kept you company on the airplane, couch, or can. By the way, you should really clean your tile. Geez sorry ope I didn't mean to be rude. You know what, I'll come over tomorrow and just clean that tile for you. Yeah no seriously I've got an hour between taking Terrance and Trish to the airport and walking the Pulaskis' pit bull. I mean it's on the way. You're just down the road about thirty minutes or so, it's really no problem. Welp! I s'pose it's about that time . . . What's in your garage now? Sure I'd love to see your snowblower still yet. Okay seriously I really better get go— Gene's doin' what now? That sounds illegal. Well tell your folks I says hi— Oh no, I couldn't stay for another . . . Well, if you insist. Want me to grab you one too? That was rhetorical—already got. Cheers. Hey, since I'm staying, you want to do this quiz, or no?

Q1: When driving in the Midwest, which of these will likely obstruct your travel?

a. Deer

b. Trains

c. Tractors

d. Horse-drawn Amish buggies

e. All of the above

Q2: Which of these is not a Midwest state?

a. Michigan

b. Minnesota

c. Iowa (which is near Minnesota and Michigan)

d. Idaho (which is near Oregon and the Pacific Ocean)

e. Wisconsin

Q3: What food groups does ranch dressing go on?

a. Breads, cereals, rice, pasta, noodles and other grains.

b. Dairy

c. Vegetables, nuts, and legumes

d. Fruit

e. All of the above

Q4: Do people in the Midwest have accents?

a. No. We talk normal.

Q5: When should you apologize?

a. Never

b. When you did something wrong

c. Ope, sorry

d. Only when you get caught

e. In heaven, later

Q6: The point of the card game euchre is to:

a. Score ten points

b. Take as many tricks as possible

c. Learn to spell *euchre*

d. Unleash emotional/mental warfare on friends and family

e. All of the above

Q7: How long is "too long" to drive somewhere?

a. 30 minutes

b. 1 hour

c. 3 hours

d. 14 hours

e. When you hit an ocean

Q8: Which of these is not an urban legend/cryptid from the Midwest?

a. The New Jersey Devil

b. The Michigan Dogman

c. Loveland Frogmen of Ohio

d. Wendigo

e. Sinkhole Sam

Q9: Which Midwest state has the most lakes?

a. Wisconsin

b. Minnesota

c. Michigan

d. Debatable; depends which one I'm from and/or which I'm in when you ask me

e. Not Nebraska

Q10: When leaving a gathering, how far in advance should you announce your departure?

a. Don't; just Batman out of there

b. 15 to 30 minutes

c. 1 hour

d. About 3 hours

e. The day before the event

Answers: 1. e, 2. d, 3. e, 4. a, 5. c, 6. e, 7. e, 8. a, 9. d or e, 10. d or e

How'd You Do?

Self-score and total your correct answers.

0–2 correct   Ope! Better read this book again . . . and buy a copy for a close friend so you can study together.

3–5 correct   Not bad, but there's still some work to be done. Better read this book again . . . and buy a copy for a close friend so you can study together.

6–7 correct   Impressive. You've clearly spent time here. Buy a copy for a close friend.

8–9 correct   You're a heartland authority with a bit more to learn. Buy copies of this book for friends.

Perfect 10   You're an eminent Midwesterner! Host a Midwest party for everyone you know . . . and give them each a copy as a party favor!

Short essay

In the space provided below, write two thousand to five thousand words exploring everything that's amazing about the Midwest . . . or just write your grocery list.

_____

_____

_____

_____

_____

_____

_____

_____

_____

_____

_____

_____

_____

_____

_____

_____

_____

_____

_____

_____

_____

_____

_____

_____

_____

_____

_____

_____

_____

_____

Lexicon

Language is the road map of a culture. So much of visiting or living somewhere is knowing and trying the local tongue. For the end of this Midwest guide, here's a convenient compendium of some of the more regional phrases and words you'll come across.

ain'-a-hey =
isn't it so

ass over teakettle =
falling head over heels, but not in love

badtree =
battery

B-Dubs =
BW3s = Buffalo Wild Wings

Beeyemites =
people who live in Birmingham, MI

believe you me =
believe me

blinker =
turn signal

Booyah! =
exclamation of victory/joy, also a stew

borrow me =
lend me

brat holder =
sunglasses holder in car

brewski =
beer

Bring Your Tractor to School Day =
exactly what it sounds like, *and* a real thing

bubbler =
water fountain

buggy =
shopping cart

carmel =
caramel

Casimir Pulaski =
day off school

catty-corner =
diagonal

cayote (two syllables; silent e) =
coyote

cheese =
major food group; more important than fruit

cheese toastie =
grilled cheese

chilly =
below 30°F

clicker =
TV remote control

c'mere once! =
come here quickly

concrete =
ice cream (*see* Freddy's)

Coney =
hot dog with chili and cheese

cornhole =
party game to play with close friends

Counciltucky =
what folks in Omaha call people in neighboring Council Bluffs

couple-two-three =
some

crawdads =
freshwater lobster

crick =
creek

cripes =
not taking the Lord's name in vain

cripes alfrighty =
not taking the Lord's name or the word *almighty* in vain

davenport =
couch

detasseling =
summer job

dinner =
lunch (*see* supper)

doorwall =
sliding glass door

Dorothy Lynch =
ranch dressing in Nebraska

dragging =
driving up and down Main
Street

'druthers =
preferences

duck, duck, gray duck!
= duck, duck, goose

the El =
train that runs through
Chicago

euchre =
second-greatest card
game on planet (next to
sheepshead)

expressway =
highway

Farm & Fleet =
a retail store found
throughout Wisconsin,
Illinois, Iowa, and Michigan

farmer wave =
lift two fingers off the
steering wheel as you pass
other driver

F.I.B. =
F#^%$^ Illinois Bas&^%d

Fleet Farm =
one-stop shop for all things
Midwest

fudgie =
tourists in the Upper
Peninsula

glovebox =
compartment in your car

going downtown =
going to Chicago

government cheese =
bad

grabowski =
good guy/gal, salt-of-the-
earth blue-collar type

green pepper =
mango

gym shoes =
sneakers

hair binder =
elastic hair tie

hey =
method of ending
sentence (eg: "Pass me that
pie, hey")

hog heaven =
all is good

home =
flyover country

Hoosier =
someone from Indiana

Hot dish =
casserole

hot minute =
long time

humdinger =
good time/place

Illinoi =
Illinois

ink pen =
pen

isa horse apiece =
it's the same thing

jeet =
"Did you eat?"

Keep 'er movin' =
life keeps movin', and you
should too

Kroger's =
Kroger (take away 's.
See also: Meijer, Aldi, JC
Penney, Jewel-Osco,
and so on)

Kybo =
porta-potty

LSD =
Lake Shore Drive

main drag =
a busy road

Michigan sauce =
chili

Michigander =
person from Michigan

Minnesota =
a state where they say
Minnesota

minnisota =
a small can of pop

no yeah =
yeah

ope =
my bad, sorry, damn!
(see page 43)

opening day =
start of hunting season

orange barrels =
highway trimming

padiddle =
car with a missing/broken
taillight or headlight

pert'near =
close (as in time or
distance)

please =
excuse me

pop =
soda

Puthergoin-eh! =
let's get going

put that up =
put something away

recombobulation =
getting reorganized

red beer =
beer mixed with tomato
juice and a piece of bacon
(don't judge until you try)

sack =
grocery bag

sammich =
sandwich

schnockered =
drunk

scoop the loop =
driving around to kill time

sheepshead =
card game

sheephead =
fish you catch when you're
trying
to catch walleyes

shelterbelt =
row of trees

shorts weather =
May through April

skeeter =
mosquito

snow day =
three feet of snowfall

spendy =
expensive

start-with-me-last =
still thinking

stick =
shtick (שטיק)

stop-and-go light =
stoplight

sundog =
circular rainbow formed
around the sun on cold days

supper =
dinner

sweeper =
vacuum cleaner

tavern =
sloppy joe sandwich

tenderloin =
breaded deep-fried pork
on a bun

tennies =
all sneakers

The Bridge =
Mackinac Bridge

The City =
Chicago

The Region =
the northwest Indiana area
near Chicago

The Soo =
the Sault St. Marie area

then =
method of ending a
sentence (e.g.: "Pass me
that pie, then.")

Three Cs =
Cincinnati, Columbus,
Cleveland

three-way =
spaghetti with chili
and cheese

tough tomatoes =
go f*ck yourself

tree =
three

troll =
people from Lower
Michigan when traveling
into the Upper Peninsula

Uff da! =
"I accept my fate."

unthaw =
thaw, defrost

up nort' =
the cottage, cabin, or lake
house

walleye =
tenderloin of the lake

warsh =
wash

washroom =
bathroom

Watergate =
type of salad

whip a shitty =
U-turn (or, what
Michiganders call a left
turn)

winter =
late September to a couple
weeks after Easter

with =
add onions

wrassle =
wrestle, struggle

yakked =
vomited

yeah no =
no

yeah no seriously =
yes!

You betcha! =
yes

youse =
a group of people

Yooper =
someone from Michigan's
Upper Peninsula

you're fine =
don't worry about it

yums =
snacks

Midwest language is always moving and changing. Just like a river. And on this language river is you. Tubing. Yes, your beer cooler can be in this analogy. You may hear a new phrase. Write it down. Share it. Enjoy it. Now watch out for deer. Yes, they swim.

_____
_____
_____
_____
_____
_____
_____
_____
_____
_____
_____
_____
_____
_____
_____
_____
_____
_____
_____

Acknowledgments

First I want to acknowledge that the land I've written about is the original homeland of the Ho-Chunk, Miami, Odawa, Potawatomi, Menominee, Anishinabe, Otoe, Ioway, Missouri, Kickapoo, Sauk, Mesquaki, Peoria, Dakota, Lakota, Nakota, Assiniboine, Mandan, Hidatsa, Arikara, Ponca, Omaha, Pawnee, Osage, Arapaho, Kaw, and Kiowa Tribal Nations and current home of so many more. They've cared for this land we all love for thousands of years, and continue to do so.

Saying I wrote *The Midwest Survival Guide* is like saying a Bloody Mary is just vodka. Nobody's trying to drink twelve ounces of straight vodka at 10:00 A.M. This isn't *The Russian Survival Guide.* Point being, I didn't write this book alone. I relied heavily on other writers, researchers, consultants, artists, chefs, book lovers, friends, family, and fans. My hope has always been to reflect the larger Midwest culture, and I know that's impossible for one guy to do. So I'd like to take some time and thank every ingredient in this Bloody Mary. From the stuffed olives under the ice to the chicken leg garnish speared on top, every ingredient was absolutely necessary. We all worked together to make this concoction. I hope you enjoyed it. Now I'd like to thank the ingredients.

Mom and Dad—The stuffed olive and bacon-wrapped Brussels sprout garnishes (respectively). They added taste and sustenance. My mom, a former journalist and current mother of twelve, has spent countless hours editing my papers and giving me feedback over the years. This book was no exception, and her insight was invaluable. My dad, former worm salesman and father of twelve, has always been a source of ideas. Especially the weird ones. Some he may not want the world to know about. Don't worry, Pop, no mention of your bird-in-the-box . . . in this book.

Matt Van De Water—My ice. He's been there from the beginning, providing structure for the cocktail of my life and always keeping it cool. Somehow he hasn't melted away in the constant stirring of schedules and deadlines. If it weren't for Matt, this book would still be "an idea I'd like to do at some point." I have a tendency to throw deadlines lifelines. That's where Matt steps in to make dreams a reality.

Claire Harris—The pickle. Crisp and sweet and makes any hangover better. Claire is my literary agent. But she's more literary than agent. So literary she probably hates that sentence. Claire is a creative. A book lover. She has great instincts and ideas. I first met Claire at Colectivo Coffee on the lakefront in downtown Milwaukee. It was shortly after the first *Manitowoc Minute* came out and she wanted to discuss ideas for a book. She had way more faith in me than I had in myself. She hung with me through bad ideas and continued brainstorming until eventually we landed on this idea. I wouldn't be doing this if not for Claire.

Geoffrey Girard—The tomato juice. A Bloody Mary wouldn't be bloody without the tomato juice, and this book wouldn't be a book without Geoff. I had never written a book before and I relied heavily on Geoff's decades of experience. He offered me an outline, a vision, creative structures, and countless hilarious punchlines. Geoff's collaborative nature made this book a joy to write. Geoff lives in Cincinnati and provided great insight on the southern edge of the Midwest. He's also an avid euchre player, which is how he got the job in the first place.

Cassie Jones and Jill Zimmerman—The celery salt and pepper. Don't think of making a bloody without celery salt and pepper. They bring out the flavor. Cassie is my editor at William Morrow, but editor doesn't adequately describe Cassie's role. She's a Wisconsinite through and through. Her suggestions and insight gave this book coherence and flow, and she always kept us on track. Her fingerprint is all over *The Midwest Survival Guide*. And I also want to mention Jill Zimmerman, who worked on everything from text to images to countless other details. Her notes were always helpful and somehow she made sure all the images ended up in the right places. A minor miracle if you ask me. And thanks to the rest of the team at William Morrow, including Julie Paulauski, Ryan Shepherd, DJ DeSmyter, Rachel Weinick, Leah Carlson-Stanisic, Yeon Kim, and Andrew DiCecco.

If this were the Oscars they'd definitely be playing the music by now. But then again, they don't serve Bloody Marys at the Oscars.

Vanessa Montano—Just like the hamburger garnish on top of a Bloody Mary, Vanessa made this book look pretty with her illustrations. She's a fellow Midwesterner, and her love of the region came through in her work. The image requests ranged from a Bob Dylan and Prince road trip to deer stuck in a four-way-stop traffic jam. There was no request too weird for Vanessa. Somehow she managed to take simple ideas and make them pop in ways I could have never imagined.

To my family—The Worcestershire sauce. Because there's a couple two-tree-hundred dashes of all you in this book. My siblings: Andy (who helped edit and write), Billy (who helped locate my mug shot for the arrest story), Betsy, Maggie, Addie, Mary Kate, John (who helped write and added photos), Emily, Nora, Bridget (who helped write and design graphic cards), and Ellie. Nana Fehr, Grandpa TG, Grandpa Bob, Grandma Sue (who spent several phone calls with me recounting stories for this book), aunts and uncles and everyone I forgot . . . thank you for letting me use your names and inspirations. Some names I changed to protect the living. Others I didn't because I forgot. If you're upset, this is me asking forgiveness for not asking permission. Please don't sue—I'll do the dishes next time I come for supper.

Josie Lee, Dr. Gene Tesdahl, and Stacey Parshall Jensen—The half corn on the cob, venison jerky, and pickled asparagus, respectively. You can't write a book about the Midwest without representing Indigenous culture, and the diversity of the Midwest. As a white fella from the Milwaukee suburbs, my perspective is very limited. I relied on Josie, director of the Ho-Chunk Nation Museum and Cultural Center, to provide creative insight, accurate history, perspective, ideas, and suggestions. Gene balanced out the comedic nature of this book with historical perspective and guidance. And Stacey ensured the final text fairly and respectfully depicted this diverse region.

Chef Yia Vang—The hot sauce. If you listen to my *CripesCast* interview with Yia, that hot sauce will make sense. The story Yia shared of his parents' immigration is incredible. My entire childhood I knew the Midwest had many Hmong immigrants, but I'm embarrassed to say I didn't know the Hmong people helped America in the Vietnam War. I think Yia's account speaks to the rich diversity often overlooked in the Midwest.

The Midwest Gallery artists. The squeaky cheese curds of *The Midwest Survival Guide*. The gallery is possibly my favorite part of the book. It shows us an array of Midwest perspectives I could have never depicted in words. First off, I'd like to thank everyone who submitted art. I was blown away by the creativity seeping from every corner of the Midwest. I think we could do an entirely different book on Midwest art alone. Gigi Berry, Bill Brien, Louis Copt, Tim Gallenbeck, Desiree Kelly, Joe Kintz, Abby Naumann, Henry Payer Jr., Christopher Sweet, Naimah Thomas, Dustin Twiss, and Brendan Wentz, I can't thank you enough for making your art. It's an honor to share it in this book.

All those who submitted recipes, you are the boundless flavors of smoked meat sticks. Sure, you *could* enjoy a bloody without the assorted meat stick varieties you won at the meat raffle, but why would you? I'd like to thank LeRoy Butler, Carolynn Ficke, Kathy Fischesser, Cindy Grunik, the Held family, Josie Lee, Carol Jean Peters, Yia Vang, and Agnes Walker for sharing your culinary delicacies with us.

I'd also like to thank the following pickled peppers that brought an extra zip to our tongue and sweat to our brow. Colleen Muraca created the Midwest Glossary images and cracked me up with each one. Thanks to Max Larsen for shooting last-minute photos. Liz Bemis helped us find images and other graphics. And the Eble family offered many insightful chicken-raising tips.

Finally, I'd like to thank the fans. You are the glass—the vessel that allows this Bloody Mary to be something more than just a mess on the floor. Thanks to all of you, the fans, for submitting ideas over the years. I've done my best to act like a sponge and absorb your ideas and squeeze them onto these pages. Thank you for your generous support over the years. You make me feel like the luckiest guy in the Midwest.

Photography and Illustration Credits

Lifebrary/Shutterstock, Inc.: i

Thanakorn/Adobe Stock: iii, 41, 286 (deer)

Visions-AD/Adobe Stock: v

Mint Images/Adobe Stock: vi

Depositphotos Inc.: x, 6, 13, 16, 24 (A and B), 50, 69, 70, 83, 85, 87, 89, 93, 101 (all images), 110, 111, 112, 115 (all images), 116 (all images), 136 (all images), 149, 161 (B), 172, 179, 180, 181 (A), 193, 199, 203 (all images), 204 (all images), 211 (A and B), 212 (A), 214 (A and B), 216 (A), 217 (A and B), 220 (A), 221 (A and B), 223 (A), 225 (A), 228 (A and B), 229 (A and B), 231 (A), 232 (A and B), 233 (A), 234 (A and B), 236 (A and B), 237 (A and B), 245 (E), 250 (background), 260 (A, B, and C), 261, 262 (A and B), 263, 264, 265 (A, B, and C), 267 (A and B), 269 (A and B), 288

Vanessa Montano: xv, xvi, 12, 15, 30, 32, 34, 36, 38, 40, 52, 55, 56, 57, 58, 59, 60, 61, 62, 63, 67, 68, 72, 77, 84, 86, 91, 94, 97, 98, 102 (illustration), 118, 126, 128, 131 (all illustrations), 132 (all illustrations), 145, 152, 156, 159, 163, 168, 170, 173, 183, 186, 196, 200, 209 (illustration), 240, 248, 249, 257, 270, 275

EugeneF/Adobe Stock: 1

Maxim Grebeshkov/Adobe Stock: 2

mariosforsos/Adobe Stock: 4

Claire M. Harris: 11, 64, 182 (B)

David E. Jackson: 19

Destina/Adobe Stock: 20

New Africa/Adobe Stock: 25, 95

Yabobchuk Olena/Adobe Stock: 28

master1305/Adobe Stock: 35

BGStock72/Adobe Stock and fad82/Shutterstock, Inc.: 37

Courtesy of the author: 45, 51, 109, 113, 117 (A and B), 133, 134, 135, 137, 141, 151, 157, 177, 189, 190 (A and B)

Courtesy of Manitowoc Minute, Colleen Muraca, and Bridget Berens: 43, 46, 47, 48

Daisy Daisy/Adobe Stock: 53

Fanfo/Adobe Stock: 54

Igor/Adobe Stock: 73

Cavan Images/Adobe Stock: 74, 76

Austin Bauer: 80

Tom Malloy: 81

Mediaparts/Adobe Stock: 88

mtatman/Adobe Stock: 96

gawin/Adobe Stock: 99

green308/Adobe Stock: 102 (background)

Andrey Popov/Adobe Stock: 106

John Berens: 119, 220 (b), 227

Naimah Thomas, naimahthomasart.com (@naimah_creates): 120

Desiree Kelly: 121 (A)

Tim Gallenbeck (@Bearded_Border): 121 (B)

Henry Payer Jr. (photo by Aaron C. Packard): 122 (A)

Brendan Wentz: 122 (B)

Christopher J. Sweet, facebook.com/csweet-dzine: 123

Louis Copt: 124 (A)

Gigi Berry, Gigi's Flair Emporium in Minneapolis: 124 (B)

Abby Nami (@abby.nami.official): 124 (C)

Joe Kintz: 124 (D)

Photography and Illustratiion Credits